REFL...

F...

SUN...

YEAR **C**

IAN ADAMS
JUSTINE ALLAIN CHAPMAN
ANGELA ASHWIN
JEFF ASTLEY
ALAN BARTLETT
JOHN BARTON
ROSALIND BROWN
JOANNA COLLICUTT
STEPHEN COTTRELL
STEVEN CROFT
MAGGI DAWN
ALAN GARROW
PAULA GOODER
ALICE GOODMAN
PETER GRAYSTONE
JOANNE GRENFELL
MALCOLM GUITE
HELEN-ANN HARTLEY
CHRISTOPHER HERBERT
SUE HOPE
EMMA INESON
MARK IRELAND
GRAHAM JAMES
CHRISTOPHER JONES
PAUL KENNEDY
JOHN KIDDLE
JANE LEACH
JANE MAYCOCK

BARBARA MOSSE
DAVID MOXON
ROSALYN MURPHY
MARK OAKLEY
HELEN ORCHARD
MARTYN PERCY
MICHAEL PERHAM
JOHN PERUMBALATH
SUE PICKERING
JOHN PRITCHARD
BEN QUASH
CHRISTINA REES
SARAH ROWLAND JONES
DAVID RUNCORN
JEANETTE SEARS
TIM SLEDGE
TOM SMAIL
MARTYN SNOW
HARRY STEELE
ANGELA TILBY
FRANCES WARD
KEITH WARD
MARGARET WHIPP
CATHERINE WILLIAMS
JANE WILLIAMS
LUCY WINKETT
CHRISTOPHER WOODS
JEREMY WORTHEN

Church House Publishing
Church House
Great Smith Street
London SW1P 3AZ

ISBN 978 1 78140 039 5

Published 2018 by Church House Publishing
Copyright © The Archbishops' Council 2018

The opinions expressed in this book are those of the
authors and do not necessarily reflect the official
policy of the General Synod or The Archbishops'
Council of the Church of England.

Liturgical editor: Peter Moger
Series editor: Hugh Hillyard-Parker
Designed and typeset by Hugh Hillyard-Parker
Copy edited by Ros Connelly
Printed in Great Britain by Ashford Colour Press Ltd

What do you think of *Reflections for Sundays*?

We'd love to hear from you – simply email us at

publishing@churchofengland.org

or write to us at

Church House Publishing, Church House,
Great Smith Street, London SW1P 3AZ.

Visit **www.dailyprayer.org.uk** for more information
on the *Reflections* series, ordering and subscriptions.

Contents

About the authors

Ian Adams is a poet, writer and photographer. An Anglican priest, he is Tutor in Pioneer Learning at Ridley Hall Cambridge, co-founder of Beloved Life, and Spirituality Adviser for Church Mission Society.

Justine Allain Chapman has served as a parish priest and in theological education specializing in mission and pastoral care. She is currently Archdeacon of Boston in the Diocese of Lincoln. Her most recent book, *The Resilient Disciple*, is for Lent.

Angela Ashwin travels widely as a retreat leader and speaker on prayer and discipleship. She has written several books, including *Faith in the Fool: Risk and Delight in the Christian Adventure*.

Jeff Astley is an Anglican priest, and currently Alister Hardy Professor of Religious and Spiritual Experience at the University of Warwick, and an honorary professor at Durham University and York St John University.

Alan Bartlett is Clergy Development Advisor for the Diocese of Durham. He was formerly on the staff of Cranmer Hall (teaching church history, Anglicanism, spirituality and practical theology).

John Barton retired as Professor of Old Testament at Oxford University in 2014 and is now a Senior Research Fellow of Campion Hall, Oxford. He is an Anglican priest and assists in the parish of Abingdon-on-Thames.

Rosalind Brown is Canon Librarian at Durham Cathedral with oversight of the Cathedral's public ministry. A town planner before ordination, she has written books on ministry and several published hymns.

Joanna Collicutt is the Karl Jaspers Lecturer in Psychology and Spirituality at Ripon College Cuddesdon and Advisor on the Spiritual Care of Older People for Oxford Diocese. She also ministers in a West Oxfordshire parish.

Stephen Cottrell is the Bishop of Chelmsford. He is a well-known writer and speaker on evangelism, spirituality and catechesis. He is one of the team that produced *Pilgrim*, the popular course for the Christian Journey.

Steven Croft is the Bishop of Oxford and writes widely on scripture, leadership and mission.

Maggi Dawn is Associate Professor of Theology and Literature, and Dean of Marquand Chapel, at Yale Divinity School in the USA. Trained in both music and theology, she was ordained in the Diocese of Ely, and holds a PhD from the University of Cambridge.

Alan Garrow is Vicar of St Peter's, Harrogate and an Honorary Academic at the Inter-disciplinary Institute for Biblical Studies at the University of Sheffield.

Paula Gooder is Director of Mission Learning and Development in the Birmingham Diocese. She is a writer and lecturer in biblical studies, author of a number of acclaimed books, and a co-author of the *Pilgrim* course. She is also a Reader in the Church of England.

Alice Goodman is the Rector of Fulbourn and the Wilbrahams in the Diocese of Ely, and the author of *History is Our Mother: Three Libretti.*

Peter Graystone works for Church Army, developing projects that take Good News to people who have no real experience of Church. He edits the website Christianity.org.uk and reviews theatre for the *Church Times.*

Joanne Grenfell is Archdeacon of Portsdown in the Diocese of Portsmouth, where she works with inner-city, outer-estate, and rural/coastal fringe parishes, as well as supporting strategic development, pioneer ministry and schools work in the area.

Malcolm Guite is Chaplain of Girton College, Cambridge. An acclaimed poet, he lectures widely on theology and literature. His many books include *Sounding the Seasons: Seventy Sonnets for the Christian Year*.

Helen-Ann Hartley is the seventh Bishop of Waikato in the Diocese of Waikato and Taranaki, New Zealand. She was ordained priest in the Diocese of Oxford and served as Director of Biblical Studies at Ripon College Cuddesdon.

Christopher Herbert was ordained in Hereford in 1967, becoming a curate and then Diocesan Director of Education. He was an incumbent in Surrey and, later, Archdeacon of Dorking and then Bishop of St Albans. He retired in 2009.

Sue Hope is the Vicar of St Paul's Shipley and an Adviser on Evangelism for the Diocese of Leeds.

Emma Ineson is the Principal of Trinity College Bristol. Before that she was Chaplain to the Bishop of Bristol and has also been Chaplain to the Lee Abbey community in Devon.

Mark Ireland is Archdeacon of Blackburn and co-author of six books on mission-related themes, most recently *Making New Disciples: Exploring the paradoxes of evangelism* and *How to do Mission Action Planning*.

Graham James has been Bishop of Norwich since 1999. Previously he was Bishop of St Germans in his native Cornwall and Chaplain to the Archbishop of Canterbury. He has served on the House of Lords Select Committee on Communications, and remains the Church of England's lead spokesperson on media issues.

Christopher Jones was widely respected across the Church of England, spending eight years as Home Affairs policy adviser for the Archbishops' Council until his death in 2012.

Paul Kennedy is Rector of St Vedast-alias-Foster in the City of London, having served previously as Rector East Winchester and Area Dean. He is also a Benedictine oblate at the Anglican Alton Abbey and blogs at http://earofyourheart.com/wp/

John Kiddle is Archdeacon of Wandsworth and was previously Director of Mission in St Albans Diocese. Before that he worked in parish ministry in Watford. He served his curacy and was a vicar in Liverpool Diocese.

Jane Leach is a Methodist Presbyter. She has been the Principal of Wesley House, Cambridge since 2011. Jane teaches practical theology in the Cambridge Theological Federation and contributes regularly to Radio 4's *Thought for the Day.*

Jane Maycock is a priest in the Diocese of Carlisle, with experience in parish ministry, as a Director of Ordinands, theological educator, writer and retreat centre chaplain.

Barbara Mosse is a writer and retired Anglican priest. She has had experience in various chaplaincies, worked for a number of years as a spirituality adviser, and has taught in theological education. Her books include *The Treasures of Darkness* and *Welcoming the Way of the Cross.*

David Moxon KNZM is the Archbishop of Canterbury's Representative to the Holy See and Director of the Anglican Centre in Rome. He was formerly Archbishop of New Zealand.

Rosalyn Murphy is Vicar of St Thomas' Church, Blackpool. She is a writer in biblical studies, often bringing a liberation and womanist theological perspective to her research.

Mark Oakley is Chancellor of St Paul's Cathedral, London, and a Visiting Lecturer in the Department of Theology and Religious Studies, King's College London. He writes on the relationship between faith, poetry and literature.

Helen Orchard is Team Vicar of St Matthew's Church in the Wimbledon Team. She was previously Chaplain-Fellow at Exeter College, Oxford and before ordination worked for the National Health Service.

Martyn Percy is the Dean of Christ Church, Oxford. From 2004 to 2014 he was Principal of Ripon College Cuddesdon, and prior to that was Director of the Lincoln Theological Institute.

Michael Perham was Bishop of Gloucester from 2004 to 2014. He was one of the architects of the Church of England's *Common Worship* and also wrote extensively about worship and spirituality. He died on Easter Monday 2017.

John Perumbalath is Archdeacon of Barking in Chelmsford Diocese. He has served as a theological educator and parish priest in the dioceses of Calcutta (Church of North India) and Rochester.

Sue Pickering is a spiritual director, retreat leader and writer. A clerical Canon of Taranaki Cathedral, Sue finds inspiration in family, friends, 'ordinary' life, contemplation, creation, gardening and quilting.

John Pritchard retired as Bishop of Oxford in 2014. Prior to that he was Bishop of Jarrow, Archdeacon of Canterbury and Warden of Cranmer Hall, Durham.

Ben Quash is Professor of Christianity and the Arts at King's College London, the author of the 2013 Lent Book *Abiding*, and Canon Theologian of Coventry and Bradford Cathedrals.

Christina Rees CBE is a writer, broadcaster, communications consultant and practical theologian. For many years she was a member of the General Synod and Archbishops' Council and a leading campaigner for women's ordination.

Sarah Rowland Jones was a mathematician, then a British diplomat with postings in Jordan and Hungary, before ordination in the Church in Wales. After 11 years as researcher to successive Archbishops of Cape Town, she returned to Wales, and is now the Dean of St Davids.

David Runcorn is a writer, speaker, spiritual director and theological teacher. He is currently Associate Director of Ordinands and Warden of Readers in the diocese of Gloucester.

Jeanette Sears formerly taught Christian Doctrine and Church History at Trinity College Bristol. She is now a freelance writer and carer. Her latest novel is *Murder and Mr Rochester* (www.jeanettesears.com).

Tim Sledge is vicar of Romsey Abbey and Area Dean. Prior to this he was Mission Enabler in the Peterborough Diocese. He is author of a number of books including *Mission Shaped Parish* and *Youth Emmaus*.

Tom Smail was a leading Scottish theologian, preacher and writer. He was Vice-Principal and Lecturer in Doctrine at St John's College, Nottingham.

Martyn Snow is the Bishop of Leicester, having previously served as Bishop of Tewkesbury and as a parish priest in Sheffield. He has also worked with CMS in West Africa and has a particular interest in the world Church and in developing mission partnerships.

Harry Steele is an Ordained Pioneer Minister in the Church of England, currently serving as the Bishop's Interim Minister in Sheffield Diocese. He serves on the national Leading Your Church into Growth Team and is chaplain to the Sheffield Sharks Basketball team.

Angela Tilby is a Canon Emeritus of Christ Church Cathedral, Oxford. A former BBC producer she was Tutor and Vice-Principal of Westcott House, Cambridge for ten years and then vicar of St Bene't's Church, Cambridge.

Frances Ward is Dean of St Edmundsbury in Suffolk. She is the Diocesan Environmental Officer, on General Synod, and a Trustee of the National Society. Her latest book is *Why Rousseau Was Wrong.*

Keith Ward is a Fellow of the British Academy, Emeritus Regius Professor of Divinity, Oxford, a Canon of Christ Church Cathedral, Oxford, and Senior Research Fellow at Heythrop College, London.

Margaret Whipp is the Lead Chaplain for the Oxford University Hospitals. She has served in parish ministry, university chaplaincy, and most recently as Senior Tutor at Ripon College Cuddesdon.

Catherine Williams is an Anglican priest working as a Selection Secretary for the Ministry Division of the Archbishops' Council. Her ministerial priorities are vocational discernment, prayer and spiritual direction.

Jane Williams lectures at St Mellitus College, London and Chelmsford, and is a Visiting Lecturer at King's College London. She taught previously at Trinity Theological College, Bristol.

Lucy Winkett is Rector of St James's Piccadilly. Formerly Canon Precentor of St Paul's Cathedral and a professional singer, she writes for the national press and broadcasts regularly on radio.

Christopher Woods is a vicar in Stepney, East London, also working in the Stepney Training and Development office. Before that he was Secretary to the Church of England's Liturgical Commission and National Worship Adviser.

Jeremy Worthen is the Secretary for Ecumenical Relations and Theology at the Church of England's Council for Christian Unity. His publications include *Responding to God's Call* (Canterbury Press).

About *Reflections for Sundays*

Reflections for Daily Prayer has nourished tens of thousands of Christians with its insightful, informed and inspiring commentary on one of the scripture readings of the day from the Common Worship lectionary for Morning Prayer. Its contributors over the years have included many outstanding writers from across the Anglican tradition who have helped to establish it as one of today's leading daily devotional volumes.

Here, in response to demand, **Reflections for Sundays** offers thoughtful engagement with each of the *Common Worship* principal service readings for Sundays and major holy days. Reflections are provided on:

● each Old Testament reading (both Continuous and Related)
● the Epistle
● the Gospel.

Commentary on the psalm of the day can be found in the companion volume, **Reflections on the Psalms**.

In addition, Paula Gooder provides a specially commissioned introduction to the Gospel of Luke, while contributions from 52 distinguished writers ensure a breadth of approach.

Combining new writing with selections from the weekday volumes published over the past ten years, **Reflections for Sundays** offers a rich resource for preaching, study and worship preparation.

An introduction to Luke's Gospel

One of the greatest gifts we have in the Gospels is the gift of four accounts: four voices (if not more) telling us the story of who Jesus was, what he did and how he lived. Each of these 'voices' helps us to see different aspects of Jesus' character. The problem we have, however, is that though the stories are told four ways, our brains often hear them as one, conflating the multiple strands and emphases into a harmonious whole. This is a natural and normal response. Our minds are much better at remembering a single narrative than they are at recalling multiple, nuanced accounts.

The great virtue of the lectionary, however, is that we are encouraged to disentangle the threads of the Gospel narratives and to hear them one at a time (or in the case of Year B, to hear both Mark and John alongside each other) so that we can hear the particular concerns or emphases that characterize that particular Gospel. As we begin a new lectionary year, therefore, it is worth pausing and reflecting on what stands out about Luke's Gospel. What its motifs, themes and concerns are. What we should be straining our ears to hear as we listen to the Gospel through the year.

It is, perhaps, easier to discern Luke's particular concerns than in any other Gospel, because Luke tells us at the start in 1.1-4 what he thinks he is doing in writing the Gospel. His opening prologue doesn't tell us everything we want or need to know but it is an excellent place to start. In it, Luke sets out who he is writing to, why he is writing, how he intends to set about it and what he hopes to achieve.

It makes sense, therefore, for an introduction to Luke's Gospel to be guided and shaped by the Gospel's own author. In the first four verses, Luke writes:

> '*Since many have undertaken to set down an orderly account of the events that have been fulfilled among us, [2] just as they were handed on to us by those who from the beginning were eyewitnesses and servants of the word, [3] I too decided, after investigating everything carefully from the very first, to write an orderly account for you, most excellent Theophilus, [4] so that you may know the truth concerning the things about which you have been instructed.' (Luke 1.1-4)*

An 'orderly account'

Luke made it clear from the very first sentence of his Gospel that he was not writing his Gospel from scratch. He was aware of other accounts of Jesus' life that have 'set down' the events of Jesus' life and have been 'handed on to us' by eyewitnesses and servants of the word. This implies that there were multiple other accounts available at the time that Luke was writing, but that he felt that they were, in some way, inadequate to the task of revealing the truth to Theophilus.

Luke even gave a clue as to what he thought was inadequate about the other accounts – a clue that is obscured by the way in which the NRSV has translated the prologue. The NRSV talks about the 'orderly account' set down by the many in verse 1 and indicates that Luke decided to write an 'orderly account' in verse 3. This makes little sense. If Luke thought the other accounts were orderly, why would he write a second orderly account? In fact, this is not quite what the Greek behind the passage conveys. The first use of 'orderly', in verse 1, translates a Greek verb (*anatassomai*), which means to compile, draw up or arrange in order. The second use translates an adverb (*kathexes*), which means in sequence, or one after the other. As you will see, these words are entirely unconnected with each other. Contrary to what the NRSV translation implies, therefore, Luke seems to think that the order of the other accounts is inadequate for conveying the truth of the good news.

A better translation might be something like: 'Whereas many have attempted to compile an account ... it seemed right to me, after investigating everything carefully from the beginning, to write it down point by point, O most excellent Theophilus.' This draws out the sense that Luke felt the other accounts were not up to scratch and he intended to do a much better job in his Gospel.

This alerts us to the importance of the order of Luke's account. Luke 1.3 indicates that Luke has carefully and deliberately laid out his narrative of the life and ministry of Jesus in an order that underpins what he is trying to say and which will, ultimately, be persuasive. This in its turn suggests that, as we read Luke, we should pay close attention – even more than we do in other Gospels – to the way in which this account is ordered, since Luke alerts us to the fact that he has researched it carefully and set it down in a particular order so that it can be as persuasive as possible. Once alert to the intentional ordering of the Gospel, it is easy to see various patterns and organisational motifs running throughout.

For example, the Gospel begins and ends in the temple (with Zechariah in chapter 1 and the disciples in chapter 24) and has as its midpoint Jesus' turning of his face towards Jerusalem (9.51). This emphasizes the point that however gentile this Gospel may be (on this, see more below), its story focuses on and around Jerusalem and its temple.

It is also interesting to note that Luke often signals themes that will emerge a little later in the text in order to prepare the reader for their importance. For example, just after Jesus set his face towards Jerusalem in 9.51 and half a chapter before the parable of the Good Samaritan in 10.25-37, Jesus and his disciples passed through a Samaritan village that did not welcome them, causing the disciples to want to rain down fire on them from heaven. This motif alerts a reader/hearer who may not have known about the historic enmity between the Jews and the Samaritans that, when a Samaritan appears half a chapter later, they should regard him with suspicion. Not only that, but the parable of the Good Samaritan, which in various ways is about the giving and receiving of help regardless of enmity, is followed immediately by the story of Martha and Mary (10.38-42). This story reminds us that activism, though good ('Go and do likewise', 10.37), should sometimes be balanced with time to sit at the feet of the master ('Mary has chosen the better part', 10.42).

All of this reminds us that, when reading Luke, we need to be even more alert than usual to what lies before and after the passage in hand. Luke has stitched his narrative together 'in order', an order that he believes will convey a message. We miss something important in the Gospel if we forget to notice the careful and thoughtful laying out of its narratives and themes.

'After investigating everything carefully... so that you might know the truth'

As we have already noted, Luke claimed that his Gospel was carefully researched (1.3). Indeed, the language he used here and in the rest of the prologue suggests that he was consciously writing as a historian of his day would have done. It was common in the Roman world to write a prologue to a history that laid out the author's motivation for writing and what they intended to achieve by doing so. For example, the Jewish historian Josephus, who wrote towards the end of the first century AD (in other words, depending on when you date Luke's Gospel, within a few decades of the writing of the Gospel) wrote a prologue in which he noted the inadequacy of other histories and laid out why he had decided to write his own history of the Jews (Josephus, *Antiquities of the Jews* 1.1-4).

This is where the connection becomes even more interesting. Josephus thought that other histories perverted the truth, so he wanted to tell the account again so that those reading might know the truth of what had happened. Like Luke, he believed that the job of a good historian was to be persuasive. This is, perhaps, one of the greatest differences between ancient and modern history. Much (though not all) modern history seeks the maximum level of objectivity. Ancient historians, in contrast, appear to hold different principles – often declaring their bias at the start of a narrative in the hope that it would then be as persuasive as possible.

Although Luke's Gospel does, in some ways, bear similarities to the writings of other ancient historians, some scholars have suggested that it is closer to an ancient biography. Ancient biographies often did not tell the whole story of a person's life. Instead, they often began with an account of a person's birth, ended with an account of their death and in between contained a sample of what they did and said, intended to give the reader a flavour of the life they had lived.

Whether intended as a history or a biography, Luke's prologue makes it clear that his narrative was designed to be transformative, to present the narrative in so persuasive a way that its readers could not help but be influenced by what Luke thought to be the truth of what he was proclaiming.

'Fulfilled among us'

Luke's language about fulfilment in the prologue is also significant. Luke did not think that the events of Jesus' life had just 'happened' – they were the culmination and fulfilment of the hopes and dreams of the Jewish people. This allows him to say that they were 'fulfilled among us'. Luke went out of his way in the Gospel to demonstrate how promises were fulfilled.

An interesting example of this can be found in the birth narratives. The Gospel opens with the foretelling of the birth of John, a birth that takes place at the end of the first chapter. This narrative is wrapped around the foretelling of Jesus' birth to Mary. This technique – known by scholars as an 'inclusio' – exists in part to demonstrate that what is promised will always come true. This reminds the reader right at the start of the Gospel to be alert to any promises that they may encounter as the story unfolds, safe in the knowledge that these promises will always be fulfilled.

This theme of prophecy and fulfilment can also be found in some of the historical books of the Old Testament – Deuteronomy, Joshua, Judges, 1 and 2 Samuel, and 1 and 2 Kings, known collectively as the Deuteronomistic histories. In those books, every promise made is seen to be fulfilled, even if the reader has to wait through three or four books for it to happen. In picking up this technique, Luke appears to be placing his Gospel in the tradition of these historical books. It is even more interesting to notice that Luke, alone of all the Gospel writers, wrote a two-volume work – Luke and Acts – or as one might say 1 and 2 Luke. This suggests that, in his mind, Luke was picking up the narrative of the story of God's people where 2 Kings left off. 2 Kings ended with God's people in exile; Luke marks the start of a grand return from exile – the redemption of Jerusalem, as Anna put it in Luke 2.38. Luke's Gospel, therefore, was not 'just' a history but the tale of the fulfilment and redemption of God's people, who had waited hundreds of years for this fulfilment to happen.

Theophilus

The prologues, of both Luke and of Acts, are, unusually, addressed to a particular person – Theophilus. The frustrating feature of this is that beyond his name we know nothing of this person. Some think that he might have been a wealthy patron who, as often happened in Rome, had commissioned Luke to write a Gospel for him. Perhaps he had heard the story of Jesus and wanted to know more? If this is true, then Luke's telling of the story as an 'old, old story' that found its roots deep in the Old Testament would have been significant, since in Roman culture the more ancient something was, the more reliable it was perceived to be. The best aristocratic families in Rome all traced their roots back to the founding of the city as a sign of their standing and trustworthiness.

There is, however, another option. Some people suggest that Theophilus was not a real person at all but a 'type'. The name Theophilus in Greek means simply 'lover of God' and therefore Luke might have been writing to anyone for whom the title 'lover of God' was accurate. If this is true, the title is an invitation to anyone who loved God to read his story and decide for themselves about the truth that he was telling.

The audience of this Gospel, then, remains elusive, but, even then, is not quite as elusive as the author himself. Throughout this introduction, I been calling the author 'Luke' because that is what Christian tradition has done for around 2000 years.

The tradition arose relatively early. One of the earliest known manuscripts of Luke's Gospel (P75) dated by most people to between 175 and 225 AD has at the end of its text 'The Gospel according to Luke'. This ascription is supported in the writings of certain Church Fathers such as Irenaeus (*Adversus Haereses* 3.1.1) and Tertullian (*Adversus Marcionem* 4.2.2).

People like Ireneaus further made the link between this Luke and the Luke reported in the Pauline epistles as being the companion of Paul. In Paul's letters, Luke is variously mentioned as a fellow labourer (Philemon 24), as someone who accompanied Paul (2 Timothy 4.11) and as a physician (Colossians 4.14). The link is also sometimes made, though less convincingly, with the Lucius mentioned in Romans 16.21 who is related to Paul. This tradition seems to be upheld by the number of times in Acts that the author slips into the plural when talking of Paul and what he did, implying that the author of Acts was there with Paul acting as his companion (e.g. 'When he had seen the vision, we immediately tried to cross over to Macedonia, being convinced that God had called us to proclaim the good news to them', Acts 16.10).

If this Luke (the author of the Gospel) and that Luke (the companion of Paul) are one and the same person, then two further pieces of information become available.

First, Luke, the companion of Paul, is said in Colossians 4.10-14 to have been a physician and a gentile. However, these two well-known 'facts' are not easily verified from the Gospel. Luke shows no more interest in human physiology or in the acts of healing than any other of the Gospel writers.

Second, and even more intriguing, is the fact that, other than a few inaccuracies of geography, Luke's Gospel reveals a very good knowledge of Judaism and its practices and, even more important, a deep knowledge of the Old Testament in both Greek and Hebrew (we know this because at times the Greek version – known as the Septuagint or LXX – differs considerably from the Hebrew text; sometimes Luke is clearly quoting from one and sometime from the other). If Luke was a gentile, he knew the Scriptures very well indeed and was able to quote from them adeptly and accurately. This suggests that if he was a gentile, he might well have been a God-fearer – a gentile drawn to Judaism but who hadn't converted to it.

As with all the other Gospel writers, Luke remains something of a mystery. He might have been a companion of Paul, might have been a physician and might have been a gentile, but, as most good writers do, he focused so hard on pointing us, the readers, to his subject that he faded into obscurity behind his text. Luke's prologue tells us a lot about Luke's Gospel – why he wrote it; how he went about writing it; what he was trying to achieve and what effect he wanted it to have on its readers – but very little at all about who Luke was or when he was writing.

Conclusions

Luke's prologue is a consciously elegant opening to the Gospel. Scholars note that these first four verses (mirrored only by the final two verses of Acts) are written in careful and perfectly honed Greek. It would be hard to conceive of an opening that was more polished than this one. In doing so, Luke alerts us to its significance. The prologue is, if you like, reading notes for the Gospel. If you want to know what to look for as you read, Luke has provided the key at the start.

Of course, the prologue does not alert us to the many theological themes that are important in Luke, such as Luke's emphasis on care for outsiders of all sorts or the unfolding of the themes of salvation and testing. These are themes that begin to unfurl as the Gospel progresses. In the prologue Luke focuses simply on one theological theme: knowing the truth about what you have heard. This theme underpins all the others and sets us on the right path for appreciating Luke's grand narrative, which stretches from the beginning to the end of the Gospel: the revelation of Jesus, the bringer of salvation.

First Sunday of Advent

Jeremiah 33.14-16
Psalm 25.1-9
I Thessalonians 3.9-end
Luke 21.25-36

Jeremiah 33.14-16

'The Lord is our righteousness' (v.16)

The name 'The Lord is our righteousness' (*Yahweh-Tsidkenu*) appears twice in Jeremiah. In chapter 23, it is the name given to the Davidic king whom God will raise up as a righteous branch and who will 'deal wisely, and shall execute justice and righteousness in the land' (Jeremiah 23.5). Here, it is the new name given to Jerusalem when that king appears, enabling the country to be saved and the city to live in safety. There is a relational link between the nature of the leadership and the identity of the city.

Relationship is a key aspect of righteousness in the Hebrew Bible. To be righteous implies a correct relationship to the will of God, expressed through obedience to the covenant; it also implies a correct relationship with other people, demonstrated through upholding justice and peace within the community.

We may not often think of ourselves as righteous. Perhaps we are more likely to use the term in a derogatory manner with the prefix 'self-' referring to someone sanctimonious, but we have been made righteous by Christ (Philippians 3.9). It is not just a king anticipated long ago who bears the name *Yahweh-Tsidkenu*, but it has been given to us too. The new name of every Christian is 'Christ is my righteousness'. The beginning of the Church year, when we anticipate the advent of the Righteous One, provides an opportunity to explore what it means to be righteous in our own context, and to foster relationships that will bring about justice and peace in our cities and communities.

Reflection by **Helen Orchard**

Jeremiah 33.14-16
Psalm 25.1-9
I Thessalonians 3.9-end
Luke 21.25-36

1 Thessalonians 3.9-end

'... may the Lord make you increase and abound in love'
(v.12)

This chapter is a wonderful manifestation of the power of the written letter in the early Christian world. Paul has grieved at not being able to be physically present with his new converts. He has worried about them, anxious that in his absence they might have turned away from the faith under the pressure of public hostility and persecution. But now Timothy has brought encouraging news, and Paul writes to express his joy that the Thessalonian converts are still standing firm and growing in faith and love.

The letter is the way in which Paul continues to build up the relationship, while still longing for and praying for an opportunity to visit them in person. Face to face is, of course, the heart of relationship, where 'with unveiled faces' (2 Corinthians 3.18) Christians behold the glory of God in one another. When Paul speaks of restoring 'whatever is lacking in your faith', he may be speaking not of a deficiency in their faith but more of a completion that would be brought by his presence.

Christians are meant to build one another up and support one another, appreciating the gifts of others and the ways in which others are different. How might the exchange of cards, messages and greetings at this time of year help to build people up in faith and mutual concern?

Reflection by **Angela Tilby**

Jeremiah 33.14-16
Psalm 25.1-9
I Thessalonians 3.9-end
Luke 21.25-36

Luke 21.25-36

'...the kingdom of God is near' (v.31)

Today, we hit one of biblical criticism's old chestnuts. Jesus appears to say, here and elsewhere, that the kingdom would come – the Son of Man would return – before some of his contemporaries ('this generation') had died. I've heard many thoughtful (and some specious!) attempts to explain these words. My own modest conclusion is that Jesus probably did say something like this but, in a straightforward, literal sense, it didn't happen.

This is not the place for lengthy exploration, but I am left with two thoughts. The first is the sense that Christ's 'return' is always imminent. This could feel like a straitjacket – better not be tipsy when he returns! Or we could take it as a call to action. We live in hard times for the Church. Ministry is often a struggle. The language of 'spiritual warfare' resonates with my experience of parish life. So I hear Christ saying: 'Don't be distracted. Be at "action stations", ready to respond energetically to whatever comes at you.'

More deeply, it feels like the kingdom is close again. Out of the current struggles of the Church in the West, a new Church will be born to serve the kingdom in new ways. For this task, we need to pray to see clearly and to be ready to move swiftly.

Reflection by **Alan Bartlett**

Baruch 5 *or* **Malachi 3.1-4**
Canticle: Benedictus
Philippians 1.3-11
Luke 3.1-6

Second Sunday of Advent

Malachi 3.1-4

'I am sending my messenger to prepare the way before me'
(v.1)

They say that there are two ways to try to remove a dragon from its lair so you can steal its treasure. Some knights take the direct approach and try to slay the dragon; others use cunning and coax the dragon out. The same can be true of any problem, including warning people of coming judgement.

The messenger is to prepare the way. Exactly what this involves we are not told, but we can guess, given that the Lord will come suddenly to the temple; he will be like a refiner's fire and fuller's soap; he will sit as a refiner and purifier of silver. The messenger's task then is to warn people. But there are different ways of doing this.

Christians take this passage in Malachi to refer to the birth of John the Baptist. John certainly took the direct approach. He didn't mince his words and made the consequences of not listening abundantly clear.

Through the rest of the New Testament we see other ways of being a messenger. Sometimes it is about persuasion (2 Corinthians 5.11); sometimes it involves argument (Acts 17.17); sometimes it is like snatching someone from a fire (Jude v.23). Deciding what is right for any given context and people is one of the primary skills all followers of Jesus Christ need to learn. For we have all been commissioned as messengers (Matthew 28.18-20).

Reflection by **Martyn Snow**

Second Sunday of Advent

Baruch 5 *or* Malachi 3.1-4
Canticle: Benedictus
Philippians 1.3-11
Luke 3.1-6

Philippians 1.3-11

*'And this is my prayer, that your love may overflow
more and more' (v.9)*

Aesop tells of a wren who hid in the feathers on the eagle's back, to win the competition to decide who was the king of birds. When the eagle had flown to the greatest height that he could, the wren flew just a little bit further.

This illustrates a paradox in the relation between comparatives and superlatives: 'betters' and 'bests'. The trouble with superlatives is that they suggest an end-point. And once such a point is imagined, we find ourselves thinking (like the wren) what a little bit beyond it might look like. The 'little bit more' makes the 'most' look like it has fallen short.

God is never an end-point. In God there is always more. Paul conjures up this mind-blowing abundance in this passage. He instructs his hearers to 'determine what is best', but 'what is best' (life with God) is known in the experience of a love that 'overflows more and more'. In such a love there is no satiation point and the delight never palls.

Even the eagle tires, and even the wren who goes that little bit higher would tire too if forced to keep going up. But God's perfection – God's 'bestness' – is not like that. As C. S. Lewis' children found as they moved into the 'real Narnia' at the end of *The Last Battle*, heaven has no borders and no limits: there is no end to going 'further up and further in!'.

Reflection by **Ben Quash**

Second Sunday of Advent

Luke 3.1-6

*'... the word of God came to John son of Zechariah
in the wilderness' (v.2)*

You can't do things by half measure if you are trying to talk about John the Baptist! As a friend of mine once mused: remember God's chosen people are not God's frozen people! The word is out, on the move, and where John is concerned, it's moving at quite a pace! Luke's Gospel might actually have once started with these verses, in a manner similar to Mark. Luke's use of named political leaders to date the ministry of John reminds us that his story is set in the realities of the Roman Empire with its means of imperial administration, and this is a recurrent emphasis in his text.

John is introduced as a prophet – one to whom the word of God came – but his own words emphasize that his role is one of preparation for another. John's heralding message is not for polite murmurings, you might say. It is an announcement that there is a changed state of affairs. The political, social and cultural scene has changed beyond recognition; watch out, take note, be encouraged, join in, because this is a message that requires all of us to play our part as disciples.

Luke includes the names of two characters that will play an important role in the later part of the story, Pilate and Herod. This is a reminder of the connections that we ought to be making. You can't compartmentalize the story; there is a 'big picture' that must be borne in mind.

Reflection by **Helen-Ann Hartley**

Third Sunday of Advent

Zephaniah 3.14-end
Canticle: Isaiah 12.2-end*
Philippians 4.4-7
Luke 3.7-18

Zephaniah 3.14-end

'The Lord, your God, is in your midst' (v.17)

Into the confusions of our bad judgement, the paranoia of our fear and the delusions of our misplaced hope, God himself enters with joy. This is the Advent hope: daughter of Zion, sing and exult with all your heart, the Lord has taken away all his judgements, the holy one is in your midst. 'The Virgin is with child,' says Isaiah, 'and will bear a son and you will name him Emmanuel.' This is the Christmas message: God is with us – the basis of our hope and the source of our deliverance. God will remove every disaster and restore all our fortunes. It won't be as we expect or according to our schedules. But it will be glorious. The writs against us will be torn up. The pleadings of our heart will be answered. We will behold and receive God in the only language we really understand: the language of another human life.

And this will be challenging. God will be just as forgiving with those who have hurt me as with those I have hurt. God will ask me to hold them and help them. God will bring everything into light. Like an artist patiently bringing to completion the emerging portrait on the canvas, God will work on me. God is becoming what we are so that we can know and receive what God is.

Reflection by **Stephen Cottrell**

Zephaniah 3.14-end
Canticle: **Isaiah 12.2-end***
Philippians 4.4-7
Luke 3.7-18

Third Sunday of Advent

Isaiah 12.2-end

'Shout aloud and sing for joy' (v.6)

To draw water with joy from the wells of salvation and to give thanks to God, singing praises and shouting aloud of the greatness of the holiness of God, is indeed the highest form of human worship: 'God listens to me when I pray, but God loves me when I sing.' This is to be the calling and destiny of the people. This will come from a deep appreciation of God's saving grace and liberating comfort. This is to name the worth-ship of God: to celebrate the great value that God is to us and within us, because we have been ransomed, healed, restored and forgiven. As the Jesuit theologian Teilhard de Chardin once said: 'Worship is ... to lose oneself in the unfathomable, to plunge into the inexhaustible, to find peace in the incorruptible ... to give of one's deepest to that whose depth has no end.'

The message of hope in the act of worship described is not for a special clique or a single city. It is a proclamation of God's name in all the earth. Those who sing do so for the whole world, and so we are reminded that worship in a particular congregation is actually centred in God's concern for everyone and every nation. This worth-ship of God finally enriches our own worth as part of the great worth of all that lives and breathes.

Reflection by **David Moxon**

Third Sunday of Advent

Zephaniah 3.14-end
Canticle: Isaiah 12.2-end*
Philippians 4.4-7
Luke 3.7-18

Philippians 4.4-7

'Do not worry about anything' (v.6)

'Do not worry about anything' is a command much easier said than done. On one level it is obvious. God is sovereign and will provide for all my needs, so there should be no need to worry. The trouble is, it's not always that easy to allow that head knowledge to invade my heart and mind.

Anxiety, stress, fear are things that beset us so readily, and it is so difficult to stop worrying by ourselves. I remember when I was ill a few years ago and I was told that 'worrying would only make it worse'. That made me even more anxious!

Paul seems to have cracked it. He has learned to be content in every situation. 'Rejoice!' has become his byword. But he goes on to say that he has 'learned' to be content (Philippians 4.11). That implies that it was not always so. For Paul, the absolute belief that there really is no need to worry is hard won from living through the good times and the very, very bad. Paul has learned that God is faithful, and his resurrection perspective helps him to see the challenges of life in the light of eternity.

Not worrying is something we cannot easily do by ourselves. But we can learn over time to trust God, increasingly bringing everything (large and small) to him in prayer, letting the knowledge that he is near seep into our hearts and souls bringing peace, gradually allowing him to turn our worry into his contentment.

Reflection by **Emma Ineson**

Zephaniah 3.14-end
Canticle: Isaiah 12.2-end*
Philippians 4.4-7
Luke 3.7-18

Third Sunday of Advent

Luke 3.7-18

'... the axe is lying at the root of the trees' (v.9)

I once saw a preacher ask the congregation to move seats. Slowly, and resentfully, they did so, but it took a long and sluggish time. The preacher continued, 'If it's taken so much effort just to change seats, imagine what it's going to take to change your life'.

I suspect John the Baptist would have approved. He preached in the wilderness, and people had to make the effort to go out of their way to hear him. That was the first step. The second, he said, was to repent. This does not mean simply apologizing. It means making a U-turn in life, showing in practic ways that you mean what you say about regrets and the need for amendments. Only in the space that opens up in such recognition can God's forgiveness change the full stops of your life into commas.

Only Luke spells out John's ethical teaching. John focuses on those who are in positions where exploitation can be too easy or can go unchallenged – those with wealth, authority and power. John is preaching the uncomfortable truth that the social form of love is justice, and that we all need judgement – a reality check on ourselves – in order to be liberated into lives of integrity. Only by understanding love better will we be prepared for the Lord. John is fulfilling Zechariah's hope that he would 'turn the hearts of ... the disobedient to the wisdom of the righteous' (Luke 1.17).

Reflection by **Mark Oakley**

Fourth Sunday of Advent

Micah 5.2-5a
Canticle: Magnificat *or*
Psalm 80.1-8
Hebrews 10.5-10
Luke 1.39-45 [46-55]

Micah 5.2-5a

'... and he shall be the one of peace' (v.5)

In 701 BC, Sennacherib, the Assyrian Emperor, invaded Judah and appointed Hezekiah as a vassal king. Sennacherib is best remembered now as the creator of Nineveh, and some claim he created the Hanging Gardens, traditionally located in Babylon.

Many biblical scholars believe the first three chapters of Micah are contemporary with Sennacherib's invasion of Judah. Later chapters in Micah, including chapter 5, were probably composed during or just after the Jewish Exile to Babylon in the sixth century BC.

So, it's a bit confusing. But a powerful theme runs through the entire book: Israel should obey the law of God and not go a-whoring after other gods. In fact, what the people of Israel should do, according to the author(s) of Micah, is straightforward; they are required 'to do justice, and to love kindness, and to walk humbly with your God' (Micah 6.8).

It is a lovely summary of what constitutes ethical behaviour. But that behaviour has a future theological dimension. As Micah says, a king will arise who will embody those moral precepts and peace will prevail across the earth.

The early Church believed that that prophecy was fulfilled in Jesus. But, two thousand years later, we know that peace does not yet prevail. How can we handle the dilemma? Perhaps by saying that we live between 'now' and 'not yet': Christ is with us now; fulfilment is still to come. Our task is to live faithfully in those two dimensions.

Reflection by **Christopher Herbert**

Micah 5.2-5*a*
Canticle: Magnificat *or*
Psalm 80.1-8
Hebrews 10.5-10
Luke 1.39-45 [46-55]

Fourth Sunday of Advent

Hebrews 10.5-10

'I have come to do your will' (v.7)

The prophets and psalmists of the Hebrew Scriptures have already begun to sow the seed of the knowledge that animal sacrifice is not really what God is interested in. These kinds of sacrifice are attempts to placate God, almost to divert God's attention from the behaviour they are trying to atone for. They acknowledge the problem, but refuse to see that the solution cannot be applied externally. What the sacrifices do not do is to change the hearts and wills of the people who offer them. But that is what God longs for.

The quotation from Psalm 40 makes the point: Jesus has come to do God's will.

And so everything changes today. Now, we know that what God offers is a relationship in which we can work with God, knowing him intimately, being part of his purposes for the world. We can't hide behind rituals and ceremonies any more; God has come close, to know and be known.

If that is frighteningly open ended, it is also liberating. We no longer have to worry about whether our sacrifice has 'worked' to keep God satisfied, because no more sacrifices are required. All that is asked of us is that we come to God, in the company of Jesus, and say the words that he has taught us, 'I have come to do your will'.

Reflection by **Jane Williams**

Fourth Sunday of Advent

Micah 5.2-5*a*
Canticle: Magnificat *or*
Psalm 80.1-8
Hebrews 10.5-10
Luke 1.39-45 [46-55]

Luke 1.39-45 [46-55]

'... blessed is she who believed' (v.45)

Today's passage relates the joyful meeting between Mary and her older relative Elizabeth, as together they give thanks for their pregnancies and the divine significance of the children they will bear. Luke describes a very specific timescale: Mary's pregnancy is in its earliest stages, while Elizabeth's is five months advanced. Mary stays with Elizabeth for three months, and returns home a short time before Elizabeth gives birth.

There is huge divine importance in this meeting, but by being so specific about the time, Luke also conveys its practical significance. Mary must surely have valued the reassurance and wisdom of the older woman, and Mary's company must have been a welcome relief to Elizabeth, who to this point had endured her pregnancy in seclusion and with a mute husband! This practical reality makes Elizabeth's words especially heartfelt: '... blessed is she who believed that there would be a fulfilment of what was spoken to her by the Lord'.

What does belief mean for us? We sometimes think doubt is a betrayal of faith, but this has never been the case. Even Jesus had moments of struggle – 'My God, my God, why have you forsaken me?' (Matthew 27.46). Faith without doubt is not faith, but a kind of certainty that we cannot have this side of heaven. As Paul famously stated, 'Now I know only in part; then I will know fully, even as I have been fully known' (1 Corinthians 13.12).

Reflection by **Barbara Mosse**

2 Samuel 7.1-5, 8-11, 16
Psalm 89.2, 19-27
Acts 13.16-26
Luke 1.67-79

Christmas Eve

24 December

2 Samuel 7.1-5, 8-11, 16

'Are you the one to build me a house to live in?' (v.5)

There is something cussedly contrary about us humans. The American playwright Thornton Wilder once said: 'When you're safe at home, you wish you were having an adventure; when you are having an adventure, you wish you were safe at home.'

It was a theme known to the earliest Jewish people. One of their foundational stories related how as a group of nomadic tribes they had wandered in the desert where, they claimed, God had wandered with them. Unsettled, they were always moving on, yet were brought eventually to the Promised Land where there were cities, villages and farms; places where, adventuring over, they could settle down.

Their subsequent history was of a constant tension between their nomadic origins and their need for stability. The same tension was reflected in the desire to settle God down as well, to build a place for him to dwell in. Yet, by definition, God is beyond such human contrivance. It is absurd to assume that the God of the infinite reaches of the Universe can be domesticated, even in the most beautiful of temples – unless, of course, he himself chooses to be so limited.

At the birth of Christ we believe that this is exactly what happened. God's self-limitation, however, was neither into a place nor into a building, but was in and through a person. And thereby he was let loose in our world in a new and wondrous way, a way that has no boundaries.

Reflection by **Christopher Herbert**

Christmas Eve	2 Samuel 7.1-5, 8-11, 16
	Psalm 89.2, 19-27
24 December	**Acts 13.16-26**
	Luke 1.67-79

Acts 13.16-26

'... to us the message of this salvation has been sent' (v.26)

To many people in society, Jesus makes this one brief appearance in their lives, at Christmas, in a carol service, a nativity play or a nostalgic memory. Today's reading takes a much longer view, as Paul demonstrates to his hearers in the synagogue at Antioch how the birth of Jesus fits into the big picture of God's purposes. In particular, Jesus comes from the royal line of David, the iconic king of Israel. Paul then zooms through history to John the Baptist, who was the forerunner, the early warning, of the promised Saviour. Paul was trying to get his Jewish audience on board by telling them their own story, but adding a thrilling new chapter.

The world is excited by tomorrow's event, but the Church is excited by the whole story and the way in which this child grew up, fulfilled his destiny and launched the kingdom project through his life, death and resurrection. The Church has a magnificent story to tell, one that encompasses everything from creation to the world's final curtain. But what that story does for the world it also does for each person, setting our story in the context of the flow of God's love through the length of our days.

Jesus is for life, not just for Christmas.

Reflection by **John Pritchard**

2 Samuel 7.1-5, 8-11, 16
Psalm 89.2, 19-27
Acts 13.16-26
Luke 1.67-79

Luke 1.67-79

'... the dawn from on high will break upon us' (v.78)

Tonight many of us will do something very strange. We will sit in a church in the middle of the night. What part of us will draw us there to do that? Might that part of us be, somehow, our better part?

In the City of London between 1400 and 1560, it was forbidden to wear party masks in the street during Christmas. There had been too many muggings. This seems an appropriate way of celebrating the season when God takes off his mask to reveal himself in a stable outhouse. To come to church tonight might be a first step towards acknowledging that our masks eat into our faces, and we need help to live without them in our longing to be free.

Zechariah lays out before us what a more God-distilled life will look like. We will be removed from hate and immersed in an experience of mercy. We will put aside our fears and will be people who understand the beauty of forgiveness. In this way we will be better equipped to bring light and peace into the lives of those around us. This was his hope for his own son John. It may be our hope for ourselves too as, honestly admitting our poverty and dislocation, we seek in the darkness a new birth within.

Reflection by **Mark Oakley**

Christmas Day

25 December
Principal Feast

[1] *Set I readings:*
Isaiah 9.2-7
Psalm 96
Titus 2.11-14
Luke 2.1-14 [15-20]

Isaiah 9.2-7

'Prince of Peace' (v.6)

In the midst of chaos, war or busyness, we long for a peace that marks an end and, after a pause for rest, heralds a new beginning.

Isaiah depicts the reign of the Prince of Peace as bringing an end to oppression. He frees humanity by breaking the burdensome yokes, which he depicts as bars heavy across the shoulders of the oppressed. The Prince of Peace, unlike Atlas, the Titan, who was condemned to hold up the sky with his shoulders, carries the authority for governing the world easily. The authority rests upon his shoulders and as Wonderful Counsellor he can fulfil the responsibilities of governing not only to end war and injustice, but also to establish peace. This is because the peace of God grows from the inside out.

We often imagine ourselves with the cares of the world on our shoulders and can find it difficult to lay them down. Jesus called those who felt burdened or heavy laden to go to him. He promised rest, an easy yoke and a light burden (Matthew 11.30). When we can pause and rest, we can more easily glimpse God, and see light in darkness. This emerging hope enables a new beginning in us and for our world. Christ's peace grows within us and becomes established as we grow in love.

This peace is a gift given to be shared.

Reflection by **Justine Allain Chapman**

[1] *There are three sets of readings for use on Christmas Night and Christmas Day. Set III should be used at some service during the celebration.*

Set I readings:
Isaiah 9.2-7
Psalm 96
Titus 2.11-14
Luke 2.1-14 [15-20]

Christmas Day

25 December
Principal Feast

Titus 2.11-14

'... the grace of God has appeared' (v.11)

On Christmas Day it may feel as if we need a little more excitement than renouncing impiety and worldly passions, or living lives that are self-controlled, upright and godly. But in the letter to Titus we're in the rapidly developing world of the early Church, where the earlier passion of an explosive new movement is giving way to the needs of the Church to organize itself for the longer term, and to regularize Christian behaviour in a way that's seemly and sustainable in times of persecution.

However, these more prosaic practices are set in the context of two of the most dynamic, life-changing doctrines of the faith, namely the astonishing fact that the grace of God has appeared in human form, and the clear expectation that Christ will come again. We have to pray that the message that the divine Author walked on stage at a precise moment in historical time and showed us the best that humanity can ever be, will never fail to thrill us. Many will be unmoved by this glorious truth today, wandering past without interest, but, as Dorothy Sayers wrote, 'If this is dull, then what in heaven's name is worthy to be called exciting?'

The grace – and truth – of God has appeared, and nothing will ever be the same again.

Reflection by **John Pritchard**

Christmas Day

25 December
Principal Feast

Set I readings:
Isaiah 9.2-7
Psalm 96
Titus 2.11-14
Luke 2.1-14 [15-20]

Luke 2.1-14 [15-20]

'... there was no place for them in the inn' (v.7)

This moment in the nativity story is traditionally interpreted as one of outsiders finding no welcome in a foreign town. As such, it is a story that can reflect the feelings and needs of outsiders, foreigners, minority groups, refugees – all who are excluded by society.

But there is another way to read it. The word for 'inn' – *kataluma* – can be translated as 'guest room'. And in first-century houses that have been excavated in the Holy Land, the stable or animal room is not an outhouse, but located at the centre of the house, where the warmth of the animals would radiate through the home.

If Joseph and Mary returned to the town of their origin, and were put up by family, then the guest room would have been full to the brim with people. No place for a baby to be born. But at the centre of the family home was the animals' room. Warm, dry and the only quiet room in the house, it was the best possible place for this young woman to bring her baby into the world.

Were they excluded and representative of outcasts and refugees everywhere? Or was their welcome into the warmest room in the house a lesson in offering Christ the best we have, however humble that may be? Whichever way you read the story, it tells us something about receiving Christ into our lives.

Reflection by **Maggi Dawn**

[1] Set II readings:
Isaiah 62.6-end
Psalm 97
Titus 3.4-7
Luke 2.[1-7] 8-20

Christmas Day
25 December
Principal Feast

Isaiah 62.6-end
'See, your salvation comes ...' (v.11)

There is a restlessness about these verses. Watchmen are appointed on the walls of Jerusalem and they are people of prayer. They act as 'remembrancers' – a slightly archaic political term. In England in the 12th century, the role of King's Remembrancer was created by Henry II to ensure that the king remembered who owed him tax. It still exists as a senior judicial post, and in 2014 Barbara Fontaine was the first woman appointed to the role.

Ancient customs often have modern equivalents. The God who knows every prayer before it is uttered still longs for his people to be remembrancers. The coming of Jesus, born in circumstances of great humility, has inaugurated a kingdom that God is building. It is a kingdom in which salvation comes and forsaken people are redeemed. Everyone who prays, 'Your kingdom come,' today acts as a remembrancer for God.

Creating that kingdom does not come quickly. Working so that the poor and desolate can be renamed with delightful names is laborious but it comes steadily, like the rebuilding of ruined Jerusalem all those centuries ago. Idling away time is not an option. Get building!

The 20th century Japanese reformer Toyohiko Kagawa lived and worked in the slums of Japan. This was his restless reflection: 'I read in a book that a man called Christ went about doing good. It is very disconcerting that I am so easily satisfied with just going about.'

Reflection by **Peter Graystone**

[1] *There are three sets of readings for use on Christmas Night and Christmas Day. Set III should be used at some service during the celebration.*

Christmas Day

25 December
Principal Feast

Set II readings:
Isaiah 62.6-end
Psalm 97
Titus 3.4-7
Luke 2.[1-7] 8-20

Titus 3.4-7

'... according to his mercy' (v.5)

The theologian Sam Wells has helpfully brought our attention to the fact that the Christian faith can be thought of in terms of God – and therefore us too – being 'for' people. Actually, the vital word that is used throughout the Gospels, and especially John's, is 'with'. Emmanuel is 'God with us'. Wells argues that 'for' is a great word, but it doesn't overcome misunderstanding; it doesn't deal with alienation, loneliness or isolation. In a lot of ways 'with' is harder than 'for' because we have to be alongside someone, look at them, hear them, hold them. To be 'with' is the heartbeat of God.

It is good to be reminded by the letter to Titus that it is this God and this God's love that are our only hope. Whereas our bodies can often heal quite nicely by themselves, our souls are not so skilled. They need to be healed from outside, by a love that reaches out and touches us back into wholeness. God did this in Christ, it says, not because we deserved it but because God is mercy, goodness and loving-kindness. God pours himself out to make us heirs, part of the family and inheritors of love. Religion loves debates but never forget, we are told, that this 'saying is sure'.

Both this letter to Titus and the Christmas season celebrate a great truth – that God can never be the object of our knowledge but must always be the cause of our wonder.

Reflection by **Mark Oakley**

Set II readings:
Isaiah 62.6-end
Psalm 97
Titus 3.4-7
Luke 2.[1-7] 8-20

Christmas Day

25 December
Principal Feast

Luke 2.[1-7] 8-20

' ... to you is born this day' (v.11)

In the mass of hype and excessive consumerism that make up the present-day experience of Christmas for most people, it seems increasingly difficult to celebrate the birth of the Christ-child in its simple, truthful essence. What is it, precisely, that so stirs our emotions at this time?

For those of us fortunate enough to have happy experiences of childhood Christmases, the memories will be good, but the baby in the manger may only be one feature among many – the Christmas tree, Santa, carols, family, presents and delicious food. And for those whose memories of Christmas are not happy, they may dread the festive season where everyone else seems to be enjoying themselves and they feel left out in the cold. But whether happy or unhappy, the memories we hold can prevent us from stripping away the inessentials and appreciating the *real* gift that God offers us with the coming of Christ into our world.

Perhaps the angel's message to the shepherds offers us a way forward: 'to you is born this day ... a Saviour, who is the Messiah, the Lord.' The angel addresses us today as urgently as he did the shepherds. Whatever our present situation, or our memories, whether good or bad, Christ is born, today and every day, for you and for me.

Let us seek God, using words from the beautiful carol *O Little Town of Bethlehem*, 'cast out our sin and enter in; be born in us *today*.'

Reflection by **Barbara Mosse**

41

Christmas Day

25 December
Principal Feast

¹ *Set III readings:*
Isaiah 52.7-10
Psalm 98
Hebrews 1.1-4 [5-12]
John 1.1-14

Isaiah 52.7-10

'How beautiful ... are the feet' (v.7)

When Joseph and Mary reached the stable at Bethlehem, they must have been weary. The journey from Nazareth, even with the use of a donkey for a pregnant woman (an assumption made in many nativity plays), was a long one. Our feet frequently bear the burden of a long walk.

It's estimated that in an average lifespan most people will walk 20,000 miles, and sometimes a great deal more. It's the rough equivalent of walking round the world. Our feet have a lot of walking to do, though we tend to take them for granted.

The word in Hebrew, *na-ha*, which we translate as 'beautiful' does not mean pretty or alluring. It's more to do with being appropriate and fitting, entirely aligned with God's purpose. Our feet are beautiful when they do the right work, God's work. In Isaiah, it's the feet of heralds that are beautiful because they are proclaiming a message of freedom for the people of Israel. At Christmas, we think of angels heralding the birth of Jesus Christ. In Romans 10.15, Paul takes this verse and applies it to those who are sent into the world to preach the gospel.

The good news of Jesus Christ, first glimpsed in Bethlehem at the time of this birth, has been carried on foot to every part of the globe in Christian mission. Where have our feet taken us in the service of Christ? And where have we still to travel?

Reflection by **Graham James**

¹ *There are three sets of readings for use on Christmas Night and Christmas Day. Set III should be used at some service during the celebration.*

Set III readings:
Isaiah 52.7-10
Psalm 98
Hebrews 1.1-4 [5-12]
John 1.1-14

Christmas Day
25 December
Principal Feast

Hebrews 1.1-4 [5-12]

'... in these last days he has spoken to us by a Son' (v.2)

Here is the Big Claim on which all other claims of the Christian faith depend. The writer of the letter to the Hebrews dares to say that if we want to know what God is like, here's the answer: it's a Son, a human being who's 'the exact imprint of God's very being'. And on Christmas Day we spell that out even more scandalously: the answer is a few hours old and lies in a cattle feeding trough. Oh and by the way, says the writer, it was through him that God created the worlds (v.2).

If that doesn't leave us breathless, what does? The main comparison that the writer makes in the early chapters of Hebrews is between what the angels do and what the Son does, just as he later compares what the Jewish sacrificial system did and what Jesus did. These may not be things that keep many of us awake at night these days, but in Jewish culture these were vital issues. How was God to be known, and how were human beings to be put right with God?

The technicalities are for different days. On this supreme day it's sufficient simply to stand back and be amazed at God's audacity in pouring God's life into a fragile human form. But this is just the first page of God's autobiography; there's huge excitement to come. Keep reading.

Reflection by **John Pritchard**

Christmas Day

25 December
Principal Feast

Set III readings:
Isaiah 52.7-10
Psalm 98
Hebrews 1.1-4 [5-12]
John 1.1-14

John 1.1-14

'...yet the world did not know him' (v.10)

At the end of the Christmas midnight eucharist in Norwich Cathedral, the great west doors are flung open and John's prologue is read. The gospeller faces the city beyond. There are usually a few Christmas revellers taken by surprise, but since it is around 1 o'clock in the morning, the city is dark and fairly quiet. John's poetic and glorious words about God speaking to the world in Christ ring out – and meet no response. It's a potent symbol. 'He was in the world ... yet the world did not know him.'

The prologue is about the Word. In Jesus, God spoke in all his fullness, holding nothing back. As the distinguished American professor Thomas Gardner says in his remarkable book *John in the Company of Poets*: 'When God spoke Jesus to the world, Jesus was everything he intended to say.'

Behind the gospeller at the midnight eucharist, a huge congregation suggests that even in secular Britain there are those drawn to the 'Word made flesh'. In the prologue, John quickly modifies his assertion that the whole world does not recognize Christ, reminding us that 'to all who received him ... he gave power to become children of God'. At the end of that Christmas eucharist, John's words hang in the air, helping us realize how frequently we live between recognizing Christ and not knowing him, poised between darkness and light. We know, too, we are being addressed directly by the God who speaks in Jesus everything he intended to say.

Reflection by **Graham James**

1 Samuel 2.18-20, 26
Psalm 148*
Colossians 3.12-17
Luke 2.41-end

First Sunday of Christmas

1 Samuel 2.18-20, 26

*'His mother used to make for him a little robe
and take it to him each year' (v.19)*

Trustingly, Hannah gives her son into Eli's care. Samuel is a gift from God, an answer to Hannah's desperate prayer for a child, and her response makes it clear why God sees her and gives her her heart's desire. Although Hannah longs above all else for this gift of a child, she knows that gifts are to be shared, and she gives him back to God (1 Samuel 1.28). The little robe that she makes for him every year is a testimony that she does not do this easily: she carries Samuel's measurements in her heart, even though she sees him so rarely.

Eli blesses Hannah and Elkanah for the 'gift' they have made to God, little realizing how costly that gift was to be for him personally. He spoke lightly of Hannah's sacrifice, but did not expect God to require any such thing from him and his sons.

There are such Christmas echoes in the story of Samuel's start in life: Hannah's song in chapter 2 is a forerunner of Mary's Magnificat; Samuel, like Jesus, grows up in a borrowed family. Perhaps above all, Samuel hints at the nature of God's great gifts. Jesus comes to claim the world and to change all who encounter him; those of us who, like Eli, think of faith as a comfortable sideline should beware.

Reflection by **Jane Williams**

First Sunday of Christmas

I Samuel 2.18-20, 26
Psalm 148*
Colossians 3.12-17
Luke 2.41-end

Colossians 3.12-17

'Above all, clothe yourselves with love' (v.14)

This passage contains a good deal of material that seems to pre-date Paul's letter. It consists mostly of short sayings about community life and worship, used here to emphasize the importance of the disciplines of common life in the body of Christ.

The passage raises the question of how Christian communities today interpret and inhabit the ethics of life in Christ. Do the details of passages like these establish the basis for right relations between people for all time? Do these passages point to key principles for relationships that need translation for new contexts? What are these key principles?

The history of the Church demonstrates that answers are not easily arrived at. Here, however, Paul offers two key ways of orienting ourselves to the endeavours of common discernment and day-to-day Christian living: we should embed our life in meditation on the Scriptures, ensuring that we listen to the discernment of each – and, above all (even when we disagree and find each other hard to understand), we should clothe ourselves with love and a commitment to the whole body.

What opportunities do you have to meditate on the Scriptures with those with whom you profoundly disagree?

Reflection by **Jane Leach**

I Samuel 2.18-20, 26
Psalm 148*
Colossians 3.12-17
Luke 2.41-end

First Sunday of Christmas

Luke 2.41-end

'Why were you searching for me?' (v.49)

This is the only story of Jesus' youth that we have, and it includes Luke's reporting of the first words of Jesus: 'Why were you searching for me? Did you not know that I must be in my Father's house?' Mary has had an awful time – losing her son in the travellers' caravan – and now she is spoken to as if she is not wanted. Simeon's prophecy is already coming true: 'a sword will pierce your own soul' (Luke 2.35).

Luke, however, is revealing the lessons being learned by Mary and Joseph, because they are truths he wants us to understand too. First, Jesus has a natural authority, found in his questioning as much as in any easy answers. As we see later in the Gospel, this boy who scrutinized the religious authorities begins to teach with a persistently figurative style, where the meaning of his stories tends to hover poetically rather than come in easily to land. Such a conversational exploration of the soul was first learned in his Father's house.

The second truth is that Jesus is at home in the temple. Later, Jesus will return there to throw out those who had forgotten it was a place of prayer (Luke 19.45-46). In Luke's Gospel, Jesus prays often. It is the source of his insight. When he tackles the temple traders, he does it out of obedience and love for the one he knows most intimately through this relationship, his Father, and it reflects that early, close, but sometimes painful, relationship with those who loved him most in Nazareth.

Reflection by **Mark Oakley**

Second Sunday of Christmas

Jeremiah 31.7-14
Psalm 147.13-end
Ephesians 1.3-14
John 1.[1-9] 10-18

Jeremiah 31.7-14

*'They shall come and sing aloud on the height of Zion,
and they shall be radiant over the goodness of the Lord'
(v.12)*

We shall soon be celebrating the Epiphany or 'revealing' of Christ's glory in the world, when wise men from the East arrive in Bethlehem and worship the child Jesus as soon as they see him. Today's reading gives us a different glimpse of glory, from an Old Testament perspective. Here Jeremiah promises hope and restoration to the Israelites exiled in Babylon (in the sixth century BC). This poetic passage presents a utopian picture of a vulnerable community (including the blind; the disabled and the pregnant) returning to their own land and finding prosperity and peace after great suffering. The Hebrew verb 'to be radiant' means both 'to flow along' and 'to become bright', suggesting a joyful procession of people who reflect something of the divine light themselves as they recognize God's goodness at work.

Jesus manifests God's radiance, although not in the triumphant or spectacular ways that many expected. His birth, baptism, miracles and even his suffering reveal the divine glory for those with eyes to see (cf. John 2.11, 13.31), and the purpose of his entire ministry is to free us from our own 'exile' experiences of guilt, legalism or despair.

As we ponder the inner healing and new life that Jesus offers, our best response is to seek to be transparent to his light ourselves.

Reflection by **Angela Ashwin**

Jeremiah 31.7-14
Psalm 147.13-end
Ephesians 1.3-14
John 1.[1-9] 10-18

Second Sunday of Christmas

Ephesians 1.3-14

'Blessed ... in Christ with every spiritual blessing' (v.3)

Where is your favourite place? Somewhere you feel relaxed, safe and 'away from it all'? Or perhaps somewhere you are invigorated and find excitement and challenge?

As we begin Ephesians, we are immediately drawn into the favourite place of its author. That place is 'in Christ'. After the initial greeting in verses 1-2, we are plunged into a beautiful and complex prayer of blessing, which extends to verse 14. One of its most striking features, lost in translation, is that it is one continuous sentence in Greek. Even divided up, it is rather overwhelming to read, with its effusive and repetitive language encompassing the full sweep of salvation history. We have here a meditation that begins before the creation of the world, rejoices in the redemption gifted to us in the Beloved and anticipates the summation of all things in the fullness of time. In all that is written about predestination, adoption, wisdom and will, we are returned continually to that favourite place 'in Christ', which – with its variant, 'in him' – is used eleven times in this passage. It is in him that we are blessed, elected, redeemed, sealed and gathered up. It is the place of surest repose and ultimate challenge, to which we can always return, wherever we are actually located.

Reflection by **Helen Orchard**

Second Sunday of Christmas

Jeremiah 31.7-14
Psalm 147.13-end
Ephesians 1.3-14
John 1.[1-9] 10-18

John 1.[1-9] 10-18

'... we have seen his glory' (v. 14)

In this magisterial introduction to his Gospel, the Evangelist gathers together the significant themes he is going to use to tell his story of the enfleshed Word of God. Light and darkness, life and rebirth, truth, witness, seeing and believing all make an appearance as terms that will be employed in his interpretation of the life and death of the person of Jesus Christ. Crucially, despite the fact that no one has ever seen God, what we have seen – and will see – is his glory. This is, in fact, what the only-begotten has made known to us.

Our focus during the Christmas season is on the beloved Son as the baby in the manger, who is 'of the Father's heart begotten'. But when John writes of glory, he is projecting us forward to the man on the cross, who shows us the depth of God's love in a climactic act of self-giving. This glory is not something that the Father and the Son possess in some kind of exclusive arrangement, but is shared with those to whom Jesus has been given. Not only do they see his glory, but he is also glorified in them (John 17.10ff) – and, astonishingly, as believers, we are called to make this glory our own. That glory is our destiny for all eternity, but we know, from the pattern set before us, that there is no way to glory except via the cross.

Reflection by **Helen Orchard**

Isaiah 60.1-6
Psalm 72.[1-9] 10-end
Ephesians 3.1-12
Matthew 2.1-12

The Epiphany

6 January

Principal Feast

Isaiah 60.1-6

'Arise, shine; for your light has come' (v.1)

Here is a picture of a world overwhelmed with gloom except for one brilliant patch of light. The light is shining from the Jews, newly re-established in and around Jerusalem. Gentiles in the darkness find the light of God's people so attractive that they flood towards it bearing gifts.

This passage sets echoes reverberating. Five centuries later in the Jerusalem temple, an old man realized that he was witnessing the fulfilment of God's promise: '... my eyes have seen your salvation, which you have prepared in the presence of all peoples, a light for revelation to the gentiles' (Luke 2.30-32). The old man's name was Simeon. And what had his eyes seen? They had seen Jesus.

God's plan for humankind has always embraced more than just the Jews. Jesus' family became aware of that during his earliest days. Intellectuals from gentile lands came to worship him, following a star and also bearing gifts. What were those gifts? Verse 6 sets off another echo.

However, the most telling echo is of Jesus commissioning his followers, 'You are the light of the world. A city built on a hill cannot be hidden ... Let your light shine before others' (Matthew 5.14,16). The responsibility to be the light that attracts people struggling in darkness towards God began centuries ago with the Jews. Then it passed to Jesus. He, in turn, has passed it to you and me. Our moment has come. Arise! Shine!

Reflection by **Peter Graystone**

51

The Epiphany

6 January

Principal Feast

Isaiah 60.1-6
Psalm 72.[1-9] 10-15
Ephesians 3.1-12
Matthew 2.1-12

Ephesians 3.1-12

'I Paul am a prisoner for Christ Jesus' (v.1)

The idea that good may come out of evil is one of the basic paradoxes that lie at the heart of faith. And one of the stranger things within the Christian tradition is the way in which we are constantly reminded of how death can also be the bearer of life, and that light is only truly appreciated when the darkness begins to cover us.

Paul writes from prison. It is no doubt dark, lonely and cold. If you are God's anointed to bring the gospel to the gentiles, how is God's purpose, you might ask, furthered by a spell in jail? Surely if God is God, Paul would be spared such sufferings and distractions? Doesn't this hold up the spreading of the gospel?

Yet Paul is in prison, and his situation prompts him to reflect on the ways in which the mystery of God is revealed. Many things that were hidden can now be seen. God's purpose is now known through Christ – who was himself imprisoned before his death. God uses weakness and suffering. The wisdom of God from the heavenly places will have much to teach the earthly powers.

So Paul does not lose heart. Indeed, he will go on to give thanks both for and in his sufferings. For, in dwelling on the generosity and goodness of God, we are enabled in our service of the world; and, loved by the God who remembers each and every one of us, we can feel gratitude for the sacrifice and service we give to one another.

Reflection by **Martyn Percy**

Isaiah 60.1-6
Psalm 72.[1-9] 10-15
Ephesians 3.1-12
Matthew 2.1-12

The Epiphany

6 January

Principal Feast

Matthew 2.1-12

*'Bethlehem ... from you shall come a ruler who is
to shepherd my people Israel' (v.6)*

The light of God in Jesus Christ dawns upon the world in darkness and obscurity. Matthew's account of Christ's birth offers a very different picture from that of Luke; here, we are in the realm of kings and royal courts, and there is not a shepherd in sight. Different the two Gospel accounts may be, but their message is consistent: the one 'who is to shepherd my people Israel' will not be like any king the world has so far known, and won't be found in the places that most expect to find him.

If we can shed for a moment our lifelong over-familiarity with the story of the 'three kings', the element of surprise continues. These wise men from the East who follow the star to Bethlehem could not be further away from the background expectations and worldview of the Jewish citizens of Jerusalem. So, right at the very beginning of Jesus' life, expectations of how God acts in this world and how he relates to his people are being challenged and overturned.

We may find it helpful here to ponder our own expectations as we look for the signs of God's continuing work in Christ in our own lives and the life of the world. Do we, like the wise men, have the humility to lay aside all that we think we know, and to ask God to open our eyes that we may perceive his truth?

Reflection by **Barbara Mosse**

The Baptism of Christ
First Sunday of Epiphany

Isaiah 43.1-7
Psalm 29
Acts 8.14-17
Luke 3.15-17, 21, 22

Isaiah 43.1-7

'When you pass through the waters, I will be with you' (v.2)

During 30 years in parish ministry, there have been many times when I have felt that the waters are up to my neck – sometimes when difficult pastoral situations have taken me out of my depth, sometimes because of opposition when I have challenged something that I felt was wrong, and sometimes when I have been in the wrong myself and made mistakes.

This passage in Isaiah is addressed to a people who have been through fire and water because of their disobedience to God. After the warnings of judgement in chapters 1 to 39, God speaks with great tenderness to those whom he has had to discipline and yet longs to bless. Such is his love for the exiles that he is willing to pay a hefty ransom to buy them back from the nations and bring them home.

Discipline is the costly part of discipleship, and when people we are responsible for do wrong, we need to act to put things right. God demonstrates costly love, restoring Israel's vocation to be his servant (Isaiah 43.10), but at the cost of becoming himself the servant who would give up his life as 'a ransom for many' (Mark 10.45).

As we face the challenges of today, aware of the failures of yesterday, let's hear again God's surprising and grace-filled verdict on his wayward people as a word to us personally: '... you are precious in my sight, and honoured, and I love you'.

Reflection by **Mark Ireland**

Isaiah 43.1-7
Psalm 29
The Baptism of Christ
Acts 8.14-17
First Sunday of Epiphany
Luke 3.15-17, 21, 22

Acts 8.14-17

'... they received the Holy Spirit' (v.17)

It's always a mistake to tell the Holy Spirit what to do. Peter and John were sent north from Jerusalem to Samaria to regularise the Samaritans' conversion. They had accepted the word of God and been baptised but had not received the Spirit. The couple laid hands on them and the Spirit duly came. Using this laying on of hands as evidence, some churches have tried to justify the practice of confirmation and others the need for a second baptism in the Spirit to supplement baptism in water.

The trouble is that the Spirit is not open to being regularized. At other times in the New Testament we see the Spirit being given before baptism, as with Cornelius and his friends in Caesarea (Acts 10.44-48), or we see no mention of the Spirit at all in baptism, as with Philip and the Ethiopian eunuch (Acts 8.38). Let's just admit that the Spirit does as the Spirit wants, and we have no business trying to systematize the ways of God. The point of today's passage is that this Pentecost in Samaria confirmed the next step of the young Church's mission.

What's the next step in our own mission as disciples today? What does God have in store for us?

Reflection by **John Pritchard**

The Baptism of Christ
First Sunday of Epiphany

Isaiah 43.1-7
Psalm 29
Acts 8.14-17
Luke 3.15-17, 21, 22

Luke 3.15-17, 21, 22

'... a voice came from heaven' (v.22)

Martin Luther King Jr once said that his greatest enemies in the fight for civil rights were not the extremists but the moderates who are always devoted to order more than justice, preferring the absence of tension to the positive peace of justice's presence. It should not surprise us that John, for similar reasons, was locked away by Herod. Bright lights are unwelcome if we are living largely concealed and with secretive motivations. We often remove inconvenient people with the excuse that we are protecting others.

As John's freedom is taken away, so Jesus' comes into its own and his ministry begins. Jesus slips under the water. All the voices from the riverbank are drowned out. He can hear his heart, his existence. He comes up, takes a new breath and then hears the one voice that matters, that of his Father from heaven. It is to this voice that he continues to listen in the years ahead, even when others are louder and more threatening. Our lives take shape around the voices we dance to.

A dove appears, as one once did to Noah (Genesis 8.11) confirming a covenant of love into the future. It is an embodiment of the Holy Spirit, the divine energy driving all the events of Jesus' life described in Luke's Gospel. Luke makes it clear that Jesus is baptized 'when all the people were baptized'. From the very beginning, Jesus associates himself with ordinary folk by the river and not with the studious religious bureaucrats at headquarters. Through this association, baptism becomes the sacrament in which, through Christ, we also belong to one another. For the Christian, water is thicker than blood.

Reflection by **Mark Oakley**

Isaiah 62.1-5
Psalm 36.5-10
I Corinthians 12.1-11
John 2.1-11

Second Sunday of Epiphany

Isaiah 62.1-5

*'You shall be a crown of beauty in the hand of the Lord,
and a royal diadem in the hand of your God.' (v.3)*

There is in the Belgian city of Ghent a phenomenal altarpiece. It is sometimes called 'The Adoration of the Lamb' or 'The Mystic Lamb'. Painted by Jan van Eyck and (possibly) also by his brother Hubert in the 1420s–30s, it still stands in St Bavo's Cathedral, close to the chapel for which it was originally created. And now that it has been meticulously restored, its colours glow with a radiant light.

At God's feet in the painting rests a crown. It consists of an exquisite gold filigree structure adorned with hundreds of pearls and rubies. When the crown was painted, because it was then believed that pearls and rubies contained fragments of light that had their origin in eternity, it had a special and holy significance. The altarpiece now draws to itself crowds from across the world. It is one of the greatest paintings ever created, so it is no surprise that people gaze at it in wonder.

Many hundreds of years before van Eyck created the Ghent altarpiece, Isaiah made a stupendous claim about Jerusalem. He prophesied that it would become a crown of beauty in the hand of God, a place that other nations would recognize as blessed.

The verse was adopted by Christians to express the conviction that God's beauty is not only to be discovered in Jerusalem but is also to be seen in Christ, the crown of all creation, lying at God's feet but nestled humbly in the straw of a manger.

Reflection by **Christopher Herbert**

Second Sunday of Epiphany

Isaiah 62.1-5
Psalm 36.5-10
I Corinthians 12.1-11
John 2.1-11

1 Corinthians 12.1-11

'... there are varieties of gifts, but the same Spirit' (v.4)

The immaturity of the Corinthian Church was particularly evident in the disunity of their worship. It seems they were approaching the gathered assembly as a platform for egotistical display.

Paul grants that the Corinthians were a remarkably gifted community (1 Corinthians 1.4-7). Their worship was full of flamboyant manifestations of the Spirit. Some spoke with tongues. Some gave prophetic oracles. Others brought ministries of healing and deliverance. There was nothing dull about Church life in Corinth. But their charismatic gifts had become a focus for boasting and strife.

The result was an un-Christian smugness and disunity. Paul refuses to collude with their spiritual exhibitionism. He points the Corinthians back to the true source and foundation of unity in the Church. It is the Spirit who allocates and animates each gift, distributing them for the common good and for the glory of Christ.

Beneath the richness and vitality of our own Church life, there are sometimes darker undercurrents of selfishness. Perhaps we are more concerned about our preferences, or looking for opportunities to perform, rather than seeking the welfare of the whole Body. Paul's picture of this early Church shows that these are not just the problems of a consumerist generation.

What are you looking for in the Christian community?

Reflection by **Margaret Whipp**

Isaiah 62.1-5
Psalm 36.5-10
1 Corinthians 12.1-11
John 2.1-11

Second Sunday of Epiphany

John 2.1-11

'Do whatever he tells you' (v.5)

Mary is a woman of few words in the Fourth Gospel, but the ones she utters are authoritative and effective. She states the problem and identifies the solution. The solution, as always, is her son Jesus. Hesitant though he may be to intervene in this situation, Mary has made it difficult for Jesus not to act, advising the servants to await his instruction.

We know more of Mary's character from Luke, who shows us that she is not afraid to ask questions of archangels, or to risk scandal and death by accepting her vocation. Presenting a practical human need to her son is not the hardest thing she has had to do. When we see how her request is answered, we are thankful for her initiative, which has prompted Jesus' first sign in this Gospel, revealing something of his identity. It speaks of abundance to the point of excess, of quality beyond anything that has previously been experienced and of the glorious celebration at the messianic banquet of the bridegroom and his bride the Church.

Would that we were more like Mary, the first to welcome Jesus into her life and, in this sense, the first Christian. Her every action points us to Jesus and highlights his words and deeds. To those in need she says: 'Do whatever he tells you.' As for herself, her desire is always the same: 'Be it unto me according to thy word.'

Reflection by **Helen Orchard**

Third Sunday of Epiphany

Nehemiah 8.1-3, 5-6, 8-10
Psalm 19*
I Corinthians 12.12-31*a*
Luke 4.14-21

Nehemiah 8.1-3, 5-6, 8-10

'This day is holy to the Lord your God; do not mourn or weep' (8.9)

Have you noticed how God often uses new Christians to infuse renewed hope and zeal into our fellowships and worship services? 'Baby' Christians often radiate a wellspring of joy that appears unquenchable, reminding us that 'for God all things are possible' (Matthew 19.26). Often their enthusiasm challenges our joyfulness (or lack thereof) and encourages us to rededicate ourselves to God in humble adoration.

Today's reading makes a powerful and faithful proclamation in acknowledging the ability of God's word to break yokes, while evoking tears of repentance *and* joy. Often, those who are new in Christ help us recognize just how complacent our relationship with him has become, or how we may have drifted away from God's divine plan for us. Ezra's encouraging words, 'do not mourn' affirm God's forgiveness.

Perhaps this is why the gospel holds such importance in worship and evangelism. God's word gently reminds us of *his* love and *our* sinful frailties. It pierces our hearts, brings repentance, gives ongoing reassurance and allows us to move closer to God. And, as we learn to accept God's will for our lives, those tears of repentance vanish. They are swept away by joyous celebration as we come to recognize how God's protective arm has faithfully been at work in our lives, ever present, guiding and drawing us toward reconciliation.

Reflection by **Rosalyn Murphy**

Nehemiah 8.1-3, 5-6, 8-10
Psalm 19*
1 Corinthians 12.12-31a
Luke 4.14-21

1 Corinthians 12.12-31a

'Are all apostles? Are all prophets? Are all teachers?' (v.29)

These verses from 1 Corinthians concentrate on Paul's familiar image of the Church as the Body of Christ, with all the different parts functioning harmoniously, as in a healthy human body. The image is an inspired one and particularly apt, but is so familiar to us that we are at risk of not fully hearing its message.

Today we focus not so much on Paul's teaching about the body and the functioning of its various parts, but on his questions towards the end of the chapter regarding different vocations. Is there a veiled reference here to the competitive, combative nature of the Corinthian Church that exercised Paul earlier in the epistle (1 Corinthians 1.10-17)? Are people within the church vying for the 'best' positions? Are some vocations being seen as more 'worthy' than others?

How does Paul's teaching relate to our own experience of Church life? Is there a challenge here for us and our competitive and envious human natures? Are we able to be content with the particular work God has given us to do, or do we envy the supposed 'better' role of another? Jesus chided Martha, who feared her sister Mary had a better position than her own (Luke 10.38-42). And when, at the end of John's Gospel, Peter asks Jesus about the future of the beloved disciple, Jesus' answer is blunt and uncompromising: ' ... what is that to you? Follow me!' (John 21.22).

Reflection by **Barbara Mosse**

Third Sunday of Epiphany

Nehemiah 8.1-3, 5-6, 8-10
Psalm 19*
1 Corinthians 12.12-31*a*
Luke 4.14-21

Luke 4.14-21

'Today this scripture has been fulfilled ...' (v.21)

Jesus returns from his struggle in the wilderness filled with the Spirit and able to set out with clarity the very core of his vocation as Messiah and our vocation as his followers. The so-called 'Nazareth manifesto', was already an ancient prophecy (Isaiah 61.1) when Jesus declared and fulfilled it on this day. When we hear it now, 2,000 years later, it seems just as pertinent, just as much in need of fulfilment.

Yet here is the paradox: 'Today this scripture has been fulfilled in your hearing'. Yes and no. It was fulfilled, in the sense that Christ, the one about whom the scripture was written, was there in their midst, just as Isaiah had prophesied – the prophecy had come true. But it was not entirely fulfilled then, nor has it been even now, in the sense that the tasks the Lord set his anointed – bringing good news to the poor, release to captives, freedom to the oppressed – are not yet complete. Christ began this work, but he calls his followers, his Church, to continue and complete it, in him and with him.

To be a Christian is to be in Christ, which means 'anointed', and therefore to be part of the fulfilling of this prophesy, and therein lies our hope. Every sharing of this good news, every liberation of a captive, every proclamation of God's grace, in the teeth of opposition, against all odds, is a step towards that fulfilment. Our actions in his name are also Christ's actions in us, and in him the fulfilment of all these things will come.

Reflection by **Malcolm Guite**

Ezekiel 43.27 – 44.4
Psalm 48
I Corinthians 13
Luke 2.22-40

Fourth Sunday of Epiphany

Ezekiel 43.27 – 44.4

*'This gate shall remain shut; it shall not be opened,
and no one shall enter by it' (44.2)*

Thresholds can be strange places, and when a closed door bars the way, the mystery of what lies behind is heightened.

In the Opera House in the French city of Nice, there is a door marked *'Paradis'*. It was there that Len Deighton's hero in *Yesterday's Spy* paused to collect his thoughts. He described the doorway as 'shabby'. The author extends the playful irony by placing a policeman in front of the door. And to what did the policeman and the door bar the way? Actually, it led to the top-most row of seats in the theatre, to what some call 'the gods', *'paradis'*. Mystery raised; mystery solved.

In St Peter's, Rome there is also a mysterious doorway. Called the 'Holy Door', it is normally bricked up from the inside, but in Jubilee years, the bricks are carefully removed and pilgrims stream through. The most recent opening of the doors was in 2015 when Pope Francis declared an Extraordinary Jubilee of Mercy, and stated that anyone entering through the doors would experience the love and consolation of God. In order that pilgrims did not have to trek to Rome, Pope Francis asked each diocesan bishop to designate a Holy Door in one of the major churches of his diocese.

The Holy Door is a powerful piece of symbolism that reflects the claim of Jesus that he himself is the door of the sheepfold. Gates once closed have been permanently unlocked by his death and resurrection.

Reflection by **Christopher Herbert**

Fourth Sunday of Epiphany

Ezekiel 43.27 – 44.4
Psalm 48
1 Corinthians 13
Luke 2.22-40

1 Corinthians 13

'... then I will know fully' (v.12)

Knowledge mattered to the Corinthians. It is one of the repeating themes of this letter, highlighted in Paul's introductory words (1 Corinthians 1.5). There is something deeply flawed in their attitude, however, and it is to do with the separation of knowledge from love; such knowledge 'puffs up' the person who would wield it, but love 'builds up' the temple of God, the Body of Christ (1 Corinthians 8.1).

Now Paul tells them that knowledge, even the knowledge that comes as a gift from God, 'will come to an end'. Yet when he tries to describe the fullness of life that lies ahead for us in Christ, he still reaches for the language of knowing: 'then I will know fully, even as I have been fully known'. What begins now and lasts forever – the depth of the present and the invitation of the future – is not knowledge as a thing we hold, but knowing God and being known by God. Such knowing is also loving, and such being known is also being loved – and it never ends.

Knowledge also matters to people today. Knowledge promises power: power to influence environments and organizations; power to shape our unruly hearts and their elusive attachments. Even at its best, however, such knowledge is only for a season. Our true life rests in the knowing that is also loving the One whose loving and knowing of us are beyond comprehension, and it overflows in ordinary, costly acts of love day by day.

Reflection by **Jeremy Worthen**

Ezekiel 43.27 – 44.4
Psalm 48
1 Corinthians 13
Luke 2.22-40

Fourth Sunday of Epiphany

Luke 2.22-40

'... the time came for their purification' (v.22)

They were an odd couple, two elderly people always haunting the temple precincts, seemingly forever on the lookout for something. Perhaps they had their sandwiches together and compared expectations and ailments. Perhaps they prayed together. And then, one ordinary day, the event happened. For Simeon and Anna there was a jolt of recognition, a flash of joy, as a couple appeared carrying a bundle that was obviously very precious to them. They were looking around, clearly somewhat anxious and bewildered about what to do next. Simeon and Anna leaped into action, greeting the shining moment with tender delight. Simeon took the baby in his arms.

Is it too fanciful to imagine Mary entrusting her precious child to our arms too? Christ gives himself to the world in vulnerability and humility, and in the hope that we'll respond to this trust with an open mind and heart. When we get over-confident in our understanding of God as 'almighty', it might be healthy to balance that perception with an understanding of God as 'all-vulnerable'. It opens up all sorts of conversations with those who've decided that an almighty God hasn't done much for them. Maybe a God who was carried in Simeon's arms and who 'humbled himself and became obedient to the point of death' (Philippians 2.8) might be more approachable.

Reflection by **John Pritchard**

The Presentation of Christ

in the Temple (Candlemas)
2 February *Principal Feast*

Malachi 3.1-5
Psalm 24.[1-6] 7-end
Hebrews 2.14-end
Luke 2.22-40

Malachi 3.1-5

'But who can endure the day of his coming?' (v.2)

Having read today's passage, the fiery aria in Handel's *Messiah* may well already be running through your mind, full of urgency and anxiety. The urgency is as it should have been for Malachi's hearers because, although only recently back from exile, they were already getting into a mess, and Malachi was calling them back to faithfulness. Watch out, he was saying, God's messenger will suddenly appear in the temple, and the outcome could be catastrophic.

On the day when we celebrate the Presentation of Christ in the temple as a newborn infant, Christian reflection sees the messenger as Jesus. And yet this little messenger is as far removed from the fearsome forerunner of Malachi as it's possible to be. He's still in nappies and utterly dependent on his mother. But think on! The Jesus who reappears in the temple later in the Gospel is indeed one of whom you could ask 'who can endure the day of his coming?' as he overturned the tables and all the conventions of the sacred site.

We need to beware the fluffy Christmas image of a Jesus we can control. This Jesus is indeed full of compassion, but that gift is structured around a steel core. He was well aware of the cost of his mission and the challenge he had to put to power. Our love for the world we inhabit needs, similarly, to combine the love and mercy of the compassionate Christ with the strength and purpose of the confrontational Christ.

The child in Mary's arms grew up.

Reflection by **John Pritchard**

Malachi 3.1-5
Psalm 24.[1-6] 7-end
Hebrews 2.14-end
Luke 2.22-40

The Presentation of Christ

in the Temple (Candlemas)

2 February *Principal Feast*

Hebrews 2.14-end

'... like his brothers and sisters in every respect' (v.17)

It's not easy to imagine God becoming human; it's like the national grid being put through a single light bulb – the energy and creativity of the one who made the world becoming real in a tiny baby. The cataclysmic nature of God becoming human leaps out from these verses as the writer of Hebrews describes how the colossal power of the one who is able to 'destroy death' is poured out into humanity. It's almost as if we make the journey with Jesus as we read. Imagining this movement from eternity to time-bound existence, by way of the destruction of death itself, is arguably a more dazzling description of Christmas than any infancy narrative. But the heightened language and imagery of the merciful high priest who keeps the company of angels, is balanced by the thoroughly realistic realization that human beings are simply afraid of dying. Not only that, says this wise and imaginative writer, we are enslaved by this fear. Perhaps it's the ultimate test: to confront the reality of our own death and learn to face it with faith rather than fear. The discussion of the testing of Jesus here reminds us of the Garden of Gethsemane, when Jesus did face his own death and begged for the cup of suffering to be removed from him. This is truly one whose flesh and blood, insists the letter to the Hebrews, is as ours is.

The power of this fleshly testing becomes clear; it is precisely because Jesus was tested and shared human suffering that God is able to dwell in the midst of humanity. By that dwelling, our life lived here and now, is made sacred.

Reflection by **Lucy Winkett**

The Presentation of Christ

in the Temple (Candlemas)

2 February *Principal Feast*

Malachi 3.1-5
Psalm 24.[1-6] 7-end
Hebrews 2.14-end
Luke 2.22-40

Luke 2.22-40

'Lord, now lettest thou thy servant depart in peace,
according to thy word' (v.29, KJV)

Jazz saxophonist and composer John Coltrane had a turbulent life, and a career of highs and lows. Eventually, though, through a new-found Christian faith, he found the stability to complete his best work. A Love Supreme became his finest album, but as he toured the work, one particular evening he gave the performance of his life. Everything – his playing, the band, the audience – came together in one sweet moment, the pinnacle of his life's work, the realization that he had done what he came for. As he left the stage, his drummer heard him say two words: Nunc dimittis.

Two prophets, Anna and Simeon, spent their life in the temple: praying, speaking God's words, but most of all watching and waiting for the promised salvation of God. As Jesus was brought to the temple for dedication, they both recognized that this was what they had been waiting for. Their responses were different: Anna began proclaiming the truth to all who would listen. Like Mary Magdalene at the resurrection, the first one to proclaim the revelation of God was a woman. But then Simeon spoke. All that he had waited for, all that his life's work had been leading up to, he saw in the tiny face of this infant. We will never know how he knew; he just did.

'Now, Lord,' said Simeon, 'I can die a happy man. I've done what I came for. Nunc dimittis.'

Reflection by **Maggi Dawn**

Isaiah 6.1-8 [9-end]
Psalm 138
1 Corinthians 15.1-11
Luke 5.1-11

**Sunday between 4 & 10 February
inclusive** *(if earlier than the
Second Sunday before Lent)*

Isaiah 6.1-8 [9-13]

'I saw the Lord sitting on a throne, high and lofty' (v.1)

In ancient Israel, people spoke of going to the temple to 'see God' – it was merely a turn of phrase. In 742 BC, Isaiah went to the temple and actually *did* see God, and the experience changed his life. It made him aware of how inadequate was not only his people's but also his own response to God, and it resulted in his feeling commissioned to act as a prophet. What God was about to do involved judgement, so bad that it would wipe out virtually all of Israel – though, in the event, things were not quite as bad as Isaiah thought they would be.

Christians have focused less on the message of unavoidable judgement here and more on the vision itself, the source of the formula 'Holy, holy, holy', which is used in both Christian and Jewish liturgy. For Isaiah, however, the holiness of God is inextricably bound up with the moral demands that, he believes, the people of Jerusalem have not lived up to. God's holiness means that he is a moral, and morally demanding, God, so that those who are 'defiled' by wrongdoing cannot stand before him.

When we worship this God, we need always to be aware that true worship is not a matter of warm, or even awed, feelings, but must issue in practical obedience.

Reflection by **John Barton**

Isaiah 6.1-8 [9-end]
Psalm 138
1 Corinthians 15.1-11
Luke 5.1-11

1 Corinthians 15.1-11

*'Now I should remind you ... of the good news that
I proclaimed to you' (v.1)*

The Church at Corinth is losing its way. Paul's response is to
call them to remember where it all began for them.
'Remember' is a key command in the Bible. It is more than
having a good memory. The opposite of remember is not
forgetting but to be *dis*-membered – to be broken off from
the whole. To *re*-member is to reconnect. Paul urges them,
and us – reconnect your life in the history of faith. Don't waste
all this! Christ died for our sins, was buried, was raised and
appeared to his followers.

The list of resurrection appearances of Jesus given here is
selective. One recorded here does not appear anywhere else.
For every story we are told, there are countless more: the
witness of unnamed men and women through Christian
history whose lives are changed by the risen Christ.

Picture an unbroken line of people across history, across the
world – all in their turn receiving, embracing firmly and
handing on the word and gift of the new life of Christ.
Remember them well, Paul says.

Today, as then, in our age and world, on this side of the empty
Easter tomb, Jesus still meets and transforms his world.

Reflection by **David Runcorn**

Isaiah 6.1-8 [9-end]
Psalm 138
1 Corinthians 15.1-11
Luke 5.1-11

Luke 5.1-11

'... they left everything and followed him' (v.11)

Only Luke and John tell the story of the miraculous catch of fish, but they tell the story in very different contexts. Whereas John makes it a post-resurrection episode, Luke makes it part of the story of Jesus calling his disciples. Either way, what is clear is that the miracle is a dramatic enactment of Jesus' promise that 'from now on you will be catching people'.

In Luke's version of the story, it is Peter who has the spotlight on him. Throughout Luke's Gospel it is very clear that it is the sinful not the righteous whom Jesus has come to call, but that there must be a recognition of who we have become before beginning the new journey with God. Spiritually, we see by first being seen. We love by being loved first.

So Peter sees himself and repents before being the first disciple to be called. He becomes us, as it were, not least in his later betrayal of Jesus too. Though the beginnings of our faith feel like a honeymoon and can be miraculous, we learn over time with Peter that conversion is a lifelong project. It has all the fulfilments and frustrations of a relationship, not a romance, with God.

Only in this knowledge and stability can Peter later be given the primary pastoral charge.

Reflection by **Mark Oakley**

Proper 2

**Sunday between 11 & 17 February
inclusive** *(if earlier than the Second
Sunday before Lent)*

Jeremiah 17.5-10
Psalm 1
1 Corinthians 15.12-20
Luke 6.17-26

Jeremiah 17.5-10

'... like a tree planted by water' (v.8)

We have a scrubby bush in our garden that has never grown very well; it is stunted, small and, in the middle of the summer, turns brown at the edges.

It is this bush that comes to mind when I read Jeremiah 17. We may not have a full-blown wilderness in our garden, but we do have a patch of soil under a large conifer tree that deprives the bush both of light and water. The bush struggles on year after year but it will never thrive because it has no access to the light and water it needs.

It is so easy, Jeremiah suggests, for our lives to be stunted and dry in a similar way. We, like bushes and trees, need nourishment to thrive and grow. Perhaps even more importantly than that, we need reserves: deep wells of enrichment that will continue to feed us in times of drought and famine. Putting our trust in human beings, rather than God, has the same effect on us as it does on my stunted bush in the garden. We might survive and even grow a little, but without the nourishment of a living stream we cannot thrive.

Jeremiah's evocative image here reminds us of the importance of developing deep roots that can access the resources we need in times of drought. It is trusting in God that sends our roots deep, helping to live and grow no matter what our lives bring.

Reflection by **Paula Gooder**

Jeremiah 17.5-10
Psalm 1
1 Corinthians 15.12-20
Luke 6.17-26

1 Corinthians 15.12-20

'... how can some of you say there is no resurrection of the dead?' (v.12)

We only have one side of the correspondence here. But there is a lively debate going on between Paul and some Church members at Corinth about the resurrection. That in itself is not surprising. The resurrection is so mind-blowing that if doesn't raise big questions, we surely haven't understood it. It may come as a relief to find the first Christians asking awkward questions about what they believe. It is a healthy Church that lives honestly with its questions. Christian faith is an enquiring faith, and that means being willing to be pulled and stretched beyond what we can immediately understand or make sense of.

It needs some detective work to clarify why some are having a problem with the idea of resurrection. It is very doubtful that they are dismissing it totally – though it would have sounded a very strange idea to the world of their day. Traditional Jewish belief was of a general resurrection at the end of time. However, Paul is emphatic that through the resurrection of Jesus, new life and forgiveness is breaking in now. It is no longer a distant hope.

When Christ was raised from the dead, the power of sin and death was broken for ever. The stone has been rolled away. A door to new life stands open for ever.

Reflection by **David Runcorn**

Proper 2

Jeremiah 17.5-10
Psalm 1
1 Corinthians 15.12-20
Luke 6.17-26

Luke 6.17-26

'... surely your reward is great in heaven' (v.23)

In *How God Became King*, the former bishop of Durham, Tom Wright, argues that Christians have incorrectly read the Gospels. He refers to 'credal Christianity' that jumps – as our creeds do – from the birth of Jesus to his death, from 'born of the Virgin Mary' to 'suffered under Pontius Pilate'. This jump ignores the gospel message of the life, healing and teaching of Jesus. The credal Christian message details how to get to heaven, whereas the life of Jesus demonstrates how to establish God's kingdom on earth by practising social justice and forgiveness. Many Christians have read Galatians and Romans, and emphasized life beyond this one, overlooking the radical practice taught in our four Gospels.

The Beatitudes, from the Latin for 'blessed', have been seen as looking forward to a life beyond this life and a future perfect relationship with God. The 'reward' of the beatitudes for the first-century Jews who heard them was about this life. The reward for credal Christians, if they read them, is about heavenly bliss. Jesus' emphasis is on building a just kingdom now. Poverty, especially if caused by oppression, is a scandal that needs to be reversed. Hoarding wealth and status is also scandalous, and the woes predicted for the rich and respected are resonant of prophetic warning of impending distress. This isn't about a future life; this is immanent.

The gospel does proclaim eternal life and eternal life starts now.

Reflection by **Paul Kennedy**

Genesis 45.3-11, 15
Psalm 37.1-11, 40-end*
1 Corinthians 15.35-38, 42-50
Luke 6.27-38

Proper 3

**Sunday between 18 & 24 February
inclusive** *(if earlier than the Second
Sunday before Lent)*

Genesis 45.3-11, 15

'God sent me before you to preserve life' (v.5)

We are witness to one of the most remarkable acts of reconciliation recorded in the Bible. This is a reconciliation that finally overcomes long-standing family distancing, falsehood, betrayal, envy and trickery. For the sake of reconciliation in this tragedy, Joseph steps outside the dignity, pride and security of his royal office and enters into the emotional complexity of his own family. Royal power will not heal the dysfunctions of his family, but empathy and vulnerability will. Joseph doesn't want guilt from his brothers – he wants the restoration of the brotherhood itself.

His inspiration and guide is God, who he believes has been working invisibly and unnoticed in everything that has happened in the family drama. This *shalom* of God can now be revealed. What God does is not dependent on the brothers' remorse. Joseph shares good news in terms of grace, partly because he himself has known grace in his own story. God has given abundant life through Joseph, rather than death by Joseph, and the brothers' own journey becomes the means for restoring this family to fullness of life again.

God works within a situation, however sinful it has become, and constantly pours out the possibility of justice and grace. Even though the brothers have an evil goal, this is outmanoeuvred by the larger sway of God's providence and good purpose – bringing life rather than death. Such are the ways of God in the world.

Reflection by **David Moxon**

Genesis 45.3-11, 15
Psalm 37.1-11, 40-end*
1 Corinthians 15.35-38, 42-50
Luke 6.27-38

1 Corinthians 15.35-38, 42-50

*'How are the dead raised? With what kind of body
do they come?' (v.35)*

The hypothetical question sounds reasonable enough: if we are indeed to be raised from the dead, what kind of body will we have? But the question provokes a strong retort: 'Fool!'

The difficulty lies in understanding the radical difference between this life and the resurrection life. The latter is not simply a longer or more intense version of the former. There are differences as well as similarities.

The illustration Paul uses here is both homely and immensely powerful: it is the analogy of seed. He continues the agricultural metaphor of 'first fruits' from earlier in this chapter (v.20) but with a very different meaning. As everyone knows, a seed is as different as can be from the plant it will become. Different seeds may look alike, but the plants themselves can be vastly different from one another and from the seed that gives them life.

So it is with the resurrection body. Our resurrection life will not simply be a continuation of this life. It will be radically different in its nature and in its glory.

The seed picture continues into one of the rhetorical high points of the chapter: a series of sharp contrasts between this mortal body and the resurrection life. A foolish question leads Paul to unpack indescribable mysteries.

Reflection by **Steven Croft**

Genesis 45.3-11, 15
Psalm 37.1-11, 40-end*
1 Corinthians 15.35-38, 42-50
Luke 6.27-38

Luke 6.27-38

'Be merciful, just as your Father is merciful' (v.36)

As the sun set on the British Empire in India, Gandhi, himself a Hindu, was taking inspiration from Jesus. He said that 'Jesus' suffering is a factor in the composition of my undying faith in non-violence … He was one of the greatest teachers humanity has ever had', and with this *Christian* approach, he pursued a non-violent campaign against the colonial power.

Jesus' non-violence is humiliating: if you turn the other cheek, you are inviting a strike with the left hand, which was used for unclean purposes; if you give your shirt, along with your coat, you are reduced to nakedness. The humiliation is mutual both for the oppressed and the oppressor who has to act improperly with the second strike or gaze inappropriately upon nakedness. The humiliation of the oppressed shames the oppressor, just as Gandhi uncovered the shame of the empire. Like Jesus, the first Christian martyr Stephen also embodied non-violence in his death, especially in praying for his executors.

Luke recalls Jesus encouraging us to take God's attribute of mercy. The old covenant tended to emphasize God's holiness, leading to an ethic of separation and suspicion of others. The contemporary Roman ethic was, 'I give so that you give'. Generous Roman behaviour was to be rewarded, and thus the rich and powerful helped each other. The call to mercy is radically generous both to those who are different and those who are poor. Living it out prophetically and peacefully speaks truth to power.

Reflection by **Paul Kennedy**

Second Sunday before Lent

Genesis 2.4*b*-9, 15-end
Psalm 65
Revelation 4
Luke 8.22-25

Genesis 2.4*b*-9, 15-end

'... pleasant to the sight and good for food' (v.9)

Gratuity is under threat in our world. We are trained in more and more aspects of our lives to justify our expenditure – of effort, of time, of money – in ways that are quantifiable and goal-oriented – that are, in other words, narrowly utilitarian.

In this passage, Adam is invited into God's delighted work of naming the creatures. He is a participant in the generous dynamic of blessing that is at creation's very source. He finds himself surrounded by a world of trees, planted by the Lord God, and these God-given trees are *first* described as pleasant to the sight, and only *second* as good for food.

Perhaps there is a hint here of what our world has lost. The pleasure of the eyes may not be a bare necessity of life, but when our only priority is with how we can make things work to serve our needs, we make lives that are hard to live and impossible to enjoy. The gratuitous 'excess' in things is not just some trivial 'icing on the cake' compared with the mechanics of production and consumption; it is a witness to why it is worth producing and consuming at all. We can live in a way that corresponds to this 'excess' in things by enjoying and not just using them.

Adam and Eve changed their relationship to that 'gratuitous' tree that was not for their use when they began to suspect it might do something for them.

Reflection by **Ben Quash**

Genesis 2.4*b*-9, 15-end
Psalm 65
Revelation 4
Luke 8.22-25

Revelation 4

*'... there in heaven stood a throne, with one seated
on the throne!' (v.2)*

Revelation is commonly understood as a text that seeks to predict the future. Another way of looking at it, however, is to see it as a revelation of the totality of the present, a present from which certain future consequences must necessarily flow.

Essential to Revelation's depiction of the present is the throne scene of chapter 4. The layers of symbolism in this chapter emphasize the complete sovereignty of God over all the universe. First, the throne itself is a symbol of power, and the tangential description of the one seated on the throne serves to emphasize his otherness. The significance of the 24 thrones is not immediately clear, but it is possible that they symbolize the hours of the day and God's sovereignty over time. The four living creatures represent four dimensions of the created order – wild animals, domestic animals, humans and birds – and show how all creation is orientated in worship of the one on the throne.

The message that emanates from this vision is that of the almightiness of God. Some extraordinarily challenging and painful episodes will be depicted in the remainder of the book of Revelation, but this vision provides an overarching canopy for them all. There is no event, no matter how terrible, that can evade, dislodge or undermine the ultimate power of God.

Reflection by **Alan Garrow**

Second Sunday before Lent

Genesis 2.4*b*-9, 15-end
Psalm 65
Revelation 4
Luke 8.22-25

Luke 8.22-25

'Who then is this, that he commands even the winds and the water, and they obey him?' (v.25)

In the second half of Luke chapter 8, we witness Jesus exhibiting his power in different realms. In today's reading, as he calms the storm, it is his power over the natural order. Then, in the exorcism of the Gerasene demoniac, it will be over the spiritual order. Next, we see Jesus' power over the physical order when he cures the woman with the haemorrhage and, climactically, we witness his power over death as he raises Jairus' daughter from the dead. It is an intensive and all-encompassing teaching programme for the disciples!

The watchwords for each story are fear and faith. Today's episode is a basic lesson in anxiety management for the disciples. It's just them and Jesus, together in a boat sailing across the lake. A tranquil setting – what could possibly go wrong? But, all of a sudden, the wind changes and there is trouble at sea. Panic ensues, and the disciples, even while in the presence of Christ, the source of life, fear death. Whether or not we have faced a near-death situation, we know what it is to fear. It is debilitating, and faith can seem to evaporate. Perhaps it is worth reflecting on the response of the disciples to their plea. In the ensuing calm, they are still afraid, but now for a different reason. They fear not the power of the elements, but rather the power of Christ: a fear tinged with awe. This is the fear which will lead to love; the love which, when made perfect, casts out all fear (1 John 4.18).

Reflection by **Helen Orchard**

Exodus 34.29-end
Psalm 99
2 Corinthians 3.12 – 4.2
Luke 9.28-36 [37-43*a*]

Sunday next before Lent

Exodus 34.29-end

'... whenever Moses went in before the Lord to speak with him, he would take the veil off' (v.34)

Today's reading is part of a strange story. It begins with Moses bargaining with God, saying that as God has asked him to lead his people out of Egypt, surely now, after years of wandering, the time has come for some clarity. In spite of their sins, will God continue to accompany his people? God replies that he will go with them. Uncertain about that response, Moses pushes the bargaining even further and asks (daringly) that he might see God's glory. God replies that he will indeed reveal himself to Moses, but will not reveal his face. Moses is ordered to meet God on Mount Sinai. He is to come alone.

On the mountain God reveals his name. It is like the previous epiphany at the burning bush where God revealed himself as 'I am'. Yet again, God makes a solemn promise that he will be with Moses and will lead the people to the Promised Land. Moses stays on the mountain for a long time and is so marked by his encounter with God that his face radiates God's holy beauty.

He returns down the mountain, and there another significant thing happens. Moses veils his face – and this is the important point – *except* when he goes into the tent of meeting and talks with God. Then there is no veil; he comes to God just as he is. In worship, Moses' inmost self meets the 'I am' of God.

There's a message there for all of us about honesty in prayer.

Reflection by **Christopher Herbert**

Sunday next before Lent

Exodus 34.29-end
Psalm 99
2 Corinthians 3.12 – 4.2
Luke 9.28-36 [37-43*a*]

2 Corinthians 3.12 – 4.2

'… but when one turns to the Lord, the veil is removed' (3.16)

If you want to impress your friends when you are visiting a church or an art gallery, try this. Look out for an image of Moses (you will be able to tell that it's Moses because there will be two lumps like horns on his forehead) and when you spot it, say 'I do believe that that is Moses'. Your friends will be astonished by your detailed knowledge of art …

Why is Moses almost always portrayed in medieval art with horns on his forehead? Because Jerome, when composing the Vulgate Bible, misread the word for 'radiance' and translated it as 'horned', and ever since Moses has been lumbered with that unhelpful iconographic attribute.

Ways of thinking, even when they are incorrect, have a habit of lasting for a long time.

One of St Paul's thought-practices, presumably learnt when he was honing his early skills in rhetoric, was to couch his argument in terms of pairs of opposites. In today's reading, his binary conceptual system is working overtime. It focuses on the 'veiled/unveiled' metaphor, which is then extended into the 'old/new' contrast, and by implication, developed further into an 'enslaved/free' disparity.

It can be a useful method of thinking, because living in a complex society, we value anything that supplies apparently neat and easy solutions. But it needs watching – otherwise the end result can be the creation of oversimple stereotypes. And we have seen in twentieth-century history some of the awful consequences of that.

Reflection by **Christopher Herbert**

Exodus 34.29-end
Psalm 99
2 Corinthians 3.12 – 4.2
Luke 9.28-36 [37-43a]

Sunday next before Lent

Luke 9.28-36 [37-43a]

'... they saw his glory' (v.32)

The transfiguration of Jesus is the pivot of the gospel story, the central event in the Lord's earthly life, both completing his ministry in Galilee and pointing ahead to his passion. This is emphasized in Luke's version where Moses and Elijah speak with Jesus of his *exodos* – his departure. This word can mean death – departure from life – but it also echoes the exodus from Egypt, suggesting that the death of Christ will bring freedom to many.

After the transfiguration, Jerusalem becomes the only direction of travel. The disciples were drowsy, possibly asleep during the actual moment of the transfiguration, but they saw its after-effects and experienced the cloud that overshadowed the event. After the questioning of the previous verses, the transfiguration finally reveals Jesus' heavenly origin. For us, such a realization may come as a fleeting experience in worship or prayer. The icons that are so much a part of Orthodox spirituality remind us that God's glory is located in the face of Jesus Christ, but, earthbound as we are, we are only occasionally able to glimpse it.

Reflection by **Angela Tilby**

Ash Wednesday

Principal Holy Day

Joel 2.1-2, 12-17 *or* Isaiah 58.1-12
Psalm 51.1-18
2 Corinthians 5.20*b* – 6.10
Matthew 6.1-6, 16-21 *or* John 8.1-11

Joel 2.1-2, 12-17

'... return to me with all your heart' (v.12)

One of the questions I ask myself on Ash Wednesday is always: 'How long will I wear the cross on my forehead?' When will embarrassment, functionality or rain get the better of the ash placed there this morning? I always feel it's a test of my loyalty, and I usually fail sometime before lunch. God's people in Judah in the seventh century BC failed too, but for them it was more serious because they were soon going to be subject to the awesome Day of the Lord, embodied in a dark, Mordor-like army sweeping down from the north. In the face of this calamity, Joel begs the people to return to the Lord with all their heart, and to rend their hearts and not their clothing. The deeper truth is always that God wants to save God's people and restore their prosperity.

As we enter Lent, it's good to hold on to that perspective. God is never out to get us! But the ash on our foreheads (made from the burning of last year's palm crosses) reminds us that we are dust and to dust we shall return, so we should turn away from sin and be faithful to Christ. It's an annual reminder that our best intentions as Christians can easily turn to ashes, and being faithful to Christ is the only remedy. Quite simply, we are called to live our lives daily in the direction of God, and it behoves us to set that compass bearing every day – preferably early on before the army of selfish motives, lazy morality, and routine hedonism sweeps down from the north.

Reflection by **John Pritchard**

Joel 2.1-2, 12-17 *or* **Isaiah 58.1-12**
Psalm 51.1-18
2 Corinthians 5.20*b* – 6.10
Matthew 6.1-6, 16-21 *or* John 8.1-11

Ash Wednesday

Principal Holy Day

Isaiah 58.1-12

'... to loose the bonds of injustice' (v.6)

When Matthew told the story of the Magi padding across the deserts in search of a king, he suggested that their quest and the very structures of the universe, the stars and planets, were somehow conjoined. It was a story of entrancing simplicity, which has inspired artists and poets ever since. Storytellers have augmented the message: Balthasar, Melchior and Caspar were only so named in the fifth century, for example. Later still they became the carriers of other meanings. It was said that they represented the then three known continents – Asia, Europe and Africa – and the three ages of humankind – old age, middle age and youth. But even with each of these playful embellishments, the core message remained the same. This journey was of cosmic significance. Heaven and earth were of a piece.

Exactly the same idea about the relationship between heaven and earth is to be found in today's reading. Real fasting requires the fast to be not simply a reflection of local cultural or religious norms, but instead it should have universal substance. Outward forms are not enough; what is needed is a radical change of moral perspective. Those who suffer injustice are to be freed from their fetters, the oppressed should be released from their yoke, the hungry are to be fed and the naked clothed. It was a message that Jesus himself also proclaimed, a message not just for the religiously inclined few but for all humanity.

Reflection by **Christopher Herbert**

Ash Wednesday

Principal Holy Day

Joel 2.1-2, 12-17 *or* Isaiah 58.1-12
Psalm 51.1-18
2 Corinthians 5.20b – 6.10
Matthew 6.1-6, 16-21 *or* John 8.1-11

2 Corinthians 5.20*b* – 6.10

'... we entreat you on behalf of Christ, be reconciled to God'
(5.20)

The messages are clear. Yesterday's pancakes reminded us in the West that our souls, like the batter in the frying pan, have become fat and flat. We have lots to live with but little to live for. Today we are marked with ash, the stuff that is left over when the fire has gone out. This season asks for some self-scrutiny as to whether life is in balance, whether we have things out of proportion and how we might confront this properly in a time for amendment.

In his letter to the Corinthian Christians, Paul outlines those things we should be focused on at such a time. He identifies, for instance, patience, kindness, genuine love, truthful speech and purity. These are things that increase as you share them. The more you give of them, often courageously, the more you ultimately receive of them. They are unlike money or power, where if I win, you lose. In all the things that matter most in this life, the truth is that the more I share, the more is shared with me, and this helps to restore the balance in our relationships and with God.

Paul tells his suffering companions that although they are poor, they are making many rich. This insight is at the heart of Lent. Although there is a poverty within us, a history of regret and a hunger for God, we are, with the gift of grace, still able to offer momentary reflections of that grace to others. How we can better do this, with a resuscitated soul, is not a bad project for Lent.

Reflection by **Mark Oakley**

Joel 2.1-2, 12-17 *or* Isaiah 58.1-12
Psalm 51.1-18
2 Corinthians 5.20*b* – 6.10
Matthew 6.1-6, 16-21 *or* John 8.1-11

Matthew 6.1-6, 16-21

'... shut the door and pray ... in secret' (v.6)

This passage forms part of Matthew's treatment of the Sermon on the Mount found in chapters 5 to 7 of his Gospel. In today's text, Jesus pinpoints certain tendencies in human nature with devastating clarity – tendencies that are easily recognizable today, over 2,000 years later. In Jesus' day, people parading their prayer, fasting and almsgiving were clearly a common sight. These activities, potentially good and beneficial in themselves, were being used to garner the praise of other people rather than that of God.

Do we sometimes fall into the same trap? It's a fine line that we tread. For instance, if I attend an Ash Wednesday service today and emerge with a striking ash cross on my forehead – what then might I do? Will I leave it in place, as a witness to my Lord? Or maybe I'm secretly hoping others will notice and approve of my supposed holiness. But perhaps I wash it off as quickly as possible, feeling slightly embarrassed and not wanting to expose myself to the risk of ridicule. As with so many other situations, our motives are likely to be mixed, and God alone knows the secrets of the heart.

As individuals and as Church fellowships this Ash Wednesday, it's worth taking some time, before God, to examine the motives for our actions. Does our right hand know what our left is doing? Do we do the things we do for God – or for public approval?

Reflection by **Barbara Mosse**

Ash Wednesday

Principal Holy Day

Joel 2.1-2, 12-17 *or* Isaiah 58.1-12
Psalm 51.1-18
2 Corinthians 5.20b – 6.10
Matthew 6.1-6, 16-21 *or* **John 8.1-11**

John 8.1-11

'Jesus said, "Neither do I condemn you."' (v.11)

The only one who had the right to condemn the woman found in adultery, did not. Even without any assurance from her that she would not sin again, he let her go. He must have recognized that such a traumatic, literally near-death, experience would change her forever, especially being met by grace at her moment of greatest jeopardy.

There has been much speculation about what Jesus was writing on the ground. Was he playing for time, urgently praying to the Father for wisdom? This would fit in with his claim never to do anything of his own will but instead what the Father wanted him to say. Was he writing the names of the sins of the woman's accusers – PRIDE, HATRED, ENVY, GREED, LUST…? They made the mistake of thinking their sins were not visible, unlike the woman's. But they were visible to the Father, and visible to Jesus.

Here we can see a wonderful demonstration of the oneness of the character of the Father and Son. It is as if, instead of the sins, LOVE, GRACE, FORGIVENESS, ACCEPTANCE are being written in the air as Jesus speaks.

Put your name in the following sentence as you pray and see where the Spirit takes you:

'Jesus was left alone with _____ standing before him.'

Reflection by **Jeanette Sears**

Deuteronomy 26.1-11
Psalm 91.1-2, 9-end*
Romans 10.8*b*-13
Luke 4.1-13

First Sunday of Lent

Deuteronomy 26.1-11

'A wandering Aramean was my ancestor ...' (v.5)

The closing chapters of Deuteronomy reiterate compelling themes from the entire Pentateuch, reminding God's people of their roots, and rehearsing a rich manifesto for life in the new covenant community.

Chapter 26 grounds this new way of life in two telling liturgies – the presentation of first-fruits to God in today's reading, followed by the dedication of the third-year tithe to the poor and disadvantaged (in verses 12-15). Through both rituals, the people's expression of gratitude and celebration prompts a holistic response of obedience, generosity, and praise.

At the heart of the liturgical action is a deeply moving account of Israel's story, beginning with a wandering Aramean. In our own days of mass migration, we are acutely aware of the threat to life and livelihood, faith and identity, faced by countless thousands of displaced people across the world.

If we belong to the privileged community of those who are free to 'possess' a home, and to feel 'settled' in it, then Deuteronomy reminds us that our human good fortune is a very precious gift of God. We have a corresponding duty to be good stewards of his manifold grace (1 Peter 4.10), seeking ways to serve one another with whatever gift each of us has received.

What basket of blessings do you have to lay before the altar of your God?

Reflection by **Margaret Whipp**

First Sunday of Lent	Deuteronomy 26.1-11
	Psalm 91.1-2, 9-end*
	Romans 10.8*b*-13
	Luke 4.1-13

Romans 10.8*b*-13

'... confess with your lips ... and believe in your heart' (v.9)

In the chapters leading up to today's reading, Paul has been wrestling with the relationship between the law and faith. Earlier in this chapter he says: 'Christ is the end of the law so that there may be righteousness for everyone who believes' (Romans 10.4). Here now is his assertion that all that is needed is confession of faith and belief in the heart. In fact, the connection is made *inwards* then *outwards*: lips to heart, and heart to mouth.

There is something very physical about faith that we often miss if we are too focused on the word. The ability to profess our faith is made through the physical action of speaking, and we cannot but be moved within by what we proclaim.

Paul's point then, as he goes on to say, is that we are all the same and we all have the ability to profess faith. Thus salvation is for everyone – Jew and gentile – and Paul remains passionately optimistic that precisely that will come about. What matters is not the law, but Christ. Again, part of the fabric of Paul's argument is the theme of the freedom that faith in Jesus brings. While we may now take that assertion for granted, Paul's reflections here present a radical argument.

Reading these words is an invitation to us to reconsider the ways in which we might take our faith for granted. As we confess our faith, how does that confession work its way out in the physicality of our life and the way in which we lead it?

Reflection by **Helen-Ann Hartley**

Deuteronomy 26.1-11
Psalm 91.1-2, 9-end*
Romans 10.8*b*-13
Luke 4.1-13

First Sunday of Lent

Luke 4.1-13

'... serve only him' (v.8)

Almost still wet from his baptism, Jesus goes into the wilderness. At his baptism Jesus had heard the one voice that matters, but now other voices come in and seek to tempt him away from this orientation of spirit that gives truth to his ministry. He has been claimed as God's beloved Son but now has to practise what has been proclaimed.

Often in the Gospels, it is when people are praising Jesus that he quickly finds the need to go away alone. Flattery can curdle our integrity. We can too easily begin to believe the false things said about us and even try to live up to them. So, here, the devil tries to seduce Jesus by reminding him who he is and what he is capable of. Temptations to misuse power, to follow the way of the world and to seek dramatic status rather than humble service of God and neighbour – these are all close to the bone for those who have an authority that appears unique. The devil knows what he is doing. He also quotes Scripture a lot – showing that mere quotation of the Bible is never enough to get near God's truth. We must always read the love between its lines too.

The devil fails in his attempt to get Jesus to surrender to self-assertion. His last suggestion is that Jesus go up to the pinnacle of the temple and throw himself off to show how the angels will protect him. Not succeeding, the devil departs 'until an opportune time'. This will be Gethsemane and will result in Jesus being on a cross, not a temple, and deserted, not upheld, by his followers. Even at the end, he refuses to sacrifice humility and its demands.

Reflection by **Mark Oakley**

Genesis 15.1-12, 17-18
Psalm 27
Philippians 3.17 – 4.1
Luke 13.31-end

Genesis 15.1-12, 17-18

'O Lord God, how am I to know that I shall possess it?' (v.8)

Since God first spoke to Abram and set him going on his journey (Genesis 12.1), Abram has done what God told him, faithfully. He has behaved as a servant should, and followed orders, and he has prospered. But now, suddenly, there is a new level of honesty between God and Abram, and as Abram reveals more of his true self, so he learns more about God.

Abram tells God what he really feels: nice as God's promises of land and protection are, they are hollow to Abram because he has no son. So even if God does indeed give him everything, he knows that the gift will be temporary, not his to pass on.

The solemn and frightening ritual that follows assures Abram that God has put his own reputation and honour at stake in this promise he has made. Abram will never forget the 'deep and terrifying darkness' in which God came to meet his greatest fear.

God's covenant with Abram is entirely one-sided: nothing is asked of Abram in return for what God promises. So Abram learns that we do not need to bargain with God. It is not that God did not know before this that Abram wanted a son, but perhaps that Abram didn't know that it was all right not just to obey God, but also to show God the truth about himself.

Reflection by **Jane Williams**

Genesis 15.1–12, 17–18
Psalm 27
Philippians 3.17 – 4.1
Luke 13.31-end

Philippians 3.17 – 4.1

'... stand firm in the Lord in this way' (4.1)

Philippi had a large number of Roman citizens, but Paul is reminding the small Christian community there that their citizenship is primarily in heaven, even if they are Romans. They are to avoid the excesses of pagan society around them ('their god is the belly') and to stand firm in their conviction that the ways of heaven are to be brought to bear on the things of earth, not the other way round. Moreover, the Lord of heaven will complete the process when he comes to transform the world, including our problematic bodies, to reflect his life and glory.

It's hard for Christians in a culture of excess to avoid the acid of materialism eating away at our convictions and values. The trick is to reverse the process, as it was for the Philippians. Heaven should permeate earth, not earth, heaven. It's important to be reminded regularly of the Big Picture, the way things really are, and that the kingdom of God is always our touchstone and the person of Jesus is always our point of reference. That's one reason we go to church. It's hard to swim against so unrelenting a tide. Only keeping a clear vision and staying close to our 'brothers and sisters' will enable us to stand firm.

Where will the pressures on you come from today? How might you reverse the tide?

Reflection by **John Pritchard**

Second Sunday of Lent

Genesis 15.1-12, 17-18
Psalm 27
Philippians 3.17 – 4.1
Luke 13.31-end

Luke 13.31-end

'... you were not willing!' (v.34)

Jesus knows how hard it is for us as human beings to fulfil our potential as children of God. We give God our hearts, then take them back again; we tell Jesus we will follow him, then we divert down the nearest primrose path as something 'other' distracts us from the One who is the Way. The door to kingdom life is narrow – we can enter fully only if we are prepared to give God our bulky baggage: failures and fears, pride or greed, successes and achievements, the ongoing impact of emotional pain, the defences and masks we've adopted and, most of all, our need to be in control.

Jesus yearns over Jerusalem, longing to save its people from the suffering that is to come, but they have a long history of spurning God's messengers and are not willing to turn and find life.

Jesus yearns over us too. He knows that occasional, superficial connection with God isn't enough to build the deeply trusting relationship that makes possible the dismantling of a lifetime's armour of avoidance of pain so our spiritual life may grow and our service of others deepen.

Just as a mother hen offers her life to protect her young, so Jesus will soon offer himself in an act that will ultimately make possible true spiritual intimacy for all humanity – that we may live with and in him forever.

If we are willing ...

Reflection by **Sue Pickering**

Isaiah 55.1-9
Psalm 63.1-9
I Corinthians 10.1-13
Luke 13.1-9

Third Sunday of Lent

Isaiah 55.1-9

'... you that have no money, come, buy and eat!' (v.1)

The person who has no money is the one who is here called by God's prophet to 'buy'. The people who do have money can buy nothing of worth. This is the paradoxical logic of worshipping a God who created everything that there is *ex nihilo* – from nothing. Perhaps it is why the prophet's message about free grace is framed by a celebration of creation: the gratuitous abundance and beauty of the natural world.

Only when you know that nothing that you think is yours to bargain with is really yours will you be equipped to unlock God's storehouses and be nourished and refreshed from them.

God's creation of the universe from nothing means that we have nothing to bargain with. Everything has come from God. Knowing we have nothing to bargain with is not an endpoint, however, on account of which we sink back and give up. Knowing we have nothing to bargain with is a beginning: the beginning of a transformative spiritual journey in which we learn to be radical receivers, set in motion by our gratitude in a way that allows us to contribute to God's kingdom.

'Just as I am, without one plea', as the hymn has it. Compassion and pardon are the bread and wine and milk that God offers us. All Isaiah asks us to do in order to purchase them is to 'return', admitting our empty-handedness. Only empty hands have room to receive. 'O Lamb of God, I come!'

Reflection by **Ben Quash**

Isaiah 55.1-9
Psalm 63.1-9
I Corinthians 10.1-13
Luke 13.1-9

1 Corinthians 10.1-13

'... our ancestors were all under the cloud' (v.1)

Who do you think you are? Where do you come from? Television programmes where celebrities explore their family trees – sometimes with surprising results – have become very popular. At this point in 1 Corinthians, Paul wants to remind his readers who they are by talking about their family, their 'ancestors'.

This may have come as something of a surprise to the gentiles among them – probably the majority. If they had been asked to describe their family tree, they might not have thought beyond biology. Paul's point, however, is that neither biological family, nor geographical and social location, define who we are in Christ. We are part of another family, another city, another history: the response to God's calling.

Advent encouraged us to identify with some of the great figures from Israel's past, especially the prophets preaching justice and announcing hope. It may come as a surprise to us to discover that our ancestors include the faithless as well as the faithful, those consumed by resentment and disappointment as well as those who walked in trust and gratitude. All were under the cloud – and Paul repeats the word 'all' four times. All received God's grace in astonishing ways, yet not all were able to keep the gift. For us too 'on whom the ends of the ages have come', the gift opens out onto a journey marked by testing, as God leads us deeper into faith in divine faithfulness. Knowing who we are will help keep our feet on the ground – and keep us moving forwards.

Reflection by **Jeremy Worthen**

Isaiah 55.1-9
Psalm 63.1-9
1 Corinthians 10.1-13
Luke 13.1-9

Third Sunday of Lent

Luke 13.1-9

'... unless you repent' (vv.3, 5)

People ask Jesus about the murder of Galilean pilgrims, perhaps wondering if he will reinforce the prevailing viewpoint that people suffer because they have sinned. Instead, Jesus points to two causes: the ruthless power of the Roman occupying forces for whom religious rituals provided opportunities for unchecked violence, and the risk – both literal and metaphorical – of building structures on flawed foundations. Jesus knows that the people of Jerusalem face annihilation unless they begin to live out his teaching, standing on the firm ground of God's love and justice.

The only thing that could possibly overcome the power of Rome then – or the effects of global financial mismanagement or systemic greed now – is the power of prayer released in ever-increasing circles of influence as more and more people, whom God has named as his own, put God at the centre of their lives.

This transformation from self-centred to God-centred living doesn't happen quickly. The fig tree story reminds us of two things: first, the hope-filled patience of the 'gardener', the Spirit of Jesus who nurtures our souls until we begin to bear that sacred fruit of love, joy and peace (Galatians 5.22); and second, that the consequences of failing to follow Jesus are as withering and inevitable as the axing of a barren tree.

What needs to be transformed in you, in me, in our communities? And what are the consequences if no changes are made?

Reflection by **Sue Pickering**

Fourth Sunday of Lent

Joshua 5.9-12
Psalm 32
2 Corinthians 5.16-end
Luke 15.1-3, 11b-end

Joshua 5.9-12

'... they ate the crops of the land of Canaan that year' (v.12)

The Israelites had crossed into the Promised Land, but when they did so they were not yet God's covenant people. The original generation that passed through the Sinai region rejected God many times on their travels. As a consequence, they were forbidden to enter the land, but the new generation who entered the land had not yet received the sign of the covenant. Hence they paused for the adult males to be circumcised into the faith of Abraham (Joshua 5.7-8). From this point they were ritually pure, a holy people, fit to celebrate the Passover.

The fact that they entered the Promised Land before they were ritually pure suggests that grace always precedes conversion and commitment. God is always ahead of us, opening the way, inviting us onward. It is only when we know something of the grace of God that we are challenged to active discipleship.

That discipleship needs discipline and nourishment. While the Israelites were crossing the Sinai, they were sustained on the provisional manna. Once in the land, they ate the crops of the land. They would need their strength for the holy war that lay ahead.

We, too, if we are to be fit for the Christian struggle against evil and injustice, need to reflect on our baptismal call and to feed on the nourishment of word and sacrament. Otherwise, the immediate task ahead will defeat us.

Reflection by **Angela Tilby**

Joshua 5.9-12
Psalm 32
2 Corinthians 5.16-end
Luke 15.1-3, 11*b*-end

Fourth Sunday of Lent

2 Corinthians 5.16-end

'... in Christ God was reconciling the world to himself' (v.19)

There are times when Paul's skill with words takes your breath away. This is one of them. In just nine words he summarizes the entire history of salvation and the meaning and trajectory of God's relationship with the Creation and with humankind.

Writing of such succinct, precise beauty does not come about by chance; nor is it a fluke. It comes from years of disciplined attention, from careful study of the rules of rhetoric, from diligent practice, from deep study of the scriptures and from prayer. It deserves the epithet 'inspired'.

Think of it: just nine words. Now compare that with all the windy sermons you have heard or with all the books you have read or with all those word-infested late-night conversations you have had with friends and fellow-students.

And if Paul's nine words describe the truth of the deep nature of God, it follows that we, the disciples of Christ in our generation, should be part of the same work of reconciliation.

Consider then those places where the world is fractured. Perhaps on a global scale we can find ways as reconcilers to bring peace. Or, at a personal level, we can ponder any discordant relationships that need healing (how can we be reconcilers there?). Deeper still, we can reflect on those areas of our own personal lives that bubble with unresolved anger or guilt. If God is reconciling the world, wherever reconciliation is needed, there God already is.

Reflection by **Christopher Herbert**

Fourth Sunday of Lent

Joshua 5.9-12
Psalm 32
2 Corinthians 5.16-end
Luke 15.1-3, 11b-end

Luke 15.1-3, 11b-end

'Then he became angry and refused to go in' (v.28)

All his life the older brother has had at his fingertips the benefits of his father's character and resources and yet he is unable to recognize what is rightfully his until his errant sibling returns. He sees their father's joy but does not share it, angered by the welcome, envious of the extravagant celebration, alienated by a false sense of injustice.

The younger son 'woke up' to his need of his father's mercy and made the journey home, rehearsing words of confession and regret that were rendered unnecessary by the father's unequivocal embrace. He knows he is not worthy, yet his father's response sweeps away any sense of shame or failure and instead wraps him round in vestments of delight.

But the older son has yet to 'wake up' to the reality that all the father has is his. He has yet to learn how to ask for what he needs; he has yet to believe that his father's love is truly unconditional. And so, instead of being a participant in the feast, he is a disgruntled observer, held back by his own ignorance of his father's true nature: love in its fullest expression.

Sulking and self-righteous, the older brother in all of us struggles to recognize the grace of God in which we 'live and move and have our being' (Acts 17.28).

Are you, am I, *really* awake to the generous love God lavishes on us here and now?

Reflection by **Sue Pickering**

Exodus 2.1-10 *or* 1 Samuel 1.20-end
Psalm 34.11-20 *or* Psalm 127.1-4
2 Corinthians 1.3-7 *or* Colossians 3.12-17
Luke 2.33-35 *or* John 19.25-27

Mothering Sunday

Exodus 2.1-10

'He was crying, and she took pity on him' (v.6)

However high the walls may rise between communities, there are likely to be occasions when encounter still happens, so that common humanity can become the exceptional ground for communication and cracks may even begin to appear across them. The decision of Moses' mother to put him in a papyrus basket has nothing to do with wanting to attract the attention of Egyptians: a pragmatic hiding place away from living quarters, and literalistic (even parodic?) compliance with Pharaoh's chilling command. Yet the basket becomes the place where Egyptian meets Hebrew, suffering evokes pity, pity leads to care, and care brings lasting interchange between the two communities, focused on a single person but with effects that will change them both irrevocably.

Pharaoh's daughter's life would have been carefully designed to ensure she never heard the cries of the oppressed Israelites. But somehow, those cries impinge on her world, and she responds with a simple act of compassion. Moreover, she recognizes immediately that she does not possess by herself, for all her riches, the means to provide the care that is required: help for the Hebrew must involve the Hebrews, without her just walking away and leaving the situation to them.

Are there people around you who are suffering, but whose cries you never hear? Are there cries you are hearing today, and which call on your compassion? Might you be called to act and take a share of responsibility, not alone but with others, including those whose cries these are?

Reflection by **Jeremy Worthen**

Mothering Sunday	Exodus 2.1-10 *or* **I Samuel 1.20-end**
	Psalm 34.11-20 *or* Psalm 127.1-4
	2 Corinthians 1.3-7 *or* Colossians 3.12-17
	Luke 2.33-35 *or* John 19.25-27

1 Samuel 1.20-end

'Hannah conceived and bore a son. She named him Samuel'
(v.20)

… only ten words, but as in a well-constructed poem, each word pulls its own weight. Consider what those ten words convey: Hannah's longing for a child; her anguished silent prayer; her vow to dedicate the child to the service of God; the mystery of conception; the labour of childbirth; and then the choice of a name for her baby son: 'Samuel', which means 'Name of God' and 'God has heard'. It's the ambivalence of the name which is such a delight; it's a cry of joy from a mother that spirals up into the universe, an exclamation of the profoundest gratitude.

The story of the angel's greeting to Mary has deliberate echoes of the Samuel story; except that in the case of Mary it was the angel Gabriel who determined the name of the child: '…you will conceive in your womb and bear a son, and you will name him Jesus' (Luke 1.31). And the name's meaning? It can be understood as 'God is a saving cry' – that is, if one calls, God will rescue, and 'God saves/rescues/delivers'. It is no wonder that having pondered the meaning of the name for several months, when Mary met her cousin Elizabeth, she burst into a song of exultant praise: 'My soul magnifies the Lord' (Luke 1.46). Only poetry will do for the miracle of birth. But after poetry comes something deeper still, a soul-shudder of silent wonder.

Reflection by **Christopher Herbert**

Exodus 2.1-10 *or* I Samuel 1.20-end
Psalm 34.11-20 *or* Psalm 127.1-4
2 Corinthians 1.3-7 *or* Colossians 3.12-17
Luke 2.33-35 *or* John 19.25-27

Mothering Sunday

2 Corinthians 1.3-7

'God … who consoles us in all our affliction' (vv.3-4)

The passage chosen here for Mothering Sunday is one that describes God as 'the Father of mercies and the God of all consolation'. Perhaps those who chose this passage were thinking of consolation as a quality chiefly belonging to motherhood, but that is not how this text describes it. There are a number of other biblical texts where the maternal references to God are much more obvious. The image of God as a bird sheltering his chicks under the shadow of his wing occurs in a number of places in the Old Testament, and Jesus himself takes up this image when mourning over Jerusalem in Luke 13.34. Two references from Isaiah make the maternal association even more explicit: 'now I will cry out like a woman in labour' (Isaiah 42.14); 'As a mother comforts her child, so I will comfort you' (Isaiah 66.13).

The fourteenth-century English mystic and writer Julian of Norwich wrote movingly in her *Revelations of Divine Love* about 'Jesus our mother'. Skilfully, she avoided the trap of trying to 'fix' God as one gender or another. She knew that God is beyond gender, but that masculine and feminine language helps us express those particular qualities we see reflected in God's dealings with us.

As we give thanks for our own mothers, we return to Julian for the last word: 'All the debt that we owe to fatherhood and motherhood – because of God's fatherhood and motherhood – is fulfilled in truly loving God, a blessed love which Christ prompts in us' (translator: Barry Windeatt, p. 131).

Reflection by **Barbara Mosse**

Exodus 2.1-10 *or* 1 Samuel 1.20-end
Psalm 34.11-20 *or* Psalm 127.1-4
2 Corinthians 1.3-7 *or* **Colossians 3.12-17**
Luke 2.33-35 *or* John 19.25-27

Colossians 3.12-17

'... clothe yourselves with love, which binds everything together in perfect harmony' (v.14)

I have never known my mother, and so today is always a bit awkward for me as I tend to reflect on a relationship that has been absent in my life. But all of us have the experience of losing people we love, of painful separations and partings. Into our bitter-sweet world of love and loss, we hold onto the promise of faith that the love from God's heart never leaves or diminishes. I love you, says God, for always. I know the cost we bear in loving but please don't be afraid.

When St Paul tells the Colossians how they should treat each other he might well have been describing the necessary qualities of a loving parent – compassion, patience, forgiveness, love – these are all needed if any household is to hold together. He also reveals that Christians should teach each other and, from time to time, help people see clearly how they might be manipulating truth or hurting themselves or those around them. Today, he might have been equally questioning as to how we treat people on social media and those we never meet face to face.

Paul seems to be saying that the Church is a school for relating, and in this school there must be a lot of singing. Harmony is only ever reached in life, as in music, if we can hear our brothers and sisters as well as know the song that lies deep within ourselves. Finally, he reminds them that everything in their community and in their lives must be done for God – not for me or my tribe or my politics or my preferences – for God only and, in that way, we will be doing it in the name of Jesus Christ.

Reflection by **Mark Oakley**

Exodus 2.1-10 *or* 1 Samuel 1.20-end
Psalm 34.11-20 *or* Psalm 127.1-4
2 Corinthians 1.3-7 *or* Colossians 3.12-17
Luke 2.33-35 *or* John 19.25-27

Mothering Sunday

Luke 2.33-35

'... a sword will pierce your own soul too' (v.35)

If you've ever sat with a mother who has lost her child, you'll know something of the agony of Mary. There's no sorrow like a mother's sorrow. I wonder if Mary took it in. She probably did, or how does it come to be recorded? Simeon's reflection over the years had led him to a sober understanding of the destiny of the Messiah when he finally appeared. Jesus would arouse fierce opposition as he lived and ministered with deep integrity and revealed the inner thoughts and motives of those who held power in the land. And that would inevitably involve Mary in the dark consequences of such a ministry. A sword would pierce her heart.

The collective pain of the world is sometimes too huge to contemplate. It's enough to face our own. But if you were to ask a large sample of people, the vast majority would say that life has still been wonderfully worth it. Mary would experience the sheer joy of having a son like Jesus who enriched every part of her life in those hidden years beyond our gaze. Her anguish at the end is terrible to contemplate, but Mary too would never have said that it wasn't worth having given birth to her beautiful son. Joy and pain come together in this life, but as a wise priest said on a retreat I once attended, 'Never let the sorrows of this world hide from you the joy of Christ risen.' Mary would have known that joy too.

Reflection by **John Pritchard**

John 19.25-27

'Then he said to the disciple, "Here is your mother."' (v.27)

After the fierce heat in the ruins of Ephesus, the reputed site of the Virgin Mary's house shaded by over-arching trees on a nearby mountain is a joy. It is quiet, enfolded into itself, a place of peace and tranquillity revered by Christians and Muslims alike.

The house was 'discovered' by a French priest in the late nineteenth century. He had read the works of a mystical German nun, Blessed Anne Katherine Emmerich (1774–1824), who had never been to Ephesus but had had a vision of the structure and location of the house. Her visions, recorded during her lifetime, were published after her death.

Why a house of Mary in that place? Because Mary, it is said, went with the apostle John to Ephesus. There a small church was built in his honour and was rebuilt in a much grander style by the Emperor Justinian in the sixth century. The ruins of that substantial basilica are still visible. And, by the way, it is also claimed that some people had made pilgrimages to the site of Mary's house long before the house itself was 'discovered'.

So, from possibly a fragment of a memory of the early Church, legend has been piled on legend and Mary's relationship as 'mother' to John has taken gentle and substantial form.

But isn't this how we humans are? As Winston Churchill once said: 'We shape our buildings and afterwards our buildings shape us.'

Reflection by **Christopher Herbert**

Isaiah 43.16-21
Psalm 126
Philippians 3.4b-14
John 12.1-8

Isaiah 43.16-21

'I will make a way in the wilderness ...' (v.19)

Unlike the carefully manicured lawns of Oxbridge colleges, which have alert porters to guard them from straying tourists and undergraduates, the lawns of university campuses in the USA are regularly criss-crossed by students. And there is a name for the beaten paths that emerge most clearly and consistently as the grass is worn away: 'paths of convenience'. These paths tell you important things about the routes that those who live in the place most want and need to travel.

The university authorities have two options at the end of each academic year. They can re-seed them, in the hope that a new generation will find a different way to travel from A to B. Or they can acknowledge the value of the paths of convenience, give in, and pave them!

The route that God most wants and needs to travel takes him across surprising terrain that few would normally cross: not precious grass, but the terrifying waters of ocean chaos, and the deadly expanses of desert wilderness. He chooses this way to reach the prison where his children are being kept, in order to set them free. It is, you might say, a path of *in*convenience, but for God it is travelled in love. It is worth thinking about how poorly the paths we usually take compare with God's; our love of convenience makes us poor travellers whose footsteps need re-seeding.

Reflection by **Ben Quash**

Fifth Sunday of Lent

Isaiah 43.16-21
Psalm 126
Philippians 3.4*b*-14
John 12.1-8

Philippians 3.4*b*-14

'For his sake I have suffered the loss of all things, and I regard them as rubbish, in order that I may gain Christ' (v.8)

> *'That's me in the corner*
> *That's me in the spotlight*
> *Losing my religion.'*

So sang REM in their mournful 90s hit, but here St Paul is not so much mournfully losing his religion as gleefully throwing it away! For what he 'regards as rubbish' in this passage is not discarded sin or error, but discarded religious achievement and status. Every distinguishing mark and sign of election, excellence and distinction is cast aside in order that he may begin again with Christ. And he wants to begin at the same point on the scale, the zero point, as every other needy human being.

This is indeed *kenosis* – or 'self-emptying' (Philippians 2.7) – in practice: a debonair detachment from the very status and respectability that, for so many, is the unacknowledged goal of religious life.

'No one can claim already to have heard the gospel', said Karl Barth, the great Swiss reformed theologian, in one of his startling aphorisms, for even faith can turn into an ego-inflating work when we cling to the status it confers.

To grasp the One who has grasped us, we must let go of everything else – even, and especially, our religious achievements and reputation.

Reflection by **Malcolm Guite**

Isaiah 43.16-21
Psalm 126
Philippians 3.4*b*-14
John 12.1-8

John 12.1-8

'The house was filled with the fragrance ...' (v.3)

All four Gospels contain this story in various forms. Because of where John places it in his narrative, he suggests that Mary's act of love comes out of gratitude to Jesus for bringing her brother back to life. John also uniquely places this incident immediately before Jesus enters Jerusalem, where Jesus will be hailed as 'King of Israel' (John 12.13, 15), hinting that Mary's gesture is also an anointing before he takes his place on the throne of his cross.

The act of anointing Jesus' feet, when taken in its literary and cultural context, displays Mary's utter devotion to Jesus. The ointment she uses is precious and, since there is no indication that Mary belonged to the wealthier classes (the meal was served by Martha rather than a servant), the ointment was apparently a major expenditure. It is also significant that Mary wiped Jesus' feet with her hair, since well-kept hair contributed to a person's dignity in the ancient world. Women took pride in long hair, which was considered attractive, and damage to one's hair was considered degrading. In this act she heightens the sense of self-effacement already reflected in her willingness to serve him as a slave as she washes his feet.

Only Judas cannot see the intensity of the love that is being ritualized through such intimacy. Only Judas cannot smell the fragrance brought into the room. It is Mary who beautifully reflects the reckless generosity of God that day and not the pinched moralism of the betrayer.

Reflection by **Mark Oakley**

Palm Sunday

Liturgy of the Palms:
Luke 19.28-40
Psalm 118.1-2, 19-end*

Luke 19.28-40

*'As he rode along, people kept spreading their cloaks
on the road' (v.36)*

It has long been noted that the cloaks strewn in the path of Jesus, as he rode on a donkey into Jerusalem, would have been the rags of the poor. He was riding into that holy city as the champion of the suffering and the oppressed. He had shared – and would soon come to share again – the full weight of their oppression, even to death. They knew him as someone who had ministered to them in their suffering and weakness, who had endured hardship like theirs and who had welcomed them and offered them hospitality when they had found every other door closed and every other table full of other guests. Jesus was known to be a hope-bearer, the incarnation of God's love for all people without distinction or prejudice, the one who came to bring freedom rather than bondage, joy rather than despair. And so they welcomed him as the anointed one who represented their liberation in God. Jesus was, for them, the Messiah of a kingdom that could be found everywhere and anywhere.

This procession was such a contrast to the Roman military, who would have come into Jerusalem at about the same time as Jesus, to intimidate the crowd at this annual religious festival. With Jesus, it was the blind, the prostitutes, the possessed, the disabled, the tax collectors, the Samaritans and the fishermen who were the special subject of his focus. Anyone might be included, even you and I.

Reflection by **David Moxon**

Liturgy of the Passion:
Isaiah 50.4-9a
Psalm 31.9-16 [*or* 31.9-18]
Philippians 2.5-11
Luke 22.14 – end of 23 *or*
Luke 23.1-49

Isaiah 50.4-9a

'Morning by morning he ... wakens my ear to listen' (v.4)

The verses in today's reading comprise the third of the four Servant Songs from the book of Isaiah (the others can be found at 42.1-4; 49.1-6; 52.13–53.12). The Servant as depicted here is an enigmatic, mysterious figure who is never specifically named, but in today's passage, whatever its original associations, the foreshadowing of Christ is significant and unmistakeable: 'I gave my back to those who struck me ... I did not hide my face from insult and spitting.'

But why this passage today? Are we not anticipating the later events of Holy Week, rather than focusing on Jesus' triumphal entry into Jerusalem on what has become known as Palm Sunday? We know that the crowd's joyful cries of 'Hosanna!' turned with alarming speed to 'Crucify him!' when Jesus failed to deliver the nation from the rule of the Romans. We, too, may find ourselves trying to force God to meet our expectations, rather than allowing ourselves to be moulded by his. But the Servant, who prefigures Christ, offers us a reminder that God's ways are not our ways, or his thoughts our thoughts (Isaiah 55.8).

The Gospels make clear that Jesus constantly listened to his Father, spending much time in solitary prayer (Mark 6.46; Luke 6.12). The Servant in Isaiah displays this same willingness to wait constantly on God. Are we prepared to listen to God with that same degree of attentiveness and humility, and to risk being open to what we might hear?

Reflection by **Barbara Mosse**

Palm Sunday

Liturgy of the Passion:
Isaiah 50.4-9*a*
Psalm 31.9-16 [*or* 31.9-18]
Philippians 2.5-11
Luke 22.14 – end of 23 *or*
Luke 23.1-49

Philippians 2.5-11

'[He] emptied himself ...' (v. 7)

What is the 'name above every name' that Jesus is given? It is unlike any other name in the world's long history, for it is a name that has the power to unite the whole world in worship: before this name, every knee will bow. But this power, likewise, is unlike any power in the world's long history. It is the power of radical generosity.

The name that Jesus bears by virtue of his willingness to live and die as a gift to others is a name that cannot be pronounced or written. It is the name communicated to Moses in the burning bush, signified in the 'tetragrammaton' (YHWH) and replaced in speech by many Jews and Christians with the words 'the LORD'. The 'name of Jesus', in other words, is much more than simply 'Jesus'. It is the eternal name of God. And what Paul wants to show us here is that the eternal God is a radical, intoxicatingly generous giver.

Feminist thinkers have rightly warned against using the 'self-emptying' of Jesus as a warrant for legitimating human self-abasement. It is not so much abased humanity that is celebrated here as generous divinity. Christ's 'emptying of himself' was not a suspension of divinity but an enactment of it. Perfect in power, he didn't fight those around him for elbow room, for recognition, for a piece of the action. Perfect in love, he didn't need to promote his 'name', as we do, treating it as a possession, an asset or a tool.

How shall we respond? Paul's answer is simple: make like-minded communities whose heart is generosity.

Reflection by **Ben Quash**

Liturgy of the Passion:
Isaiah 50.4-9a
Psalm 31.9-16 [*or* 31.9-18]
Philippians 2.5-11
Luke 22.14 – end of 23 *or*
Luke 23.1-49

Palm Sunday

Luke 22.14 – end of 23

'... they do not know what they are doing' (23.34).

Each of the crucifixion narratives in each of the Gospels is moving in its own way, but Luke's has an added pathos all of its own. Luke's account has its focus not just on Jesus and his death but on the disaster that awaits the people of Jerusalem in the future. He presents them as people who are sleep-walking into disaster. Their treatment of Jesus was, as Jesus observes, symptomatic of who they were, and who they were could only bring one thing – catastrophe.

This theme comes out strongly in what Jesus says to the women of Jerusalem and also in Jesus' prayer of forgiveness from the cross. Jesus warned the women of Jerusalem of the catastrophe that faced them – and indeed the whole nation; if this was how they reacted to the one who had come to love, save and heal them, how much worse would it be in the future? 'If they do this when the wood is green, what will happen when it is dry?' Jesus foresaw a desperate future for the people he loved so much, a future that they would bring on themselves because 'they do not know what they are doing'.

Jesus' words echo through the centuries, ringing as true now as they did then. Now, as then, we seem unable to understand what it is that we are doing; now, as then, we seem intent on sleepwalking into disaster. We need salvation now as much as ever.

Reflection by **Paula Gooder**

Palm Sunday

Liturgy of the Passion:
Isaiah 50.4-9*a*
Psalm 31.9-16 [*or* 31.9-18]
Philippians 2.5-11
Luke 22.14 – end of 23 *or*
Luke 23.1-49

Luke 23.1-49

'If you are … save yourself!' (23.37)

One of the features of Luke's Gospel is that, in it, we can find themes that weave their way throughout the whole Gospel (and sometimes onwards into Acts). One such theme is 'temptation' or 'testing'. Luke's version of the temptation narratives ends surprisingly and differently from the accounts in Matthew and Mark. In Luke, the devil departs but only until an opportune time. The implication of this phrasing (since the devil never returns in person) is that the devil returns in different guises throughout the Gospel. As a result, we, the readers, are to be alert to the very many times of testing that Jesus faced throughout his life.

This is nowhere more true than in the crucifixion narrative. There, three times, Jesus is 'tempted' to come down from the cross: first by the crowd; then by the soldiers and finally by one of the two criminals. The first two occasions even use the same phrasing ('if he is the Messiah of God'; 'If you are the King of the Jews') as the devil did in his temptations. Here, as in the temptations, Jesus is tempted to take a shortcut and to prove who he really is to those taunting him by doing something miraculous. With added irony, Jesus is challenged to save both himself and the people watching, while we, the readers, are all too aware that it was precisely his refusal to save himself that saves us.

Reflection by **Paula Gooder**

Exodus 12.1-4 [5-10] 11-14
Psalm 116.1, 10-end [*or* 116.9-end]
1 Corinthians 11.23-26
John 13.1-17, 31*b*-35

Exodus 12.1-4 [5-10] 11-14

'... they are to take a lamb for each family' (v.3)

Images of shepherds, sheep and sacrifice pepper the Old and New Testaments. These images are about reclaiming the purity of sacrifice, redeeming defilement. A Lamb shall be slain.

Yet although references to shepherds and lambs wind their way through many scriptural texts, they are difficult images for the Church to embrace. Most of us are far removed from the practices of shepherding. Furthermore, the notion has taken on a rather negative meaning – to describe someone as a sheep is an insult, implying they follow the crowd without question and expect someone else to be responsible for them.

The first Passover was a prelude to a journey. Now, we are all to be followers of the way, and we need to prepare and make ready. In the imagery of Passover, we encounter a journey of faith that is meant to carry us through our darkest hours. This trust, like the ways of a sheep with its shepherd, is not blind obedience. It is, rather, a radical trust that empowers us to believe that life has Christian meaning, even though our immediate experience may be telling us otherwise.

So, 'My sheep hear my voice. I know them, and they follow me' (John 10.27) is a message for Passover, and for Christian faith. But how easy can this be? Just ask any of the disciples whom Jesus called and who are there not to be served, but to serve. For the way of the Shepherd and sheep leads to both life and death; safety and sacrifice; love and loss. It is to this we are called.

Reflection by **Martyn Percy**

Maundy Thursday

Principal Holy Day

Exodus 12.1-4 [5-10] 11-14
Psalm 116.1, 10-end [*or* 116.9-end]
1 Corinthians 11.23-26
John 13.1-17, 31*b*-35

1 Corinthians 11.23-26

'This is my body that is for you. Do this in remembrance of me' (v.24)

Paul is remembering and recounting the words that Jesus used when he shared a last supper – the Last Supper – with his friends. Even though that meal happened not many years before Paul wrote his letter to the Church in the city of Corinth, the times were very different.

The Church Paul writes to is divided. The tradition at the time was to celebrate the Lord's Supper in the context of a meal, but, whereas nowadays we observe the sacrament and forget the meal, it seems that members of that early Christian community were enjoying the meal and forgetting the sacrament. The meal would have taken place in someone's home. We know, through archaeological studies, that homes then didn't have a dining room large enough for much more than ten, so if there were more people, they would have to eat in the atrium – a kind of large hallway with space, in large houses, for perhaps 50 people. It seems members of the Church were offering the use of their home, but trying to make sure their friends were in the 'dining room', whilst everyone else slummed it in the atrium. The Church was divided at the very place it ought to be expressing unity.

On Maundy Thursday, and every resurrection day, we remember that in the broken bread we encounter Jesus' body. As we, the Church, share that, we also become the body of Christ. So the Church can be broken, but it ought never be divided.

Reflection by **Harry Steele**

Exodus 12.1-4 [5-10] 11-14
Psalm 116.1, 10-end [*or* 116.9-end]
1 Corinthians 11.23-26
John 13.1-17, 31*b*-35

Maundy Thursday

Principal Holy Day

John 13.1-17, 31*b*-35
'He laid aside his garments' (v.4, KJV)

John's is at once the most cosmic and the most intimate of the Gospels, and it is the intimate details that carry the cosmic implications. So, here, Jesus lays aside his garments and kneels at his disciples' feet, but John frames this action in the fullness of Godhead. Jesus is the one who had come from God and was going to God, and so this little laying aside becomes itself the expression of his great *kenosis*, his 'self-emptying'. For he laid aside the garment and splendour of heaven, emptied himself and took the form of a servant. Every gesture is resonant: the one who covered himself with light as with a garment (Psalm 104.2) girds himself with a towel; the one whose Spirit moved on the waters of creation pours water into a basin.

Peter, like so many of us, can cope with the cosmic but not with the intimate. He is happy with Jesus high on the mountain of transfiguration with a newly made tabernacle between the two of them (Matthew 17.4), but he shrinks from this intimate touch. But here, as in all things, Jesus stoops to conquer.

> *'And here he shows the full extent of love*
> *to us whose love is always incomplete.*
> *In vain we search the heavens high above;*
> *The God of Love is kneeling at our feet.*

(Malcolm Guite, 'Maundy Thursday'
in *Sounding the Seasons*, Canterbury Press 2012)

Reflection by **Malcolm Guite**

Good Friday

Principal Holy Day

Isaiah 52.13 – end of 53
Psalm 22 [*or* 22.1-11 *or* 1-21]
Hebrews 10.16-25 *or*
Hebrews 4.14-16; 5.7-9
John 18.1 – end of 19

Isaiah 52.13 – end of 53

'... we held him of no account' (53.3)

Isaiah's vision of the suffering servant 'wounded for our transgressions, crushed for our iniquities' seems a natural reading for Good Friday. The surprise is that it's also read on Christmas Eve in churches festooned with Christmas trees.

What unites Good Friday and Christmas Eve is the indifference of the local population, whether to the birth of Jesus or his crucifixion. A few shepherds apart, Bethlehem 'held him of no account'. Joseph and Mary were homeless travellers, insignificant and unregarded. On Good Friday in Jerusalem, Mary and a few others waited at the foot of the cross, having followed Jesus after his condemnation. The life of the city was barely interrupted by yet another felon going to his execution. The central events of Christianity took place largely unnoticed by the world. Even today, the Via Dolorosa in Jerusalem is a place of commerce. For most of the year, Christian pilgrims follow the way of the cross and sing their hymns and say their prayers while shopkeepers and stall-holders tout for their business.

One difference between Christmas Eve and Good Friday is that, in most parts of the world, many more people go to church on Christmas Eve. A baby always pulls our heart strings. A convicted criminal (even an innocent one) arouses much less sympathy. If there are far fewer people in church on Good Friday, it's a helpful reminder for us that Jesus Christ was 'held of no account'.

Reflection by **Graham James**

Isaiah 52.13 – end of 53
Psalm 22 [*or* 22.1-11 *or* 1-21]
Hebrews 10.16-25 *or*
Hebrews 4.14-16; 5.7-9
John 18.1 – end of 19

Hebrews 10.16-25

'... let us consider how to provoke one another to love and good deeds' (v.24)

Time to get provocative? At this point in the letter to the Hebrews, the writer urges the readers to redouble their efforts to be Christ's people, seeking God with boldness – 'let us approach with a true heart in full assurance of faith' – and making a difference in the world. The writer's suggestion is that we should 'provoke one another to love and good deeds'. In the context of the particular first-century Christian community receiving this letter, those acts of love and good deeds might have been both effective and dangerous.

There has perhaps never been a better time to provoke one another, in Christ's name, to love and good deeds. Our world is as needy as ever for goodness and love, and the means to do this are at our fingertips. The presence of social media and the accessibility of the internet mean that we can very easily play our part in the ushering in of the peaceful kingdom of Jesus. One challenge may be around deciding where exactly we get involved. Another might be in learning to be generous to others who don't share our particular passion. The vital thing is to be open to the acts of love and goodness to which we are being called – and in our provocation itself, to be full of love and goodness.

Reflection by **Ian Adams**

119

Good Friday

Isaiah 52.13 – end of 53
Psalm 22 [*or* 22.1-11 *or* 1-21]
Hebrews 10.16-25 *or*
Hebrews 4.14-16; 5.7-9
John 18.1 – end of 19

Hebrews 4.14-16; 5.7-9

'Jesus offered up prayers and supplications, with loud cries and tears' (5.7)

On this sombre day, the writer to the Hebrews reminds us that we are never alone with our anguish; Jesus, the Son of God, has been there. He has been tested by darkness and abandonment and so has exposed God's heart to human pain. And yet that very act of obedience also means his life was somehow completed ('made perfect'), and he has become 'the source of eternal salvation' for all who approach him.

As we spend this day in the shadow of the cross, we won't have much to say. The terrifying reality of the cross is too complex and extreme to submit to the imprisonment of words. But those truths expressed by the writer to the Hebrews resonate somewhere deep within us. We will never be alone in our weakness and powerlessness; Christ has been there. And in a way we can't explain, evil is now broken-backed, and our future is secured. The truest response we can make is surely to kneel before the cross and say, 'Thank you. You did this for me.'

Those prayers and supplications, those cries and tears resound through history. But so too do the notes of a different song, heard on the wind three days later.

Reflection by **John Pritchard**

Isaiah 52.13 – end of 53
Psalm 22 [*or* 22.1-11 *or* 1-21]
Hebrews 10.16-25 *or*
Hebrews 4.14-16; 5.7-9
John 18.1 – end of 19

John 18.1 – end of 19

'There they crucified him' (19.18)

And that's it. Have you noticed how the Gospels dwell not at all on the physical details of the crucifixion? This is in stark contrast to the graphic detail of modern journalism or Hollywood films of Jesus. The reality is not being denied. Men and women in every age have found deep comfort and support in knowing that Jesus entered the utter depths of human sin and suffering – and so may we.

But we must trust the reticence we find here. As with all Bible-reading, we must attend to what we are told – to the details we are given. A narrow focus on bloody detail may even be distracting. The gift and uniqueness of this death will not be established on some imagined scale of physical pain. It is not quantity that saves. People have suffered worse, more prolonged deaths. The death of Jesus is not in competition with anyone else's.

A far greater story is being told here, one that will always elude our words and explanations. For who can possibly know what it costs to 'take away the sin of the world' (John 1.29)? The person who is dying here and why he dies is what makes this hellish day and place so improbably hopeful – a good Friday.

We stand and watch as best we can.

Reflection by **David Runcorn**

Easter Vigil

A minimum of three Old Testament readings should be chosen.
The reading from Exodus 14 should always be used.

Genesis 1.1 – 2.4*a*	Psalm 136.1-9, 23-end
Genesis 7.1-5, 11-18; 8.6-18; 9.8-13	Psalm 46
Genesis 22.1-18	Psalm 16
Exodus 14.10-end; 15.20, 21	***Canticle:* Exodus 15.1*b*-13, 17, 18**
[1] Isaiah 55.1-11	*Canticle:* Isaiah 12.2-end
Baruch 3.9-15, 32 – 4.4	
or Proverbs 8.1-8, 19-21; 9.4*b*-6	Psalm 19
Ezekiel 36.24-28	Psalms 42, 43
Ezekiel 37.1-14	Psalm 143
[2] Zephaniah 3.14-end	Psalm 98

Romans 6.3-11   **Psalm 114**
Luke 24.1-12

[1] *For a reflection on Isaiah 55.1-11, see page 95.*
[2] *For a reflection on Zephaniah 3.14-end, see page 26.*

*See page 122 for a list of the
Easter Vigil readings*

Genesis 1.1 – 2.4*a*

'God blessed them' (1.22, 28)

In the opening chapter of Genesis, the main three things God does are to *utter*, to *see*, and to *name*.

God utters in what is known grammatically as the 'jussive' mood. We don't have an exact equivalent in English to this Hebrew form, which is why we have to add the auxiliary word 'let' to the word 'be': 'let there be'. The jussive is a sort of command, but a command based on desire. God *wants* all of these abundant and particular things – 'each according to its kind' (NIV) – to *be*. Creation is an activity of desiring; God's love is its motor.

Then God sees what he has made. God is a sort of 'recipient' of the creatures that have been brought to being by his utterance inasmuch as they now appear to God. This is a first step towards something like a relationship with them.

Then, in a third aspect of God's primal work of making, there comes a further step towards the realization of reciprocity: God calls his creatures by *name*. This is a conferring of identity and of dignity on them.

Yet that is not all. In today's passage, at the point when not just 'mineral' and 'vegetable' but 'animal' creatures spring into being, there is a huge development. A new verb appears: God *blesses*, and this same blessing will soon be extended to the first humans too. No greater confirmation is needed that this world is made by and for love. It is 'very good'. Blessing is its crown.

Reflection by **Ben Quash**

123

Easter Vigil

See page 122 for a list of the Easter Vigil readings

Genesis 7.1-5, 11-18; 8.6-18; 9.8-13

'For in seven days I will send rain on the earth for forty days and forty nights' (7.4)

We have had it drummed into us so often that 'the animals went in two by two' that we can find ourselves surprised that some animals went in by *fourteens*. Seven pairs of all those animals considered clean were preserved in the ark, seven being a great, sacred number in the Bible, one that always signifies something special.

This is not the only time that the number seven appears in today's passage. After the rain has stopped, Noah waits for seven days between each sending of the dove. And in advance of the flood, intriguingly, it seems that the animals and Noah, with his family, were required by God to go into the ark seven whole days before the first raindrops began to fall. Why? Was it a time of prayer? Or of adjusting to their new circumstances? We are left to imagine.

From a Christian point of view, seven is special too, but it is not so much a number of *completion* as a number of *preparation*. The seven days of creation are followed by the eighth day of new creation, in Christ. Christ rises on the eighth day – the day *after* the Sabbath. This is why many baptismal fonts and baptistries have eight sides, because baptism achieves the new creation of Christians.

The flood has been seen as a figure or anticipation of baptism. So perhaps we can see the eighth day, the day on which the rain began, as the beginning of a new and gracious world as much as the ending of an old and wicked one.

Reflection by **Ben Quash**

*See page 122 for a list of
the Easter Vigil readings*

Easter Vigil

Genesis 22.1-18

'... your only son ... whom you love' (v.2)

According to an ancient tradition, the bare hillside of Mount Moriah where Abraham climbed with his son Isaac was the site where Jerusalem would be built (2 Chronicles 3.1). Abraham is asked to offer his only son, whom he loves, in the very place where thousands of years later, the promises to Abraham would be fulfilled.

Abraham's son carries the wood for the offering as Jesus carries his cross on the first Good Friday. Isaac is then laid on the wood as Jesus submitted to the cross.

The story of God's command to Abraham is a terrible one. It takes us deep into Abraham's heart, where his love for his son and his faith in God are tested as iron is tested by fire.

Yet the story also gives us a lens through which we can watch the passion of Jesus Christ unfold today. It is the lens of a father's heart where the Father's love for his Son endures even as the Son suffers and gives his life for the sin of the world.

Abraham's faith shines through the story. He says to his servants: 'We will come back to you'. He says to Isaac: 'God himself will provide the lamb for a burnt-offering'. This Easter, we are called to be children of Abraham, through the same faith that, through the death of Jesus on the cross, our sins are forgiven and we are accounted righteous before God.

Reflection by **Steven Croft**

Easter Vigil

See page 122 for a list of the Easter Vigil readings

Exodus 14.10-end; 15.20, 21

'Israel saw the great work that the Lord did ...' (14.31)

The discipleship that God requires of us is one that is centred on journey and risk. There is no enchanted path. The road we travel in our faith is one in which God abides with us – but it is fraught with hazards, and dangers remain. We are asked to trust. And sometimes to take extraordinary risks.

Moses has taken his people as far as he can go. Now he finds himself caught between his pursuers and a seemingly insurmountable obstacle. There is nothing Moses can do. He is trapped. It is as this point that God speaks to Moses. God sees our plight. And at the point when we are beginning to feel utterly defeated, God somehow redeems us.

Many readers today will struggle with the huge loss of life contained in this story. But in some respects, this is not a story about victors and vanquished; it is, rather, a story about how God meets us in moments of dire despair and desolation. The game appears to be up for the Israelites. They are about to be recaptured. Yet this story says that God will not give up on us. When we cry out to God, we are heard.

Sometimes it is easy to feel defeated by the overwhelming odds we face or the sheer scale of needs we are attempting to address on behalf of others. So this story shows that God can snatch a victory from the jaws of defeat. What God needs us to be is not fearful, but rather watchful and faithful. Rather than face drowning or annihilation, we may yet find ourselves on some dry land, and with an unlikely path ahead.

Reflection by **Martyn Percy**

*See page 122 for a list of
the Easter Vigil readings*

Easter Vigil

Exodus 15.1*b*-13, 17, 18

'I will sing to the Lord, for he has triumphed gloriously' (v.1)

In dark, hushed churches all over the land, people await the news of an astonishing victory. Throughout Holy Saturday the world has held its breath. Now the news of resurrection is about to break, and the image that anchors it in ancient tradition is that of the exodus, the foundational event of the Jewish faith. Just as God rescued the Israelites through the Red Sea where 'the floods stood up in a heap', so now God is about to rescue humanity through the deep waters of death that had drowned Jesus on Good Friday.

Christians have long since claimed this ancient song as a 'pre-echo' of the resurrection. We have been rescued through the deep waters of baptism and brought out to a new world that is all God's gift. But, as the Israelites were to discover, with privilege comes responsibility. They had a task to fulfil and a way of obedience to follow in a new land. So as we come through the waters of baptism and enter the new world of resurrection, we have to follow the guidelines of the kingdom given to us in the ministry of Jesus and sealed in the resurrection.

That seems to mean leaving wet footprints wherever we go, signs that we too have gone through the waters and been changed by tonight's glorious victory.

Reflection by **John Pritchard**

Isaiah 12.2-end

'With joy you will draw water from the wells of salvation'
(v.3)

Chapter 12 of the long book of the prophet Isaiah has only six verses. But it packs a punch. It is a glorious vision of Israel's restoration, remaking and renewal. At its heart is an image of water drawn from the wells of salvation. So it fits Easter Eve when, at the Vigil, there is a long-standing tradition that new Christians are baptized.

Water baptism became quickly established as the primary public ritual on becoming a Christian. Jesus spoke of bringing a gift of living water. He tells the Samaritan woman at Jacob's well (John 4.10) that the living water he offers is for everyone, not just his own people. Then at the feast in Jerusalem, Jesus says 'let anyone who is thirsty come to me to drink ... out of the believer's heart shall flow living water' (John 7.37-8).

It's not simply the washing away of sin that animates our understanding of baptism, but a much deeper and richer biblical inheritance. At the Easter Vigil, the whole story of our salvation is recalled. We are reminded that we are baptized into Christ's death so that we may rise with him in triumph. Water is the source of all life. But if we are overwhelmed by it, we will drown.

Jesus assures us that his gift is 'living water'. We cannot have too much of it, for it springs up for eternal life.

Reflection by **Graham James**

See page 122 for a list of
the Easter Vigil readings

Easter Vigil

Proverbs 8.1-8, 19-21; 9.4*b*-6

*'I walk in the way of righteousness,
along the paths of justice' (8.20)*

The idea of 'the quest' has been a staple of literature for thousands of years: think of the Epic of Gilgamesh, a Mesopotamian poem dating from circa 2100 BC, where the quest is to discover the secret of eternal life; or the quests of King Arthur and the Knights of the Round Table. More recent examples include the Indiana Jones films, and in literature, Tolkien's *Lord of the Rings*. Stories where the hero goes on a perilous journey, encounters major crises but triumphs victoriously seem to be hard-wired into the human psyche.

The parallel notion that we humans are on an existential quest for meaning, purpose and fulfilment is a foundational part of the narratives we create to structure our inner lives.

It is not at all surprising, therefore, that biblical stories too include the concept of 'quest'. In Proverbs that quest is expressed in terms of the search for wisdom, but there is a subtle and significant difference. Instead of the quest being about self-fulfilment ('pursuing the dream'), the quest is linked strongly with the concept of love. Those who search for wisdom will find, according to Proverbs, that it is discovered in and through the love of God.

The search is not just confined to our minds, or to our emotions. It is holistic: it is only as we love and are loved in return that we find the very heart and source of wisdom.

Reflection by **Christopher Herbert**

Easter Vigil

See page 122 for a list of the Easter Vigil readings

Ezekiel 36.24-28

'I will sprinkle clean water upon you, and you shall be clean'
(v.25)

There are many times when the prophet Ezekiel denounces the sin of Israel as a matter of impurity. The injustice that has led to the misery of exile is a kind of pollution. It is both analogous to, and includes, sexual sin. Like many religious people, the prophet reflects a real horror of uncleanness, of human mess and disorder obscuring God's holiness. But the prophet himself is inspired to pronounce the answer. God in his holiness will intervene to make his people holy once again, not as a concession to their bad behaviour, but simply because he is good. The cleansing water is an act of sheer grace, and it creates a change of heart; the heart of stone becomes a heart of flesh. There is a new humanity about to be born; even the desolate land will become a new Eden.

The language of sprinkling, of the new heart and life in the Spirit, anticipates Christian beliefs about conversion and baptism, and this language is often to be found in the liturgies of Eastertide.

As Christians, it is good for us to be thankful for our baptism, the permanent reminder that, however much we mess up, the cleansing water of God's grace is always welling up within. Purity is God's gift, not our achievement.

Reflection by **Angela Tilby**

*See page 122 for a list of
the Easter Vigil readings*

Easter Vigil

Ezekiel 37.1-14

'I am going to open your graves' (v.12)

The night of the Easter Vigil is a mysterious time. Old images and metaphors swirl through our liturgies reminding us that the night of resurrection was itself deeply mysterious and beyond description. It wasn't the kind of truth you captured on a fridge magnet. One of the images that has seemed to express some of the feelings associated with this night is that of the dry bones in Ezekiel's vision, the bones of devastated Israel, disorientated and despairing in their Babylonian exile. God gave those tired, scattered bones life, first by joining them together again, and then by breathing his spirit into them. It was like opening the graves of a dead people. It was resurrection.

On this night of metaphors it's also good to earth those images in our own experience. We may not, spiritually, be a heap of old bones, but we might have lost the zest of those heady days when the faith was new-born within us. Our spiritual journey tends to drift downhill rather than fall off a cliff. Familiarity might not breed contempt, but it easily encourages boredom and a lack of expectation. Each year on the night of resurrection, we have the opportunity to claim again this most heartening of news – that we can live again, and again, and again.

Reflection by **John Pritchard**

See page 122 for a list of the Easter Vigil readings

Romans 6.3-11

'... baptized into Christ Jesus' (v.3)

When the Victorians redeveloped a church where I once served, they sank a large baptistry into the floor. It's now hidden under carpeting, and most people don't know it's there. It was such a disappointment that I never got to use it!

In fact, it hasn't been used for baptisms in living memory, but it proved invaluable in the Second World War when it was kept full of water that was put to good use to extinguish an incendiary bomb that fell through the roof in 1941.

Our old self is extinguished by the waters of baptism – that at least should be in our minds, even if we're more familiar with water being poured on the forehead of a child or adult. But we mustn't lose sight of the powerful symbolism that total immersion has: of being buried with Christ and, as we resurface, also being raised with Christ.

Even if our mortal life still has years to run, and even though we're still fallible, we're no longer enslaved by sin, and resurrection life has begun. Whatever form of baptism we follow, it leaves us utterly drenched, and saturated through and through, with Jesus Christ. And from that point, we'll find his death and resurrection starting their work within us, steadily destroying death and bringing renewed, redeemed, overflowing life in every part of our being.

Reflection by **Sarah Rowland Jones**

See page 122 for a list of the Easter Vigil readings

Easter Vigil

Luke 24.1-12

'... he went home, amazed at what had happened' (v.12)

For the followers of Jesus, working out what had happened on the first Easter Sunday was a slow process. The women's initial reaction was confusion. Then they were frightened. Then they imprecisely recalled something Jesus had said. The men's first reaction was to dismiss what they were told out of hand. Only Peter afforded the women the dignity of going to see whether there was any substance to what they said. But he had no flash of insight, just puzzlement.

Resurrection is real, but it will not be hurried. The tragedies of our lives often come at speed – bereavement, breakdown of a relationship, pain. But the way God brings new life is measured.

When I am bereaved, resurrection begins when I look at a photograph of the person whose loss has wounded me, and the sight of it unexpectedly brings a joyful memory instead of distress.

When a relationship ends, resurrection begins when I realize for the first time that I am enjoying something because I am me, not because I am half of a couple.

When pain is intolerable, resurrection begins when I slip away from the body that has limited and disabled me, and step liberated into the presence of God. That, more than any other, is how God silently brings new life.

Today, as on that Sunday that changed everything, God reveals himself slowly. But his plan to make all things new is irrepressible.

Reflection by **Peter Graystone**

Easter Day

[1]**Acts 10.34-43** *or* Isaiah 65.17-end
Psalm 118.1–2, 14–24 [*or* 118.14–24]
1 Corinthians 15.19-26 *or* [1]Acts 10.34-43
John 20.1-18 *or* Luke 24.1-12

Acts 10.34-43

'I truly understand that God shows no partiality' (v.34)

This passage is like an embryonic creed, a succinct summary of salvation history: God chose the Israelites; Jesus is the Messiah; he was put to death, but God raised him to life ... and everyone, Jew and gentile, can now receive forgiveness of sins in his name. Of course, this is not necessarily an accurate report of what Peter said to Cornelius and his household. It is Luke's version of what Peter probably said, but whether historically accurate or not, the passage reveals that very early in the life of the Christian movement, summaries of the key points of the faith were being constructed. Those summaries, couched in Judaistic terms, presupposed that the hearers had some understanding of the religious beliefs of Judaism. You can only talk about the Messiah if your hearers have an inkling of what 'Messiah' means. In the case of Cornelius, it was a successful strategy, for he was already a devout and sympathetic God-fearer.

Two thousand years later, in our multi-faith context, surrounded as we are by a Babel of beliefs liberally garlanded with misinformation, how do we create the language to convey the glory of the resurrection? Shouting Christian slogans loudly or scattering gobbets of Christianity into the cacophonous realm of social media are unlikely to prove fruitful strategies.

To change the metaphor: if much of the soil is stonily unreceptive, then presumably we ought to begin by trying to create better soil. But that's a long, slow, patient process, isn't it?

Reflection by **Christopher Herbert**

[1]*The reading from Acts must be used as either the first or the second reading.*

Acts 10.34-43 *or* **Isaiah 65.17-end**
Psalm 118.1-2, 14-24 [*or* 118.14–24]
1 Corinthians 15.19-26 *or* ¹Acts 10.34-43
John 20.1-18 *or* Luke 24.1-12

Easter Day

Isaiah 65.17-end

'... be glad and rejoice forever in what I am creating' (v.18)

God is building a kingdom. The coming of Jesus announced that it was near. His resurrection from the dead made it inevitable. One day, when heaven and earth are renewed, it will become a reality so perfect that the suffering of this uncertain life will be completely forgotten.

Isaiah spells out what a vision of that kingdom can and should mean in the present as well as in the future. It means children surviving childbirth and thriving in infancy. It means people living healthily to a good age. It means stable societies free from war, famine and the other catastrophes that force people to leave their homes.

It is marked by an end to a mother's nagging fear about what the future holds for her child. It is marked by such a closeness to God that every whisper will be heard. It is marked by a world in which humans are at one with the created order – neither threatened by nor a threat to the environment.

Christians are called to be beacons, shining in today's world by working to make the values of the kingdom a reality and illuminating the path that leads to our future in heaven where it will perfected eternally. In our world of shocking inequalities, this vision is not just a comforting hope; it is an urgent challenge.

Reflection by **Peter Graystone**

Easter Day

[1]Acts 10.34-43 *or* Isaiah 65.17-end
Psalm 118.1-2, 14-24 [*or* 118.14–24]
1 Corinthians 15.19-26 *or* [1]Acts 10.34-43
John 20.1-18 *or* Luke 24.1-12

1 Corinthians 15.19-26

'... all will be made alive in Christ' (v.22)

The First Prayer Book of Edward VI in 1549 ordered at Easter the saying or singing of an Easter anthem, bringing together verses from Romans and 1 Corinthians. They have been part of Anglican devotion ever since. They include these verses from 1 Corinthians 15 (KJV): 'For since by man came death, by man came also the resurrection of the dead. For as in Adam all die, even so in Christ shall all be made alive.'

We are given an image of Jesus as the new Adam. The first Adam, who represents the old humanity, brings sin and death into the world through his disobedience – sin and death represented by a tree from which forbidden fruit is taken. The second Adam, Jesus, the one who inaugurates a new humanity, himself the fruit of another tree, the cross, conquers sin and death and restores life, opening up a way to a new and eternal life.

Bishop John V. Taylor used often to say that 'God does not care very much whether you are religious, but he does care that you should be alive'. Jesus himself spoke of coming to bring life in all its fullness. Paul is telling us that this aliveness is a fruit of the resurrection. The deadness of Adam, of the old humanity, has gone. In Christ, all is made alive. The Prayer Book of 1549 wisely added to the text three alleluias!

Alleluia, alleluia, alleluia.

Reflection by **Michael Perham**

[1]*For a reflection on Acts 10.34-43, see page 134. The reading from Acts must be used as either the first or the second reading.*

Acts 10.34-43 *or* Isaiah 65.17-end
Psalm 118.1-2, 14-24 [*or* 118.14–24]
1 Corinthians 15.19-26 *or* Acts 10.34-43
John 20.1-18 *or* ¹Luke 24.1-12

Easter Day

John 20.1-18

'Do not hold on to me' (v.17)

John's Gospel highlights the angels in Jesus' empty tomb, 'one at the head and the other at the feet'. Archbishop Rowan Williams shows the connections that may be made: 'Iconographically, it recalls ... the mercy-seat of the ark, flanked by the cherubim' (*On Christian Theology*, Blackwell, 2000). Israelite tradition held that God dwelt between the cherubim that were mounted on the ark and leant towards each other across the throne or mercy-seat. However, the ark's throne contains no image of God – God is both there and absent, seen and not seen. Archbishop Rowan calls this a 'paradoxical manifestation'.

This paradoxical manifestation is carried forward into the resurrection. We have Mary Magdalene and those on the road to Emmaus failing to recognize the risen Christ. The Jesus whom they previously knew is both there and absent. A fundamental change has taken place. The change is not to deny the reality of the resurrection but to affirm that Jesus has risen into something new, and his rising continues in the looking forward to the ascension.

'Do not hold on to me,' Jesus said to Mary Magdalene. This may be better translated as 'do not keep clinging'. Mary has to let go of her personal relationship with the physical Jesus and embrace the mystical presence/absence that now inspires the Church.

Reflection by **Paul Kennedy**

¹*For a reflection on Luke 24.1-12 see page 133.*

Second Sunday of Easter

[1]Exodus 14.10-end;15.20, 21
[2]**Acts 5.27-32**
Psalm 118.14-end *or* Psalm 150
Revelation 1.4-8
John 20.19-end

Acts 5.27-32

'And we are witnesses to these things, and so is the Holy Spirit whom God has given to those who obey him' (v.32)

Sometimes the Acts of the Apostles is referred to as 'The Gospel of the Holy Spirit', for this book tells the story of a Spirit-filled and Spirit-guided Church expanding and growing. Its message is the good news of what God has done in Jesus Christ.

In this reading, Peter again repeats the basic proclamation of the gospel: Jesus was killed, God raised him to life, forgiveness is found in him. Its method is witness through word and deed. And it is carried out by history's most unlikely collection of ambassadors – the twelve apostles and those who travelled with them. Few of them are learned or articulate by the world's standards, but it is this company of men and women who, spurred on by Jesus and sustained by the Spirit, succeed in taking the gospel across the known world and establishing Christian communities in many far-flung places. As Peter says here, it is both their witness and the witness of the Holy Spirit. All this enrages the religious leaders. But the first Christians consider it an honour to suffer for the sake of the gospel, and they carry on teaching and proclaiming Jesus as Messiah.

If, like Peter, we remain faithful, if we walk in the light of this gospel, then the same Spirit will be at work, witnessing through us. That is the astonishing Christian claim.

Reflection by **Stephen Cottrell**

[1] *For a reflection on Exodus 14.10-end;15.20, 21, see page 126.*
[2] *The reading from Acts must be used as either the first or the second reading.*

Exodus 14.10-end;15.20, 21
[1] Acts 5.27-32
Psalm 118.14-end *or* Psalm 150
Revelation 1.4-8
John 20.19-end

Second Sunday of Easter

Revelation 1.4-8

'I am the Alpha and the Omega' (v.8)

The last book of the Bible gives us a window onto God's ultimate purposes. The author of Revelation is John, a Christian visionary, whom tradition identifies as John the Evangelist, though his style is so different from that of the author of the Fourth Gospel as to make this unlikely. In spite of that, these prophecies have the stamp of authenticity. They come from the heart of a suffering and expectant Church. John is inspired by the Spirit to record a series of visions and send them by letter to the seven churches of Asia.

Christ is 'the faithful witness, the firstborn of the dead'. This testimony to the resurrection of Jesus runs through the opening chapters of Revelation. Christ has the authority of his victory over death; he has become the Alpha and the Omega, the first to return from death. John points those who are suffering persecution to the fact that they are not alone. The Lord knows what is in store for them and gives them the courage to face it.

We do not know what lies ahead for us today or in the future, but the living Christ is always near us. The resurrection is not an event in the past, but a promise for today and every day. The living Christ is always near us and tells us not to be afraid.

Reflection by **Angela Tilby**

[1] *The reading from Acts must be used as either the first or the second reading.*

Second Sunday of Easter

Exodus 14.10-end;15.20, 21
Acts 5.27-32
Psalm 118.14-end *or* Psalm 150
Revelation 1.4-8
John 20.19-end

John 20.19-end

'Jesus came and stood among them and said,
"Peace be with you."' (v.19)

I recall a priest leaving an academic seminar on the person of Christ and grumbling: 'Why can't we concentrate on the big ideas? Not "nature", "person" or even "Son", but words like "Peace"?'

The risen Christ comes back to his disciples with a conventional Jewish greeting, but now and here it overturns their world. Before his arrest, trial and passion, the Jesus of John's Gospel spoke at length to his disciples 'so that in me you may have peace', and with that peace courage, since 'I have conquered the world' (John 16.33). For the next few days, it must have been quite impossible for them to believe this. But now everything has changed. So, John can portray Pentecost come early, to show that the empowering Spirit of Peace, which is the Church's only weapon, is the direct gift of this crucified Messiah. It is his very life breath.

But Thomas – that impulsive, questioning disciple (John 11.16, 14.5) – misses it all. One can hardly imagine his despair. Nor how he felt when he finally meets his Lord, and hears for himself the 'Peace be with you'. Does he really need to reach out his hand now? Does he even need to see Jesus? Isn't that Peace always enough?

Reflection by **Jeff Astley**

¹Zephaniah 3.14-end
²**Acts 9.1-6 [7-20]**
Psalm 30
Revelation 5.11-end
John 21.1-19

Third Sunday of Easter

Acts 9.1-6 [7-20]

'Saul, Saul, why do you persecute me?' (v.4)

Paul's conversion experience has influenced the stories that people over the centuries have told about their own conversions. They too recall a moment of flashing insight. They too have felt in need of being 'led by the hand'. They too have wanted to proclaim their experience of having been overwhelmed by God. But look at this story from another angle. Look at it not so much as a prototype of 'conversion' but as a way of understanding who Christ really is. The question that Saul heard was of immense significance. Technically speaking, Saul had *not* persecuted Jesus. To the best of our knowledge Saul had never even met Jesus, let alone set the attack dogs on him. He had been witness to the killing of Stephen, one of Jesus' followers. Yet Saul recognized (and this was the amazing insight – note the words) that in killing Stephen and in going after the Christians, he was in reality attacking Christ himself. The new followers embodied the very being of Christ. They and their Lord were one.

It was, of course, a moment that changed history and one on which Saul/Paul continued to reflect deeply. It led him to see that the new way was one which was about liberation. It was about humanity becoming one with the Creator ('For all who are led by the Spirit of God are children of God', Romans 8.14). It was about recognizing that all barriers between people were now abolished.

Reflection by **Christopher Herbert**

¹ *For a reflection on Zephaniah 3.14-end, see page 26.*
² *The reading from Acts must be used as either the first or the second reading.*

Third Sunday of Easter

Zephaniah 3.14-end
[1]Acts 9.1-6 [7-20]
Psalm 30
Revelation 5.11-end
John 21.1-19

Revelation 5.11-end

'Worthy is the Lamb that was slaughtered!' (v.12)

Together, chapters 4 and 5 form the heart of John's Revelation. This is the larger reality from which every other element of the story flows. While chapter 4 serves to emphasize God's power, chapter 5 gives us an extraordinary insight into the source of that power: God's vulnerability. It is worth pausing to note that the one who controls the outcome of all history is depicted as a lamb (Revelation 5.6) who stands as if he has been slaughtered.

Chapter 5 helps to build in our imaginations an ever-expanding picture of the whole universe. At the focus of worship and the centre of dramatic tension lies the one on the throne, the Lamb and the scroll. This scroll contains the story of 'what must soon take place', as promised in Revelation 1.1, 1.19 and 4.1, the contents of which are eagerly awaited by John and those who long for God's saving justice. Through the course of chapter 5, the camera angle widens to reveal the presence of myriad angels who, like the elders and living creatures, are focused on this central tableau. As the vision expands still further, every creature in heaven and on earth and under the earth is similarly transfixed. The attention of every element of the universe is focused in a particular direction. We are invited to share their gaze and to join in the worship they offer.

Reflection by **Alan Garrow**

[1]*The reading from Acts must be used as either the first or the second reading.*

Zephaniah 3.14-end
Acts 9.1-6 [7-20]
Psalm 30
Revelation 5.11-end
John 21.1-19

Third Sunday of Easter

John 21.1-19

'Just after daybreak, Jesus stood on the beach' (v.4)

The words of the Gospels can never do justice to the reality of the resurrection. The first Easter is, simply, more than tongues can tell. But the stories we are left with contain some vital clues as to what to expect of or hope for the future Church. The number of fishes – 153 of them – hauled up in the nets is probably trying to tell us something quite important about the future of the Church. The Church will be as abundant as a fisherman's haul – and diverse, full of interesting specimens. And John, in his recounting of the breakfast, is also saying something about hospitality: that Jesus still invites us to feast with him. Even though the disciples deserted Jesus after the last supper, there are other suppers. Jesus is, in every sense, the Host. We continue to feed on him, and feed with him.

Then there is the swimming. One of the strange things about the Bible is that there is no real example of successful swimming prior to the resurrection. Water symbolizes the forces of chaos and overwhelming. But after Easter, it is different. Peter can take the plunge. The resurrection appearances invite the disciples to take risks. The Church will be advanced by those who can learn to swim, or even to try and walk on water.

There is a Venetian proverb that says 'the critic stands on the shore; but the artist swims in the sea'. In our resurrection faith, we are invited to take the plunge, not because we are rash, but because Christ now beckons us to join him in a new life of adventure and hope.

Reflection by **Martyn Percy**

Fourth Sunday of Easter

[1]Genesis 7.1-5, 11-18;
8.6-18; 9.8-13
[2]**Acts 9.36-end**
Psalm 23
Revelation 7.9-end
John 10.22-30

Acts 9.36-end

'Peter ... knelt down and prayed' (v.40)

In this part of Acts, Luke switches his attention away from Paul to Peter. Peter goes on a tour of the Christians living in Lydda (now called Lod, north-west of Jerusalem), and then he is summoned by some of the Christians to Joppa (present-day Jaffa). Here, the story that Luke tells has a number of echoes of the healings associated with the Prophets, Elijah and Elisha, as well as the healing of Jairus' daughter by Jesus. In other words, Peter is portrayed as continuing the powerful healing work of God.

There is one subtlety, however, and that concerns the woman in Joppa, named in Greek, Dorcas, and in Aramaic, Tabitha. It's a deft signal that the gospel is moving out of its Jerusalem-centred locale. And, if the echo of Elijah's healing is intentional, that too reinforces the sense of God being available to all; the woman in the Elijah story was not a Jew but a Phoenician who lived near Sidon.

The Spirit, implies Luke, is at work and is beginning to break down barriers, to liberate people from illness and even death. Could there be any greater sign of God's universal grace and purpose?

Now recall who the transmitter of God's love is – it is Peter, the very man who had denied Jesus just before the trial but to whom Jesus had appeared at the resurrection. A new world beckons ...

Reflection by **Christopher Herbert**

[1]*For a reflection on Genesis 7.1-5, 11-18; 8.6-18; 9.8-13, see page 124.*
[2]*The reading from Acts must be used as either the first or the second reading.*

Genesis 7.1-5, 11-18;
8.6-18; 9.8-13
[1]Acts 9.36-end
Psalm 23
Revelation 7.9-end
John 10.22-30

Revelation 7.9-end

'... a great multitude that no one could count' (v.9)

There is something wonderfully inclusive about the Easter message. What Jesus has done for us he has done for all humanity. As John looks towards the redeemed saints, he sees that they are a worldwide community, so large that they cannot be counted. They wave palm branches to mark the victory of the Lamb, in contrast to the palm branches that were waved on the way to his betrayal and death.

The human multitude joins the worship of heaven alongside the angels, the elders and the four living creatures, who appear in the Book of Ezekiel (Ezekiel 1.5 ff) and represent the living energies of God. These four creatures also come to represent the four evangelists, and so the four Gospels, and the gospel itself that is preached to the four corners of the earth. Nothing is beyond the scope of God's redemptive purpose.

That purpose is only fulfilled at a price, however. The dialogue with 'one of the elders' reinforces the point that earthly suffering is part of the vocation of those who follow the Lamb. We may feel we do not suffer much compared to those who are persecuted. We should nevertheless consider how our baptismal faith is strengthening and sustaining us to cope with the sufferings that inevitably come our way in the course of life.

Reflection by **Angela Tilby**

[1] *The reading from Acts must be used as either the first or the second reading.*

Fourth Sunday of Easter

Genesis 7.1-5, 11-18;
8.6-18; 9.8-13
Acts 9.36-end
Psalm 23
Revelation 7.9-end
John 10.22-30

John 10.22-30

'How long will you keep us in suspense?' (v.24)

The French philosopher Voltaire once commented that 'God made man in his own image, and man returned the compliment'. It is true that we are all very skilled at making God a convenient reflection of ourselves. It is remarkable, too, how often God agrees with us and not with our opponents ...

The same is true with Jesus. Depending on who you talk to, he can be the conservative guardian of family life and traditional values or the radical subversive who attacks the establishment and the status quo. In this passage, we find a heated conversation taking place as to who Jesus is: 'How long will you keep us in suspense?'

In John's Gospel, we find that Jesus eludes our categories and definitions. Although much in the religious temperament can make us want to define and defend what it is we believe, the danger is that our soul forgets that it is always in school. The spiritual adventure to which we are called is a constant, often painful, journey in which our full-stops are changed into commas so that another chapter can begin in us and other lessons learned. Even at the end of John's Gospel, in the Easter garden, Mary Magdalene is asked not to cling to Jesus. She needs to be able to run if she is to become apostolic.

The ancient Assyrians' word for prayer was the same as their word for the act of opening a clenched fist. We are not to be possessive of God, for time will only teach us that (as from his interrogators in verse 39 of this chapter) he has escaped from our hands.

Reflection by **Mark Oakley**

Baruch 3.9-15, 32 – 4.4 *or*
¹Genesis 22.1-18
²**Acts 11.1-18**
Psalm 148 [*or* 148.1–6]
Revelation 21.1-6
John 13.31-35

Fifth Sunday of Easter

Acts 11.1-18

'The Spirit told me to go' (v.12)

The movement of the Holy Spirit is absolutely key to understanding the entire narrative of Luke/Acts. Peter's transformation is so important to Luke that he reports it at least twice, perhaps even three or four times if we include other passages in Acts.

Here the stress is on the divine initiative in the whole experience that Peter had. The Spirit directed Peter to go, and the Spirit was also responsible for breaking down the barriers of identity. There is more than that, however, as Peter links the role of the Spirit that has inspired him in this episode with the coming of the Holy Spirit at Pentecost, the whole reason for the rapid growth of followers of Christ.

So Peter, foundational as he inevitable was for the whole Church, points to the wider narrative of God's Holy Spirit enabling the story of God to flourish and develop. Peter gives voice to a whole new language of faith that itself enabled communication of the gospel to spread.

This gift of faith fulfils the prophetic words of Jesus, and links the outpouring of the Spirit to the baptism first proclaimed by John. There is a vivid sense of prophetic heralding here that finds new voice in the story of the early Church. This, in turn, works its way out in new ways in our contemporary expression of faith.

Reflection by **Helen-Ann Hartley**

¹ *For a reflection on Genesis 22.1-18, see page 125.*
² *The reading from Acts must be used as either the first or the second reading.*

Fifth Sunday of Easter

Baruch 3.9-15, 32 – 4.4 *or*
Genesis 22.1-18
[1]Acts 11.1-18
Psalm 148 148 [*or* 148.1–6]
Revelation 21.1-6
John 13.31-35

Revelation 21.1-6

'See, the home of God is among mortals' (v.3)

The message of the last chapters of Revelation is that God chooses to make his home among us. His purpose is to dwell with us in a transformed world: 'See, I am making all things new.' The present fabric of this world is not to last for ever. God's world will be free of the chaotic elements of the human spirit, which bring us greed and violence. The evils of the world are represented here by the raging turbulence of the sea, which is why in the vision 'the sea was no more'.

The beautiful vision of the Holy City coming down from heaven assures us that the world to come is a social world, a place of true community. No wonder these words are often read at funerals. They point us to a future in which there will be no more death, no more grief. In that context, they offer huge consolation.

The promise is not only for the future, though. It speaks to us today. God promises to the thirsty the gift of water 'from the spring of the water of life'. Thirst is a metaphor for our human experience of longing for God and God's peace, justice and freedom. God has made us, knowing instinctively what we need for our fulfilment. Today in your worship, ask God to open to you the stream of life.

Reflection by **Angela Tilby**

[1]*The reading from Acts must be used as either the first or the second reading.*

Baruch 3.9-15, 32 – 4.4 *or*
Genesis 22.1-18
Acts 11.1-18
Psalm 148 [*or* 148.1–6]
Revelation 21.1-6
John 13.31-35

Fifth Sunday of Easter

John 13.31-35

'... love one another; even as I have loved you' (v.34, ERV)

Here is the whole gospel concentrated into nine words. It's not simply the *novum mandatum*, the positive commandment to love, replacing all those negative 'thou shalt nots'; it's the second clause, the 'even as', that is the true foundation of this love. There is a paradox here. We cannot be *commanded* to love. Love does not come at command; indeed 'command' is the very thing most likely to kill it. On the contrary, only love can beget love; we can only love in response to being loved, only know what love is because we are loved.

This is self-evident at the natural level. Just as a baby learns to smile in response to the smiles of its parents and learns language by being spoken to, so the very possibility of love, let alone its vocabulary and gestures, can only be learned in response to the love that finds us first, finds us before we even know what or who it is that has loved us.

And so it is with us spiritually. We love as we are loved, and Jesus makes the new commandment possible because of the utterly new and radical way in which he has loved us: absolutely, unconditionally, without reserve and to the last drop of his heart's blood.

Reflection by **Malcolm Guite**

Sixth Sunday of Easter

[1] Ezekiel 37.1-14
[2] **Acts 16.9-15**
Psalm 67
Revelation 21.10, 22 – 22.5
John 14.23-29 *or* John 5.1-9

Acts 16.9-15

'During the night Paul had a vision ...' (v.9)

It has sometimes been said 'If you want to hear God laugh, tell God your five-year plan!' In the opening verses of this chapter of Acts, we see the human-laid plans of Paul and Barnabas and John Mark, as well as their relationships, for a while, dribble into the sand. Paul has attempted a very reasonable strategy – in human terms – to go into Bithynia, a key strategic Roman province. But the spirit of Jesus did not allow the party to proceed. Instead, during the night, down in Troas, Paul has a vision of a man calling him to come to Macedonia and help. This calling to proclaim the good news in part of Greece is not what Paul had in mind originally at all. And yet this divine inspiration, which altered Paul's plan and gave him a totally new vision, saw the gospel move into the borders of Western Europe for the first time. From this move, came the first churches of the West. From this base, western Christianity was born.

Had Paul proceeded up into Bithynia, not taking the vision seriously as a call from God, he may well have become bogged down in a very unproductive and beleaguered context. A move up into north-east central Asia, at that point, may have been the wrong move at the wrong time.

We are called to discern our Christian instincts when we are given visions on this earthly pilgrimage. We are not a compass unto ourselves.

Reflection by **David Moxon**

[1] *For a reflection on Ezekiel 37.1-14, see page 131.*
[2] *The reading from Acts must be used as either the first or the second reading.*

Ezekiel 37.1-14
[1] Acts 16.9-15
Psalm 67
Revelation 21.10, 22 – 22.5
John 14.23-29 *or* John 5.1-9

Sixth Sunday of Easter

Revelation 21.10, 22 – 22.5

'... the glory of God is its light, and its lamp is the Lamb'
(21.23)

This reading weaves passages from Old Testament prophecy into a new harmony. There is no temple in the city. God and the Lamb are the temple, the place where God and humanity are finally at home with one another. The city is supremely attractive, radiant with God's presence, constantly open to the traffic of the nations who come not to take or to trade but to bring their glory to the greater glory of God and the Lamb.

The seer reinterprets Ezekiel's vision of a temple firmly boundaried to keep out what is impure or unclean. Here the river of life produces healing trees, the fruit of which cures the ills of the nations. It is no longer a matter of keeping out what is accursed; there simply is nothing accursed to be found. God does not rule over the city like an earthly king, guarding his privileges. In contrast, he is the living heart of the city – those who worship him do not serve him as slaves; they share his reign.

The vision of the city and the river of the water of life invites us to live in such a way as to prepare ourselves for heaven. But heaven is still a gift, not something we create but something we must receive. How, by our deeds and words, can we prepare ourselves, and others, for that gift?

Reflection by **Angela Tilby**

[1] *The reading from Acts must be used as either the first or the second reading.*

Sixth Sunday of Easter

Ezekiel 37.1-14
Acts 16.9-15
Psalm 67
Revelation 21.10, 22 – 22.5
John 14.23-29 *or* John 5.1-9

John 14.23-29

'… we will come to them and make our home with them'
(v.23)

Jesus prepares his disciples for his passion, building them up in the expectation that, though he must leave them, he is not abandoning them. He will ask the Father to send the Advocate, the Spirit, to continue to teach them and remind them of what he has already shown them. The promise of the Spirit makes explicit what has previously been hinted at: the mutual love within the Godhead has a threefold shape. True life springs from love, given, received and communicated.

One of the spiritual tragedies of our time is the loss of personal relationship in daily life that has come through our increasingly automated world. We are in danger of becoming spiritually autistic, isolated and empty, aware only of our own needs and incapable of recognizing the reality of other people. Christ shows us that our neediness cannot be met by grasping at what we imagine will satisfy us. Ultimately, we need to recognize our emptiness and turn away from ourselves to the love that already embraces us.

At the point at which Jesus faces utter exclusion and rejection, he assures us that the divine persons make their home with those who believe. We have our own passion to bear and may experience loneliness, trouble and abandonment, but Christ leaves us his peace, his promise that all will be well. In that confidence he signals the moment to depart.

Reflection by **Angela Tilby**

Ezekiel 37.1-14
Acts 16.9-15
Psalm 67
Revelation 21.10, 22 – 22.5
John 14.23-29 *or* **John 5.1-9**

John 5.1-9

'Do you want to be made well?' (v.6)

What an astonishing question for Jesus to ask a sick man! Ill for 38 years, the anonymous invalid by the pool of Beth-zatha had always been beaten in the rush to enter the waters by his more able-bodied peers. So he must have been desperate to be made well – *mustn't he*?

But Jesus again demonstrates his instinctive awareness of the tendencies of human nature. Why did he address *this* man, rather than the others? It was because he 'saw him lying there and knew that he had been there a long time'. We sometimes hear of people who have 'enjoyed bad health for many years'. Enjoyed what? Not the pain and inconvenience, obviously – but what about all the extra attention and freedom from responsibility illness temporarily brings? In such cases, it may take courage to seize the opportunity for health should it be offered. Such a prospect could be daunting, and may encourage the chronic sufferer to use their sickness as a protective shield.

So Jesus asks the man, do you *want* to be made well? Satisfied with the man's response, he tells him bluntly, 'Stand up, take your mat and walk'. Chronic illness is a complex issue, and not all situations will be amenable to the urging to, quite literally, 'stand on your own feet'. But this passage does perhaps encourage us to risk asking Jesus' question of ourselves: do we want to be made well?

Reflection by **Barbara Mosse**

¹**Acts 1.1-11** *or* Daniel 7.9-14
Psalm 47 *or* Psalm 93
Ephesians 1.15-end *or* ¹Acts 1.1-11
Luke 24.44-end

Acts 1.1-11

'... as they were watching, he was lifted up' (v.9)

Luke–Acts is a two-volume work. You could say that Luke is the gospel of Jesus, and Acts is the gospel of the Holy Spirit. Already we see an excited anticipation of the Spirit in verses 5 and 8. The disciples will then no longer be confused, as they have been throughout Luke. They'll be ready to stand tall and tell people the extraordinary, life-changing story of Jesus. Then the apostles will reverse the journey that Jesus took from Galilee through Samaria to Judaea and Jerusalem. They'll start their journey at the other end, going from Jerusalem through Judaea to Samaria and then to the ends of the earth – that is, to Athens and eventually to Rome.

But first comes one of the story's strangest episodes, at least to the modern literal mind. Jesus 'was lifted up, and a cloud took him out of their sight'. This was not mere primitive thinking. It was a way of saying that Jesus was finally leaving 'our space' and going to 'God's space', God's dimension of reality – though 'earth' and 'heaven' were actually both God's reality and one day would be joined together in what we call the 'second coming'. So Jesus would 'come [back] in the same way as you saw him go'.

In the meantime, the disciples committed themselves to expectant prayer, awaiting this mysterious 'Holy Spirit' and the equally mysterious 'return' of Jesus. I wonder what the return of Christ means for you and me today?

Reflection by **John Pritchard**

¹*The reading from Acts must be used as either the first or the second reading.*

¹Acts 1.1-11 *or* **Daniel 7.9-14**
Psalm 47 *or* Psalm 93
Ephesians 1.15-end *or* ¹Acts 1.1-11
Luke 24.44-end

Ascension Day

Principal Feast

Daniel 7.9-14

'His dominion is an everlasting dominion that shall not pass away ... ' (v.14)

Today we celebrate the feast of the Ascension, when Christ, his work on earth completed, returned to his Father in heaven. Daniel here uses language that anticipates passages in the book of Revelation (e.g. Revelation 19), looking beyond the end times to the fulfilment of God's purposes in the establishment of 'one like a human being' – 'His dominion is an everlasting dominion that shall not pass away, and his kingship is one that shall never be destroyed'. Over time, Christian tradition came to identify this mysterious figure with Christ, and Christ's kingship is the ultimate reality to which our celebration of the ascension points.

The language Daniel uses here demands a great deal of us spiritually, intellectually and imaginatively. It stretches us way beyond the boundaries of what we are capable of grasping humanly. We may enjoy singing familiar hymns about this mysterious reality, such as 'At the Name of Jesus' – but how frequently do we pray that God would help us to really *live* the reality of Christ's kingship in our lives?

We live in troubled times, both nationally and internationally, but when has that ever not been the case? A belief in the reality of Christ's return to his Father challenges us, in the face of all that may appear to the contrary, to hold to and believe in the ultimate fulfilment of God's good purposes.

Reflection by **Barbara Mosse**

¹*The reading from Acts must be used as either the first or the second reading.*

Ascension Day

Principal Feast

[1]Acts 1.1-11 *or* Daniel 7.9-14
Psalm 47 *or* Psalm 93
Ephesians 1.15-end *or* [1]Acts 1.1-11
Luke 24.44-end

Ephesians 1.15-end

'I do not cease to give thanks for you ...' (v.16)

At the end of our last supper together, my host Pastor Johannes prayed for me and gave thanks to God for my time with his family during that Easter's school exchange visit. I had never openly been prayed for before, and I found myself silently biting back tears, overwhelmed by a sense of belonging and being loved, both by God and by my new friends.

The writer of Ephesians returns to the theme of thanksgiving that has already dominated the letter's opening verses, bringing into yet sharper focus the hope and blessings that are embodied in Christ's followers. Thanksgiving moves into encouragement, as we are enjoined to grow in our knowledge and love of God. And encouragement moves into praise, with the writer almost losing himself in the wonder of the blessings he prays for.

Though stylized, this is no mere rhetoric; the author's thankfulness for our faithfulness and his concern for our spiritual growth enable him to carry us through with him into a deeper appreciation of the power of the exalted Christ. Gratitude builds us up in faith.

To say in person, to write, to text, or to tweet our prayerful thanksgiving for those who, whether near or far, journey with us in faith, reminds us of our inheritance among the saints and of the greatness of the gift of salvation that the risen Christ offers to each of us.

Reflection by **Joanne Grenfell**

[1] *For a reflection on Acts 1.1-11, see page 154. The reading from Acts must be used as either the first or the second reading.*

Acts 1.1-11 *or* Daniel 7.9-14
Psalm 47 *or* Psalm 93
Ephesians 1.15-end *or* Acts 1.1-11
Luke 24.44-end

Ascension Day

Principal Feast

Luke 24.44-end

'While he was blessing them, he withdrew from them' (v.51)

It is such a tantalising mixture of detail and opacity. The place of the ascension is specific – Bethany – but the rest is impenetrable. Even the oldest surviving texts of Luke's Gospel are at variance with each other. Some say that having blessed the disciples, Jesus was carried up to heaven; others, more enigmatically, omit the phrase about ascension altogether. And, of course, Mark, Matthew and John do not mention the ascension at all.

What are we to make of it?

Obviously, something had to have happened to Jesus after the resurrection. It would seem, according to the earliest accounts, that he only revealed himself to the disciples for a brief time and then was seen on earth no more. In such a scenario, talk of ascension makes some kind of sense. But ascension to where? In what form? How could the apparently material, still-wounded body of Christ de-materialize? The questions are unanswerable. We simply cannot know. We have to live with hints and guesses but mostly with un-knowing.

Perhaps the glorious opacity of the ascension echoes our own experience of Jesus? There are times when he feels very close, but other times when his absence is entirely and horribly real. And yet, paradoxically, his absence is somehow not absolute. The hints remain, the truths remain, but he feels just out of reach – there and not there at exactly the same time. 'While he was blessing them, he withdrew from them ...'

Reflection by **Christopher Herbert**

Seventh Sunday of Easter

Sunday after Ascension Day

[1] Ezekiel 36.24-28
[2] **Acts 16.16-34**
Psalm 97
Revelation 22.12-14, 16-17, 20-end
John 17.20-end

Acts 16.16-34

'Believe on the Lord Jesus, and you will be saved' (v.31)

Extreme events often make people think about their eternal destiny. A new birth can prompt a person to wonder whether there is a Creator. A severe illness can prompt a person to ask whether there is a Saviour. In Philippi, a jailer survived a tremor and assumed his captives had escaped through the smashed doors. An immediate suicide seemed preferable to a drawn-out execution.

But what drew him to faith was not extreme at all. It was the integrity of Paul and Silas who, rather than scamper, had chosen to wait for justice to be seen to be done. You and I do not need miracles or jail sentences in order to relate to this story. We don't even need to draw attention to ourselves with hymns at midnight. All we need for our neighbours to notice that people of Christian faith are distinctive is integrity. The way we dignify outsiders, the way we take responsibility for unloved areas of housing estates, the way we recognize and respond to needs – these things are observed.

When integrity has broken down barriers between Christians and unchurched people, the next step is shared experience. Out of the storage vessels came water for the jailer to clean the prisoners' wounds. Out of the same vessels came water to baptize the jailer's family. It doesn't require an earthquake for you or me to introduce someone to Jesus. It's much simpler than that.

Reflection by **Peter Graystone**

[1] *For a reflection on Ezekiel 36.24-28, see page 130.*
[2] *The reading from Acts must be used as either the first or the second reading.*

Ezekiel 36.24-28
Acts 16.16-34

Seventh Sunday of Easter

Psalm 97

Sunday after Ascension Day

Revelation 22.12-14, 16-17, 20-end
John 17.20-end

Revelation 22.12-14, 16-17, 20-end

'"Surely I am coming soon." Amen. Come, Lord Jesus!' (v.20)

Revelation ends with a promise, an invitation and a prayer.

The promise is that, even now in the present, with all the troubles and horrors of persecution, war and injustice, the final outcome of all things is assured. The Lord will come, 'See, I am coming soon'.

But we are not left simply to wait in suspense. Although wickedness continues to flourish, those who struggle to serve God are sustained by God. The gift of the water of life is available to whoever desires it. We can taste the clarity and radiance of heaven in the here and now, as a gift of God who is always prodigal with his gifts. It is in response to that invitation that the Church prays daily and urgently: 'Thy kingdom come'.

The prayer is for the coming of the Holy Spirit. In the Orthodox tradition, the kingdom simply is the Holy Spirit, and our life's purpose is to become the place where the Spirit dwells.

It is easy to lose heart in a world where so many seem obsessed by the accumulation of power and wealth. In fact, we have all that we need. We are not to add or take away from the words of the prophecy. Our task is to desire God above all else and to live from that desire. So, come Lord Jesus.

Reflection by **Angela Tilby**

Seventh Sunday of Easter

Sunday after Ascension Day

Ezekiel 36.24-28
Acts 16.16-34
Psalm 97
Revelation 22.12-14, 16-17, 20-end
John 17.20-end

John 17.20-end

'... that they may be one, as we are one' (v.22)

Today's passage comes at the end of Jesus' long prayer to the Father. It is a prayer from the heart and in the shadow of the cross. As his prayer concludes, he now intercedes for the unity of the Church, a unity that mirrors the unity of the Trinity. It is a mystical passage where Christians are encouraged to share in the nature of God.

We can struggle to understand this divine nature in which we share. Often, the Trinity is seen in a hierarchical way – the Father as the head, with the Son doing what he is told, and the Holy Spirit obeying them both. If that is our Trinitarian model, it may also be our model of the Church: one that requires a strong unifying authority. On one level, this model has attractions, offering certainty about our faith and membership, with strong adherence to inherited understandings of Scripture and tradition. However, is it 'one as we (the Father and Son) are one'?

Another way of viewing the Trinity is as a relationship where Father, Son and Holy Spirit break down possible barriers with an intimacy and equality that is sometimes likened to a dance. There is no one head, no one way of being, as the *persons* of the Trinity remain distinctive. Such a model of the Church will celebrate difference. If we disagree over Scripture, lively and loving debate can be the fruit of diversity.

Reflection by **Paul Kennedy**

¹**Acts 2.1-21** *or* Genesis 11.1-9
Psalm 104.26-36, 37*b* [*or* 104.26-end]
Romans 8.14-17 *or* ¹**Acts 2.1-21**
John 14.8-17 [25-27]

Day of Pentecost
(Whit Sunday)

Acts 2.1-21

'... there came a sound like the rush of a violent wind' (v.2)

Now we see the promised Spirit in action. We have the sights and sounds of fire and wind, reminding us of the Spirit coming on Jesus at his baptism, an event with its own sight (the dove) and sound (the voice from heaven). We're shown the power that will drive through the rest of Acts, the 'violent wind' that will take Peter, Paul and the others to the ends of the earth (Rome), changing people's lives as it sweeps through the known world. The tongues of fire symbolize the speeches that make up one third of Acts, here foreshadowed in Peter's speech that was preached to 'every nation under heaven'. A map of the places mentioned shows a complete circle around the ancient near east. The Spirit is up and running!

The question we can't avoid is why the Spirit seems only to be 'up and dawdling' in the lives of many of us. Certainly we can imagine the need for a turbocharge to start the process off at the beginning of Acts, so the effect of the Spirit may not need always to be quite so overwhelming, but still, aren't we missing something rather vital?

Perhaps we could invite God's Spirit – even tentatively, and even today – to blow through the cold, dusty rooms of our lives, and bring us a touch of the sun-drenched life of the Spirit that we see in Acts.

Reflection by **John Pritchard**

¹ *The reading from Acts must be used as either the first or second reading.*

Day of Pentecost

(Whit Sunday)

[Acts 2.1-21 *or* **Genesis 11.1-9**
Psalm 104.26-36, 37b [*or* 104.26-end]
Romans 8.14-17 *or* [Acts 2.1-21
John 14.8-17 [25-27]

Genesis 11.1-9

'... let us make a name for ourselves' (v.4)

Over 54 per cent of the world's population lives in cities at the time I am writing this, and by 2050 this proportion is expected to increase to a phenomenal 66 per cent.

Cities are perhaps the most distinctive phenomenon of modernity: mechanized, diverse, anonymous and morally ambiguous. At one level, they are magnificent reflections of human aspiration and technical capability. They are places of intense endeavour and creativity. However, they are also places of intense alienation and individualism, as their human occupants find themselves forced to compete for goods, for space, for recognition, for security.

T. S. Eliot insisted in his *Choruses from the Rock* that in order for our cities not to be wastelands, we must persist in asking the question: 'What is the meaning of this city?' Do our own creative endeavours participate in God's? The opening chapters of Genesis show God separating and also gathering: 'Let the waters under the sky be gathered together ...' (Genesis 1.9). Gathering is God's job, and when we gather – as we do in our cities – we will only create something that can endure and be fruitful when we do it with God's help.

> *'Unless the Lord builds the house, those who build it labour in vain.*
> *Unless the Lord guards the city, the guard keeps watch in vain.' (Psalm 127.1)*

Reflection by **Ben Quash**

[The reading from Acts must be used as either the first or second reading.

¹Acts 2.1-21 *or* Genesis 11.1-9
Psalm 104.26-36, 37b [*or* 104.26-end]
Romans 8.14-17 *or* ¹Acts 2.1-21
John 14.8-17 [25-27]

Day of Pentecost
(Whit Sunday)

Romans 8.14-17

'... we suffer with him so that we may also be glorified with him' (v.17)

There are two really important aspects to this passage from Romans 8. The first is Paul's description of faith as a pilgrimage: the notion that the freedom that is found in Christ requires us to go on the whole of the journey. You cannot simply bypass the gospel from birth to resurrection without paying attention to all that happens along the way. The cost of discipleship involves the reality of the cross before it bursts forth in the new life of the resurrection.

Early Christians were often described as 'The Way', which gives texture to our lives as journeys, and all that journeys imply. Perhaps this is why the complexity of flesh and spirit helps us understand the often unwieldy way our lives can be mapped out at any given moment.

The second aspect of the passage Paul has in mind is the situation of a Greco-Roman household where the eldest son was usually the heir. Adoption was sometimes used when a father was to die childless, and slaves or children of another family could be adopted. This close relationship of father to child is used by Paul to indicate the inclusive potential of the family of faith to which we belong. In that sense no one is excluded, and barriers are broken down and lives are transformed.

Reflection by **Helen-Ann Hartley**

¹*For a reflection on Acts 2.1-21, see page 161. The reading from Acts must be used as either the first or the second reading.*

Day of Pentecost

(Whit Sunday)

Acts 2.1-21 *or* Genesis 11.1-9
Psalm 104.26-36, 37b [*or* 104.26-end]
Romans 8.14-17 *or* Acts 2.1-21
John 14.8-17 [25-27]

John 14.8-17 [25-27]

'Whoever has seen me has seen the Father' (v.9)

The life that Jesus reveals on the night of his passion is a life of absolute reciprocity. This is the life of God, and the message of John's whole Gospel is that God's life has come into the world in Christ to embrace all who are prepared to believe.

Out of passages such as this comes the revolutionary Christian interpretation of monotheism: that God is one and yet the oneness of God is a relationship of mutual love, given, communicated and received. The school of love is Jesus Christ himself and for those who have enrolled in that school, Jesus is both the teacher and the syllabus, 'the way, and the truth, and the life' (John 14.6).

Discipleship is a process of transformation in Christ that embraces every part of our selves and brings our humanity to fulfilment. Philip's request – 'show us the Father' – is, in the end, idolatrous because it makes the Father an object of our curiosity and our grasping desire. We cannot reach God by thinking about him, by making him a 'fact' in our lives. The only way to know God is to embrace the way of love that Jesus reveals. Jesus calls Philip back into recognizing that the Father is only known through relationship and reciprocity. Those who follow Jesus find the Father, as those who love find that they are loved.

Reflection by **Angela Tilby**

Proverbs 8.1-4, 22-31
Psalm 8
Romans 5.1-5
John 16.12-15

Proverbs 8.1-4, 22-31

'Does not wisdom call, and does not understanding raise her voice?' (v.1)

It seems appropriate to have a reading about wisdom today, as many of us feel we need more of it if we are to begin to understand the Trinity. The priest and poet John Donne reminds us, however, that the Trinity is 'bones to philosophy, but milk to faith'. Analytical and abstract approaches to the nature of God can be overly dry, whereas faith understands that the Trinity is more than a doctrine. It is the passionately poetic expression of the truth of God's reality. It is the mystery that, if celebrated, nurtures the world.

In the book of Proverbs, wisdom is personified and calls for our attention. She speaks her origins before creation and her consequent place within it. She was like 'a master worker' busy in the workshop of the creator, helping to shape and inspirit all that is. There is also something childlike about her relationship with God. She is God's 'delight' and shares his joy in the playground of the world he has brought about.

In Christian faith, God's wisdom from all eternity was indeed personified – in Christ – and called out to us in an invitation of love. The Holy Spirit still creates through creation, working with the same love to fashion what is good and just, still calling out to us to join in.

We have a God who is, as Holy Trinity, always beyond, beside and within.

Reflection by **Mark Oakley**

Trinity Sunday

Proverbs 8.1-4, 22-31
Psalm 8
Romans 5.1-5
John 16.12-15

Romans 5.1-5

'... endurance produces character, and character produces hope' (v.4)

One of the many lessons that people living in the Western world can learn from our brothers and sisters in developing nations is how human character can become grateful and hopeful even with very little by way of financial and material provision. If we have all the consumer possessions we want, then we can often reach a 'brick wall' of hopelessness and lack of vision for the future. This can, in turn, lead to depression, breakdown of community, dishonesty and mistrust.

Of course, that does not mean we should be content for developing nations to remain in horrendous poverty, without adequate food, clean water or shelter. But it is worth pondering how those who are struggling can lead the rest of the world by example through trust in and awareness of the love of God.

The author of the letter to the Romans is encouraging early Christians who were being persecuted and finding the path of faith difficult, to persevere and not lose hope. It is part of the calling of the follower of Christ to look forward to a life when suffering has passed away and we can fully bask in the glory of the Risen Christ.

Until then, we can only glimpse such glory, which comes through endurance and patience in suffering. That is the example that people who struggle to make ends meet can teach those who have more than they will ever need.

Reflection by **Christopher Woods**

Proverbs 8.1-4, 22-31
Psalm 8
Romans 5.1-5
John 16.12-15

Trinity Sunday

John 16.12-15

*'When the Spirit of truth comes,
he will guide you into all the truth' (v.13)*

What exactly is the work of the Spirit? One of the characteristics that marked out the early Christian saints is that they understood faith to be passion. Faith, in terms of discipleship, is often not reasoned coolness; it is passion that spills over – the love that is stronger than death. It might be thought through. It may even be willed reason. But my God, it has to be willed with the very fibre of your being.

Extreme faith is not the same as *passionate* faith. The former can be unyielding, unforgiving and self-righteous. The latter is more like the work of the Spirit. True, it can still be intemperate and immodest, but it abounds in energy and love because it springs from the liberality of God. It is released as a kind of raw energy, precisely because it breaks the chains of inhibition, and springs forth from spiritual encounters that can border on ecstasy. It is passion resulting from encounter, conversion, conviction, resurrection and transformation.

The work of the Spirit, then, is one of refinement and discernment. It is often willed acts of moderation or self-control that emerge out of passionate convictions, grace and love. That's why the list of the fruits of the Holy Spirit from Galatians 5.22 is so important. Love, joy, peace, patience, kindness, self-control, humility, gentleness and faithfulness are all rooted in the passion of Christ – a putting-to-death of our desires and seeing them reconfigured through the Holy Spirit. So, excess and abundance are of God; extremism, however, is of the flesh.

Reflection by **Malcolm Guite**

Proper 4

Sunday between
29 May & 4 June inclusive
(if after Trinity Sunday)

Continuous:
I Kings 18.20, 21 [22-29] 30-39
Psalm 96
Galatians 1.1-12
Luke 7.1-10

1 Kings 18.20, 21 [22-29] 30-39

'How long will you go limping with two different opinions?'
(v.21)

The radical monotheism that we associate with Judaism seems not to have been established in Elijah's time. He asks the people why they follow both God and Baal and don't make their mind up? They are silent. Perhaps they don't understand the question? Has their religious dual citizenship, as it were, become comfortable and not at all a matter of concern? We can often be blind to the contradictions we live with as believers in God while at the same time courting the fashionable gods of the day.

Elijah puts Baal to the test. The prophets of Baal wind themselves up into a frenzy of self-mortification and movement, but with no result. Elijah just prays to his God, asking that it be made clear that he is the all-powerful and that Elijah is his servant. As throughout our tradition, from Moses to Pentecost, God is caught up in fire. He burns away dross and error. Those who come near are scorched forever.

There is an unsettling end to this story, played out in the verse that follows today's reading. Elijah, once he has proved his point, orders the prophets of Baal to be put to death in what must have been a carnage of blood and guts. It reminds us of the intensity and dangers of the religious competitions of the day and how God-fearers thought they were serving God best by murdering those who disagreed with them. Such curdled and hateful belief can still rear its head in our times.

Reflection by **Mark Oakley**

Related:
1 Kings 8.22-23, 41-43
Psalm 96.1-9
Galatians 1.1-12
Luke 7.1-10

Proper 4

1 Kings 8.22-23, 41-43

*'... your name has been invoked on this house that
I have built' (v.43)*

David had been told that he would not be allowed by God to build the temple in Jerusalem; instead his son Solomon would have that honour. In the Holy of Holies of Solomon's temple was placed the Ark of the Covenant containing the two stone tablets on which the Ten Commandments had been inscribed. In other words, the solemn covenant between God and his people was at the deep centre of the liturgical, social and political life of the chosen people.

However, as we can see in today's reading, there was a sub-theme: the temple was also built in the name of God. And that suggestion takes us right back to one of the most significant encounters in the Bible, to that moment when Moses asked what God's name was and was told that it was 'I am who I am', or, 'I will be what I will be' (Exodus 3.14).

It is the most apt and beautiful of names for it describes the very heart of God. It reveals the idea that God is Being itself, and is therefore the source of *all* being. God is also the ground of all that will be in the future: nothing is outwith his presence, neither time present nor time future. And we, who 'have' being, as it were, derive from God and are journeying towards God. We are, in truth, part of the living temple that bears God's Name.

Reflection by **Christopher Herbert**

Proper 4

Continuous:	*Related:*
1 Kings 18.20, 21	1 Kings 8.22-23, 41-43
[22-29] 30-39	
Psalm 96	Psalm 96.1-9

Galatians 1.1-12
Luke 7.1-10

Galatians 1.1-12

'I am astonished ...' (v.6)

Sometimes Paul appears arrogant. So confident is he that he is right that he dismisses all other views out of hand. Galatians 1 is a good case in point. In this chapter Paul declares that the gospel he has proclaimed is the only possible gospel and that all others are misguided and wrong.

A little background, however, makes Paul's tone here easier to stomach. As we read on in Galatians, it becomes clear that the issue at stake is not an insubstantial, unimportant issue but one that strikes at the very heart of the gospel that Paul proclaims. The issue is circumcision and whether gentiles need to be circumcised – in other words become Jews – in order to follow Jesus.

The people against whom Paul is fighting here seem to be arguing that gentiles do need to become Jewish and follow the Jewish law in order to be 'in Christ'. This goes against the very essence of what Paul has proclaimed. This is why his language is so passionate. What Paul proclaims – that Jesus offers love and redemption to everyone no matter what their background, status or gender – lies at the very heart of his faith. His tone may be off-putting, but his message remains as relevant today as it was then.

Reflection by **Paula Gooder**

Continuous:	*Related:*	
1 Kings 18.20, 21	1 Kings 8.22-23, 41-43	**Proper 4**
[22-29] 30-39		
Psalm 96	Psalm 96.1-9	
Galatians 1.1-12		
Luke 7.1-10		

Luke 7.1-10

*'Lord ... I am not worthy that thou shouldest enter
under my roof' (v.6, AV)*

Society often constructs barriers. In today's reading these barriers are many: between Jew and gentile (as the centurion will not approach Jesus in person); between occupying army and occupied Palestinian (even though the centurion built the Capernaum synagogue, for him to enter a house would cause defilement); and between the holiness revealed in Jesus and our own sinful nature. The centurion's cry 'I am not worthy' is echoed in our traditional liturgy's use of his words (see above).

It is striking that the centurion erects a barrier of unworthiness while the elders dismantle any such barrier by emphasizing his love and deeds. It's often easier to see the good in others while being all too aware of our own sinful nature.

This encounter is a foretaste of the post-resurrection Church where another centurion, Cornelius, is welcomed into the Church (Acts 10), and the Church's mission is understood to embrace all humankind. There's the Christian vocation to break down external barriers, but also a vocation to break down *internal* barriers. The Christian call to holiness is associated with wholeness and an integrated personality. This is achieved when we accept and embrace the damaged parts of our ego, seeing ourselves as Christ sees us. To both us and Christ, our own damaged nature is visible, and still he wants to come under our roof.

Reflection by **Paul Kennedy**

Proper 5

**Sunday between
5 & 11 June inclusive**
(if after Trinity Sunday)

Continuous:
1 Kings 17.8-16 [17-end]
Psalm 146
Galatians 1.11-end
Luke 7.11-17

1 Kings 17.8-16 [17-end]

'I have commanded a widow there to feed you' (v.9)

Mrs Davies was a delight. An elderly clergy widow who had spent much of her life in a beautiful remote valley in the Black Mountains of Wales, she talked to me of people whose families had featured in the mid-19th century diaries of Francis Kilvert. His parish had been neighbour to the parish cared for by Mrs Davies' husband. Her stories linking past and present entranced me.

When I first met her she was living in a tiny bungalow in Hereford, crammed to overflowing with objects and memories of her life. One day she handed me a small fossil, an ammonite and asked me to accept it as a gift. It had no monetary value, but because it was she who had given it to me I have treasured it ever since. It encapsulates her deep and humour-filled faith, her resilience, her bravery and her acceptance of all that life had thrown at her.

From the little that she had, she had chosen to give me a piece of rock. As far as I was concerned, it was pure gold.

Among those who have very little, there is frequently a generosity that is transformative. Mrs Davies was a living embodiment of the meek inheriting the earth. As the widow of Zarephath out of her poverty fed Elijah, so Mrs Davies nourished me.

Our churches are filled with such people and we are deeply blessed by their life-enriching generosity.

Reflection by **Christopher Herbert**

Proper 5

1 Kings 17.17-end

*'You have come ... to bring my sin to remembrance,
and to cause the death of my son!' (v.18)*

Today's passage begins halfway through a story. Earlier, the chapter tells of a widow of Zarapeth and her son who is on the verge of starvation. Elijah stays with them and channels the power of God so that their remaining food is miraculously replenished. But when, in today's verses, her son sickens and dies, the woman turns on Elijah. Elijah prays; God intervenes; the child is saved.

In the New Testament, Elijah is seen as a forerunner of Jesus (e.g. Mark 8.27-28), and the biblical scholar Choon-Leong Seow has commented on parallels between this incident and Jesus' raising of the widow's son at Nain told in Luke 7: 'the city gate, the plight of a widow, a son who has died, the miraculous resuscitation, the return of the son to his mother' (*New Interpreter's Bible*, Vol. III, p. 130).

Parallels there may be, but Jesus transcends the role of Elijah in every way. The woman had assumed her son's death was a punishment for her sin, and Elijah, while remonstrating with God, didn't contradict this perception. But Jesus shattered this pattern of cause-and-effect thinking. When he healed a blind man, he told his disciples that neither the man's nor his parents' sin was to blame; the mysterious reason was 'so that God's works might be revealed in him' (John 9.3). From the widow's reaction in our reading, this is precisely what this miracle of Elijah achieved.

Reflection by **Barbara Mosse**

Proper 5

Continuous:
1 Kings 17.8-16 [17-end]
Psalm 146

Related:
1 Kings 17.17-end
Psalm 30

Galatians 1.11-end
Luke 7.11-17

Galatians 1.11-end

'For I want you to know, brothers and sisters ...' (v.11)

Galatians is Paul's most passionate letter. We can almost sense the white-hot urgency with which he dictated it. Paul's Galatian converts are in danger of lapsing from his teaching because certain agitators are preaching a 'different gospel'. Galatians is a forceful defence of Christian freedom. It raises important issues about the sometimes competing claims of authority and personal experience in Christian life.

In this opening chapter, Paul lays out his credentials. He has received his mission not from human authorities but direct from God. The gospel he proclaimed to his Galatian converts was not an invention but a revelation. In support of this, he recounts his own experience of conversion from Judaism to faith in Jesus Christ. This biographical passage differs from the more distanced account in Acts 9. Paul's aim is to make clear that he has been set apart from birth for his mission. After his dramatic encounter with Christ, he does not consult with the Church in Jerusalem, but goes away to Arabia. Yet, in spite of the singularity of his experience, Paul writes as one of God's family and as one whose apostleship is recognized by other Christians.

Today's reading leads us to reflect on the paradox that, while the heart of the Christian gospel is deeply personal, we are never Christians in isolation. We are accountable to others, as they are to us.

Reflection by **Angela Tilby**

Continuous:
I Kings 17.8-16 [17-end]
Psalm 146

Related:
I Kings 17.17-end
Psalm 30

Galatians 1.11-end
Luke 7.11-17

Proper 5

Luke 7.11-17
'Do not weep' (v.13)

This is a situation in which death reigns. The horizon is filled with it. The widow of Nain has already lost her husband; now her only son too is dead. Death holds sway over her past, her present and (it appears) her future. She seems to sum up the whole lot of humanity, whose last horizon is only death.

Jesus, however, refuses to be confined by the apparent terms of the situation, the normal rules of engagement, the 'givens'. Disregarding the spectre of death, his 'Do not weep' proclaims his confidence in a plenty and life at the hands of God; he then draws nearer to death in order to show that it can be outflanked. In a way that is bold, compassionate and shocking, he touches the bier. The touching of death – whether of a body or of its vehicle – was an act of terrible self-pollution in the terms of the religious laws of Jesus' day. What was expected was withdrawal from death – keeping a safe distance. By contrast, Jesus makes a beeline for it. And, as he does so, a new, wholly unpredictable possibility springs up: 'The dead man sat up and began to speak ...'

We who are baptized have been marked by a sacrament in which – with Christ – we have taken steps into the very teeth of death. How can we live lives that affirm the plenty and life that we have received in that sacrament? How can we live as though moving away from death and towards life?

Reflection by **Ben Quash**

Proper 6

Sunday between
12 & 18 June inclusive
(if after Trinity Sunday)

Continuous:
1 Kings 21.1-10 [11-14] 15-21*a*
Psalm 5.1-8
Galatians 2.15-end
Luke 7.36 – 8.3

1 Kings 21.1-10 [11-14] 15-21*a*

'... you have sold yourself to do what is evil' (v.20)

King Ahab and Queen Jezebel are interesting character studies. Like Macbeth and his wife, each knows the other's strengths and weaknesses. But, although Jezebel's name resounds through history as a synonym for vice, it is Ahab, the much more nuanced and divided character, who actually drives the relationship. Ahab knows exactly what to do to get the reaction he wants out of Jezebel.

So, when he goes to complain to her about Naboth, he leaves out several important details in the conversation he has just had. Naboth invokes both God and the law in refusing to part with his vineyard. Both God and the law of inheritance have made the land his. But Ahab only tells Jezebel about the refusal to sell for money, making it sound a petty and unreasonable denial of the king. Then he sits back and waits for her to get him what he wants.

Ahab does recognize Elijah as God's true spokesman. He treats him with a mixture of respect and hatred that shows the fault line in his character. He does know God, but he wishes that God was more like Jezebel and would simply give him everything he wants. Ahab and Jezebel believe that kingship is about power, but, unfortunately for them, God does not agree.

Reflection by **Jane Williams**

Related:
2 Samuel 11.26 – 12.10, 13-15
Psalm 32
Galatians 2.15-end
Luke 7.36 – 8.3

Proper 6

2 Samuel 11.26 – 12.10, 13-15

'You are the man!' (12.7)

It was a chilling moment. David had stitched up Uriah and taken his wife, Bathsheba, but God had sent Nathan with a heart-rending story about a poor man and his ewe lamb, and David was exposed with those incisive words that Nathan flung at him, 'You are the man'. It was a highly effective way for Nathan to help David hoist himself with his own petard. Actions have consequences, and even if you were God's favourite, as David was, you were still subject to the laws of moral behaviour. David's saving virtue was his honesty. He made no attempt to hide his guilt. Straight off he says 'I have sinned against the Lord' – never mind poor old Uriah. So his punishment is commuted from death to the loss of his child. Bad enough, you would have thought, especially for Bathsheba.

Then comes another of those wonderful one-liners in which the Bible excels: 'Then Nathan went to his house.' He had done what he had to do. As for David, he needed to reflect, to mourn his stupidity. In a culture that encourages us to bluster our way through our failures, admitting anything except that we were wrong, it would be good if we all practised more reflection on those episodes where we have been untrue to others, to ourselves, and to God.

We would probably discover both grace and truth.

Reflection by **John Pritchard**

Proper 6

Continuous:
1 Kings 21.1-10 [11-14]
15-21*a*
Psalm 5.1-8

Related:
2 Samuel 11.26 –
12.10, 13-15
Psalm 32

Galatians 2.15-end
Luke 7.36 – 8.3

Galatians 2.15-end

'I have been crucified with Christ; and it is no longer I who live, but it is Christ who lives in me' (vv.19-20)

In this part of his letter to the Galatians, Paul expresses his despair over his back-sliding converts. He has seen for himself how deep a hold the Jewish law still has on Peter, and how easy it is for gentile converts to be pressured into accepting circumcision and the food laws 'just in case', or to gain approval from others who are doing so.

For Paul, this is a betrayal of the gospel because it makes null the saving death of Christ. His language is extreme because something extreme is at stake. Is Christianity another form of Judaism – more open and accessible to gentiles but still requiring the adoption of a distinctly Jewish identity? Or is it something different – a new movement of God to bring the gentiles into the promises God made to the Jews, and yet without requiring conformity to the law? If the second of these is true, then obedience to the law implies radical doubt in the gospel, a sinful abandonment of hope in Christ alone.

In his anguish over the fate of the Galatians, Paul articulates the mystical heart of the gospel. Through his death on the cross, Christ has become the inner life of every believer. Our selfhood is not grounded in our achievements, however worthy, but only in his grace and love.

Reflection by **Angela Tilby**

Continuous:
I Kings 21.1-10 [11-14]
15-21*a*
Psalm 5.1-8

Related:
2 Samuel 11.26 –
12.10, 13-15
Psalm 32

Galatians 2.15-end
Luke 7.36 – 8.3

Proper 6

Luke 7.36 – 8.3

'... she has shown great love' (7.47)

Yet again, Jesus eschews the social norms of his day. It is one–nil for the outcasts when Jesus, friend of tax-collectors and sinners, comes to dinner at the house of Simon the Pharisee. The story assures us beyond doubt that what counts for Jesus are the intentions of the heart.

In terms of hospitality, Simon's behaviour is lacking, but not rude. To provide water for guests to wash their feet is well attested, but it was not a normative practice; a kiss of greeting was accepted but not mandatory; anointing the feet was very unusual outside the family. Simon's manners are correct, but *merely* correct.

The woman, on the other hand, has behaved in an outrageous manner, displaying a level of intimacy that is embarrassing the host within his own house. Her actions enable Simon to make a judgement about Jesus. This 'teacher' whom he invited to dinner has proved unworthy. It doesn't take a prophet to realize what kind of woman is touching Jesus: the loosing of the hair and kissing of the feet pretty much give it away! But, despite this, it is Simon who receives censure. Jesus sees the heart of both, and it is the love and gratitude of the penitent that is cherished, whatever form that takes.

Reflection by **Helen Orchard**

Proper 7

**Sunday between
19 & 25 June inclusive**
(if after Trinity Sunday)

Continuous:
1 Kings 19.1-4 [5-7] 8-15a
Psalms 42, 43 [or 42 or 43]
Galatians 3.23-end
Luke 8.26-39

1 Kings 19.1-4 [5-7] 8-15a

'It is enough; now, O Lord, take away my life ... ' (v.4)

Elijah's had enough. He's run away scared because Jezebel is after his life and, while on the run, he seems to give up and basically tells God to finish him off. It's a nice human portrait of Elijah that we get here, someone we can identify with perhaps. God is having none of it and provides food via an angel to keep him on the journey. He still has work for Elijah to do, and to call him back to his first love of God, to inspirit his energy, Elijah is taken to mount Horeb.

The other gods of the day were thought to show their strength through natural phenomena and violent demonstrations. Here, however, Yahweh reveals himself to be different. There is a power but a gentleness to this revelation, a beauty and a terror. The 'sheer silence' in which God's presence dwells has an X-ray quality to it, penetrating and searching the world with a holiness that can't be voiced.

God is often spoken of in frightening terms as if he is a traffic warden of souls, out to get us and condemn us. The Bible so often shows that God is be feared not because he is frightening but rather because he is real. His reality exposes our masks and superficiality, and this, like silence itself, is both horrific and liberating, as at last we are shown what we have become and who we really are. Such knowledge is needed if our vocations are to be lived fully.

Reflection by **John Pritchard**

Continuous:
Isaiah 65.1-9
Psalm 22.19-28
Galatians 3.23-end
Luke 8.26-39

Proper 7

Isaiah 65.1-9

'Here I am, here I am' (v.1)

This poem begins with a depressing list of all the reasons that God could justifiably have rejected his people. And then comes a most surprising moment of hope.

Our God is one who has opened his arms and made himself obvious to everyone. Not even just those who are searching for him, but anyone. And how did the Jews who lived all those centuries before Jesus respond? They provocatively worshipped in ways that were forbidden. They toyed with necromancy and defiantly ate prohibited foods. And they claimed that this made them holier than anyone else.

Does all that wrongdoing grind you down? Then take heart because God's graciousness is greater than you could imagine. You would expect a bunch of grapes that's withered and dry to be thrown away. But, instead, God intends to use even the most unpromising resources. He will not reject those grapes but will use every last one to make wine. That is his extraordinary blessing.

Like a bruised reed that is not chopped down, but tended back to life; like a flickering candle that isn't extinguished, but coaxed into flame (Isaiah 42.3, Matthew 12.20), God will keep working on our lives with loving determination. No one is ever regarded as too useless for his purposes. He even sees the potential in a dried-up grape like me. How can I resist when he calls out, 'Here I am'?

Reflection by **Peter Graystone**

Proper 7	*Continuous:*	*Related:*
	1 Kings 19.1-4 [5-7] 8-15*a*	Isaiah 65.1-9
	Psalms 42, 43 [*or* 42 *or* 43]	Psalm 22.19-28

Galatians 3.23-end
Luke 8.26-39

Galatians 3.23-end

'There is no longer Jew or Greek ... slave or free ...
male and female ...' (v.28)

Without getting too technical, we all know that, over time, texts can acquire deeper meanings and greater significance. Verse 28 is one such text. Its original meaning was to be found in the conflict between Paul and those wishing to restrict the new Christian communities either ethnically or by ritual boundaries. Through the radical recommencement of the spiritual journey of humankind, which Christ had initiated, all were now on a level playing field. The old spiritual privileges of the Jews under the law had been abrogated. The basis for inclusion, now, was simple faith (just like Abraham).

This text reveals why Christianity was so attractive in the first century: all could belong equally. The reality of Church life was sometimes ongoing social and ethnic divisions, but the ideals of unity and equality that the Church articulated were Christ-given and deeply theological and could not be forgotten.

This passage also reveals a fundamental quality of Christianity, which, when it is suppressed in one section of the Church, bursts out elsewhere. All people are equal in Christ. Whether it is in the radicalism of the Franciscans or the Quakers, the revolutionary theories of the Liberation Theologians, or the passionate patience of women in the modern Church, we should not be surprised that spiritual and real equality keeps resurfacing. Paul knew that it came from Christ.

Reflection by **Alan Bartlett**

Continuous:
1 Kings 19.1-4 [5-7] 8-15*a*
Psalms 42, 43 [*or* 42 *or* 43]
Galatians 3.23-end
Luke 8.26-39

Related:
Isaiah 65.1-9
Psalm 22.19-28

Proper 7

Luke 8.26-39

'... they were seized with great fear' (v.37)

Encountering serious mental or spiritual illness can be a frightening experience. Sufferers may behave in a way that is unexpected, uncontrollable and threatening. In this Gospel story, everyone is afraid – everyone, that is, except Jesus. The Gerasenes are afraid of the demoniac, keeping him chained up outside the city. The demoniac himself is afraid of torment on encountering Jesus – or, rather, that which possesses him is terrified by the power of the Son of the Most High God. The dramatic exorcism itself provokes a mixed response. In the man formerly known as 'Legion', fear has given way to faith, as he sits at the feet of Jesus. But, for the townsfolk, fear has multiplied – indeed, they are 'seized with great fear'. A violent madman was just about manageable, but someone who wields such power in the spiritual realm is truly terrifying. In Jesus, they perceive a man who really is unmanageable – and they are right!

Fear as a response to God and his deeds is a well-attested aspect of biblical faith, from patriarch to psalmist to Paul. In the same way that the disciples feared the actions of Jesus when he calmed the wind and waves on Lake Galilee (Luke 8.25), wondering 'Who is this?', so the Gerasenes fear him now. The only difference is in response. Instead of being drawn into faith, they allow fear to separate them from God. They forget that to fear God is to grow to know him, and that this fear is the beginning of wisdom (Proverbs 1.7)

Reflection by **Helen Orchard**

Proper 8

Continuous:
2 Kings 2.1-2, 6-14
Psalm 77.1-2, 11-end [*or* 77.11-end]
Galatians 5.1, 13-25
Luke 9.51-end

Sunday between
26 June & 2 July inclusive

2 Kings 2.1-2, 6-14

'Tell me what I may do for you, before I am taken from you?' (v.9)

In the Jewish Scriptures, people tend to view death as the natural conclusion to a life rather than as some feared enemy. This story, from which a faith in resurrection later develops, gives the sense that Yahweh is a God of life and that there is existence with him beyond the confines of our earthly living. For those who looked for the Messiah in the time of Jesus, it was to be Elijah returned from heaven who would announce his arrival – hence John the Baptist's Elijah overtones.

Elisha is appointed as Elijah's successor, inheriting his spirit and powerful mantle. We get another important theme here – that faith in God is something that is inherited and handed down. We have a duty to pass on the truths that have inspired us and helped us through life to another generation. We cannot expect them to discover the riches of the soul for themselves. This is a day to recall all those who nurtured and encouraged your own Christian discipleship – and then to ask whom you must now help.

As faithful vocation is handed on in this passage, so the whole impression is of life, glory and expectancy. To the jaundiced of the world, everything will look rather yellow, but to the faithful, life will be constantly opened up as we are carried by grace and enabled to do good things in the time given to us.

Reflection by **Mark Oakley**

Related:
I Kings 19.5-16, 19-end
Psalm 16
Galatians 5.1, 13-25
Luke 9.51-end

Proper 8

1 Kings 19.5-16, 19-end

'... a sound of sheer silence ' (v.12)

The modern Church seems to be being offered two clichés. Either that faith has to be minutely and definitely expressed, so that there is no room for doubt or error. Or that faith is too uncertain to be defined and so cannot be – except that it is obviously true that it is too uncertain to be defined ... The story of Elijah takes us to the heart of how it is to be human in the face of God.

Elijah does not doubt the existence of God. He appears to be doubting his own effectiveness in God's service and perhaps even God's commitment to him. In exile, having fled Queen Jezebel, he is utterly spent – defeated even. He is so worn out, he just wants to die.

God does not come to him with a 'statement of faith'. Nor does God overwhelm him. God just comes to him. The encounter is indescribable – NRSV says 'a sound of sheer silence' – but Elijah knows it is God who has come to him. This is not noisy faith or thin faith; rather it is an authentic encounter with God in this world, but one that is beyond words.

And what is the first thing that God does? Not a telling off. Not a theological statement. No. God provides colleagues. Which, of course, is what worn-out and depressed Elijah needs most of all.

Authentic encounter with God will be indescribable, but it will have tangible consequences.

Reflection by **Alan Bartlett**

Proper 8	*Continuous:*	*Related:*
	2 Kings 2.1-2, 6-14	1 Kings 19.5-16, 19-end
	Psalm 77.1-2, 11-end	Psalm 16
	[*or* 77.11-end]	
	Galatians 5.1, 13-25	
	Luke 9.51-end	

Galatians 5.1, 13-25

'If we live by the Spirit, let us also be guided by the Spirit'
(v.25)

In trying to demonstrate what's distinctive about the way Christians should live, Paul sets two approaches in clear opposition: the way of the flesh and the way of the Spirit. By 'flesh', Paul doesn't quite mean what we might think; he means more like 'the way of the world', a world without Christ as the touchstone. As ever, Paul pulls no punches: those who live in a worldly way will not inherit the kingdom of God. Your choice, he says.

It's well on occasions to see the contrast laid out starkly, but the practice of 'splitting', if it becomes a habit, can lead to some pretty unpleasant behaviour – condemnation, judgementalism, etc. But Paul shows us the better way – live by the Spirit and be guided by the Spirit. If you're lost in a car in a strange town, what you need isn't a list of complicated instructions but someone who knows the place well and who'll get in the front seat beside you and talk you through the road system. We have such a guide, says Paul, the Spirit of Jesus Christ, who will ensure that we choose the streets that are marked by love, joy, peace, patience, kindness, generosity and so on. So the question is: which navigation system do we use? Are we nudged and guided by the Spirit, or by the compulsions and obsessions of the world?

Will we start each day by inviting the divine Guide to show us the way?

Reflection by **John Pritchard**

Proper 8

Luke 9.51-end

'... he set his face to go to Jerusalem' (v.51)

Today's passage begins in great solemnity. Jesus setting his face to go to Jerusalem marks a moment of intense commitment. He knows his destiny. But he still has to get there. Those who reject him at this stage of his ministry are signs and anticipations of the great rejection that lies ahead.

As Jesus takes the road to Jerusalem, so the destiny of many others is being played out. It is noticeable that Jesus is harder on the 'would-be' disciples who make the right noises but lack urgency, than he is on the Samaritans who refuse to give him hospitality. Rejection can be forgiven, but lukewarm or insincere acceptance grates because it misunderstands the ultimate nature of Jesus' call.

On the way to Jerusalem, Jesus promises no easy road, and the road we are called to follow as Christians is always the *via crucis*, the way of the cross. This is extremely challenging, especially for those of us who have been Christians for many years, or all our lives. We may have integrated our faith so well into our personalities and lifestyles that we are no longer shocked by its extreme demands. We look for our spiritual life to bring us peace but this should not be the false peace of self-satisfaction. The kingdom of God demands more.

Reflection by **Angela Tilby**

Sunday between
3 & 9 July inclusive

Continuous:
2 Kings 5.1-14
Psalm 30
Galatians 6.[1-6] 7-16
Luke 10.1-11, 16-20

2 Kings 5.1-14

'... his flesh was restored like the flesh of a young boy,
and he was clean' (v.14)

Getting into God's healing zone often means getting out of our own comfort zone, as this story shows. A slave girl has to lift her head from cleaning floors to refer her sick master to the right consultant. A king has to turn from politics to ask one of his vassals to facilitate the healing of his leading general.

It is hardest of all for Naaman and Elisha. Elisha has to learn how to be inclusive and generous to a threatening stranger without compromising his own faith and calling. He will indeed heal Naaman, but he has to seek that healing by a baptism in Israel's river and at the hand of Israel's God.

For Naaman himself, it is hardest of all. He has to go into an alien culture and submit himself to the ministry of a man whom he would have considered his natural enemy. He certainly does not like the prescription that is offered to him, with its claim that the rivers and the God of Israel have a saving power far beyond those of Syria. But the reward of such humiliation is more than healing – it is conversion to the living God.

Reflection by **Tom Smail**

Related:
Isaiah 66.10-14
Psalm 66.1-8
Galatians 6.[1-6] 7-16
Luke 10.1-11, 16-20

Isaiah 66.10-14

'I will comfort you' (v.13)

Endings are not always pleasing. The Old Testament ends with the threat of a curse if ancient laws are forgotten (Malachi 4.4-6). The book of Isaiah ends just after today's reading with a vision of the death of those who reject the Lord (v.24). In fact, when it is read in synagogues, it is customary to read verses 22 and 23 again at the end to soften the blow. In contrast, the New Testament ends with Jesus' grace resting on all believers (Revelation 22.21). It is a vision of a peaceful future that Isaiah prepares us for in verses 12-14 of today's reading.

Here is one of the precious Bible passages that encourage us to think about the actions of God in female terms. God has made Jerusalem a source of security and wellbeing. The city has become a mother with tender care for her children. She is the source of comfort, the kind that a baby can only find in a mother's arms. Body and soul flourish because the context is peace.

The prophetic poem continues with a list of what must have seemed earth's remotest places, Tarshish (Spain) to Javan (Greece). Jews and gentiles alike will be drawn to worship the glory of God. This peaceful vision is a precursor to the promise of the new Jerusalem, the very image with which the Bible comes to a climax – the glorious destiny of all who long for God's kingdom to come (Revelation 21.2).

Reflection by **Peter Graystone**

Proper 9

Continuous:
2 Kings 5.1-14
Psalm 30

Related:
Isaiah 66.10-14
Psalm 66.1-8
Galatians 6.[1-6] 7-16
Luke 10.1-11, 16-20

Galatians 6.[1-6] 7-16

'... for you reap whatever you sow' (v.7)

This is one of the more resonant biblical mantras – one that has found its way into Pentecostal hymnody, as well as many a sermon. At the heart of the phrase is a simple idea, one that echoes a frequently occurring theme of the Old Testament – the 'parents have eaten sour grapes ... and the children's teeth are set on edge' (Jeremiah 31.29).

A society that puts work, pleasure and money at the heart of its priorities will raise a generation of individualistic, distracted and avaricious children. The development of moral character and social awareness will, alas, be secondary.

Paul tells us to beware of this in the Church and in the world. Churches can foster and focus distinctive values that provide leaven in complex contexts. So, faith communities often find themselves promoting forms of goodness that secular organizations might miss. Through a simple ministry of hospitality, care and celebration, churches sometimes do more good for their communities than they can often know. Churches may simply offer regular lunches to the needy, or open house for tea and coffee at any time – the potency of the practice lies in the latency, and is significant. They open up a different side of the Church to the world. The Church, in other words, is an extension of Christ's love for the world, and helps to inaugurate that new creation that is rooted in grace and hope. So, let us sow the seeds of Christ's love, patience and gentleness where we can, for the harvest reaped will come of such faith.

Reflection by **Martyn Percy**

Continuous:	Related:	
2 Kings 5.1-14	Isaiah 66.10-14	**Proper 9**
Psalm 30	Psalm 66.1-8	

Galatians 6.[1-6] 7-16

Luke 10.1-11, 16-20

Luke 10.1-11, 16-20

'Carry no purse, no bag, no sandals' (v.4)

Jesus appoints and commissions 35 pairs of evangelists to go ahead of him into God's harvest. Why does he choose 70 people? There are several suggestions, all with Old Testament connections. They could represent the 70 gentile nations mentioned in Genesis, or the 70 members of Jacob's family who go down to Egypt representing the people of Israel, or the 70 elders chosen by Moses who receive the Holy Spirit.

The 70 Jesus selects are to travel swiftly and lightly. The message of peace they carry is urgent, and they are not to be weighed down with unnecessary paraphernalia. Nor are they to waste time with those who won't listen. Israel is ripe for harvesting and there's no time to be lost: Jesus won't come this way again. Wolves are already snapping at his heels.

Not only does Jesus call us to follow him, he also sends us out ahead of him to herald his existence and harvest the fruit of his kingdom. It's a task that requires dedication and the ability to travel lightly through life, holding onto what really matters and letting go of the rest. Jesus calls you to proclaim his kingdom. What do you need to let go of for that to happen more effectively?

We are reminded again that 'the harvest is plentiful, but the labourers are few'. In your prayers today, ask the Lord to call passionate workers into his abundant harvest.

Reflection by **Catherine Williams**

Proper 10

**Sunday between
10 & 16 July inclusive**

Continuous:
Amos 7.7-end
Psalm 82
Colossians 1.1-14
Luke 10.25-37

Amos 7.7-end

*'See, I am setting a plumb-line in the midst of my people
Israel' (v.8)*

The famous picture of the plumb-line in Amos 7 has been
speculated about for centuries. It's one of only two occasions
where it appears in the Bible (the other being Isaiah 34.11).
Nowadays, we have spirit levels to make sure our DIY projects
are in line, while surveyors use laser measurements to check
dimensions. What all these devices do is to measure against
something else. In the case of this vision of God, the Lord is
the builder, measuring Israel to see whether she meets with
approval. Even though God shows mercy, we are also
accountable to him.

This is not about 'measuring up' to standards, but balancing
what we do against God and God alone. This is hard in a
world where relativism holds sway - the notion that all points
of view are equally valid, and that all truth is relative only to
the individual. In such a world, we just measure ourselves
against ourselves, and define our morality against ourselves.
For God, having a line – a plumb-line or any other measuring
line – means that there is a clear marker, one that we do not
write ourselves, but that God has written.

Today, think of this line not as a long plumb-line, but as the
line around the heart of God – God who continually shows
mercy. When we cause God grief, it is not just that our line
does not measure up to God, but that it breaks the heart of
God, who is still seeking to align his heart to ours.

Reflection by **Tim Sledge**

Related:
Deuteronomy 30.9-14
Psalm 25.1-10
Colossians 1.1-14
Luke 10.25-37

Proper 10

Deuteronomy 30.9-14

' ... the word is very near to you' (v.14)

The Israelites' long wilderness wanderings are almost over, and today's reading forms a part of an extended speech of Moses to the people of Israel on the verge of their entry into the Promised Land. The people's history in the desert has been a chequered one, their experiences of closeness to God alternating with times of alienation on account of their disobedience.

But here and now, says Moses, is the promise of a bright new future, and the people's current situation is pregnant with possibility. In the past, it was never God who turned away from his people; rather it was the people who abandoned God. Appealing to their hidden reserves of faith, hope and courage, Moses tells them that the God they seek is much closer to them than they ever imagined; God's word is not beyond the sea or up in heaven, but 'in your mouth and in your heart for you to observe'.

There is much in this passage about the choices we make in life, and the Israelites' experience here reminds us that the decisions we make in our own particular circumstances will carry consequences, for good or ill. We are urged to *listen*: to listen to the 'still, small voice' of God within our hearts. We won't always get it right, but if we are truly seeking God's way, we will discover that God is indeed 'very near' and faithful to us.

Reflection by **Barbara Mosse**

	Continuous:	Related:
Proper 10	Amos 7.7-end	Deuteronomy 30.9-14
	Psalm 82	Psalm 25.1-10
		Colossians 1.1-14
		Luke 10.25-37

Colossians 1.1-14

*'In our prayers for you we always thank God, the Father
of our Lord Jesus Christ' (v.3)*

Children's prayers usually begin with the words 'Thank you'.
Adults' prayers usually begin with the word 'Please'. But if we
dwell in God's kingdom, we should all live with child-like
thanksgiving. Hence, Paul's letters always begin and end with
thanks. Indeed, we use the Greek word for thanksgiving –
Eucharist – as the name for the central act of Christian
worship. And it is a thanksgiving that goes on even when we
face challenge and suffering. It is the joyful refusal to submit
to the pessimism and defeat of the world. 'Endure everything
with patience,' says Paul, 'give thanks to God.'

Paul rejoices that this hope has taken root in the Church at
Colossae, and beginning his letter to them he calls them
'saints'. Now we usually reserve this word for the most holy
and distinguished Christians. But the journey of Christian
living indicates a deeper truth – that all of us are saints: not
because of our goodness or even our holiness (this is not the
point), but because of what God has done in Christ and
because we have responded. We have received the gift of a
new life and we have found ourselves re-created and re-
focused in Christ. We are holy – we are saints – because we
now live our lives in union with a holy God. Worth a 'thank
you', don't you think?

Reflection by **Stephen Cottrell**

Proper 10

Luke 10.25-37

'Go and do likewise' (v.37)

It can be difficult to receive very well-known passages from scripture freshly because we have heard them too often. The parable of the Good Samaritan is surely one of those passages. It has become a hallmark for the response to suffering that everyone recognizes as truly and distinctively Christian. The Samaritan acts without guile; he has no need, as the lawyer does, to justify himself. He is moved by pure compassion. He does not weigh up the disadvantage to himself in acting compassionately, as the priest and the Levite do when they pass by. His response is direct and human. He 'feels with' the suffering of the robbed and wounded man. Such compassion cannot be faked; it springs from the heart.

But there is more in the story Jesus tells than a paradigm of Christian love. The mercy shown by the Samaritan mirrors the boundless mercy of God. The Samaritan's spontaneous response to human need reveals God's own heart. The fact that he is not an orthodox Jew drives the point home. God's love is not limited to those of the 'right' creed or practice. God's love is manifest whenever compassion for suffering results in the relief of suffering. The story invites us to examine our own hearts. We can all feel sorry for those in obvious need. But do we do anything about it?

Reflection by **Angela Tilby**

Proper 11

**Sunday between
17 & 23 July inclusive**

Continuous:
Amos 8.1-12
Psalm 52
Colossians 1.15-28
Luke 10.38-end

Amos 8.1-12

'... a basket of summer fruit' (v.1)

Two of the prophet Amos' visions are extraordinary and must have involved 'seeing' with the imagination or the mind's eye: locusts formed by God (Amos 7.1) and a great devouring fire (Amos 7.4). The other two visions are more ordinary. The prophet's eyes rest upon some everyday object, singled out for his attention by the words: 'What do you see?' The first is a plumb line (Amos 7.7), used on every building site. The meaning drawn is straightforward. God is measuring Israel's straightness before him. The second is a basket of fruit. Here there is a play on words. The phrase 'summer fruit' and the word 'end' in Hebrew sound almost the same.

These ordinary and extraordinary visions and word plays will be taken up by the other prophets and also by Jesus, the greatest of the prophets and more than a prophet. Many of us may never experience extraordinary visions or special words from God (and for those who do, they can be a heavy burden). But we all need to be open to God's word to us today and each day through the ordinary: through the scriptures; in conversations; through a striking image; through seeming coincidence; through a basket of fruit.

The deep inner dialogue Amos enjoys with the Lord is one of the great privileges of the Christian life. Times of prayer in the day need to carry over into the whole of the day.

Reflection by **Steven Croft**

Related:
Genesis 18.1-10*a*
Psalm 15
Colossians 1.15-28
Luke 10.38-end

Proper 11

Genesis 18.1-10*a*

*'I will surely return to you in due season, and your wife
Sarah shall have a son' (v.10)*

In an encounter related in Chapter 17, God promises Abraham
a son by his 90-year-old wife Sarah (Genesis 17.16). In response,
Abraham falls on his face and laughs. Now we hear that
promise through a human story. We encounter Abraham
bursting with action, as he looks up, runs, bows down, hastens
into the tent and organizes hospitality that vastly exceeds the
'little bread' he has offered. Why? Because three men have
suddenly appeared in the midday heat, and oriental courtesy
and hospitality are called for. Abraham does not recognize
them as divine beings, or indeed that the Lord himself is
among them, but they bring their amazing message, and this
time it is Sarah who laughs (Genesis 18.12).

Again, Abraham and Sarah are faced with the magnitude of
God's grace. The question that Sarah goes on to ask herself –
'Is anything too wonderful for the Lord?' – is one that we also
can ponder when we are tempted to live parsimoniously
because we cannot comprehend the extent of God's
generosity and purposes to bless the whole world.

The letter to the Hebrews reminds us that sometimes we can
entertain God's messengers (angels) without realizing it, while
the Collect prays that the light of Christ will shine in our hearts
and reveal the knowledge of God's glory in Jesus Christ. Pray
that prayer for anyone you know who is discouraged by
events that weaken their faith. Perhaps God will answer that
prayer by sending an unrecognized angel.

Reflection by **Rosalind Brown**

Proper 11

Continuous:
Amos 8.1-12
Psalm 52

Related:
Genesis 18.1-10*a*
Psalm 15
Colossians 1.15-28
Luke 10.38-end

Colossians 1.15-28

'... in him all things hold together' (v.17)

This great hymn to Christ in Colossians has the same cosmic resonance – indeed hints at the same final coherence – as the prologue to John's Gospel. It lifts us out of our littleness. The next time your PCC is bogged down in a discussion of stationery, or the minutiae of the coffee rota seems to loom larger than it should, it would be well to recite, in awe-struck tones, these verses of Colossians: all-inclusive, and all-transforming, that great phrase 'all things' is repeated again and again. Nothing and no one is beyond God's presence, or the reach and scope of his concern.

But there is more: this passage is not only about presence and coherence, about all things holding together in Christ; it is also about peace and reconciliation. It is not only that Christ reconciles things on a cosmic scale, bringing together, as he does, the very things we contrast and oppose – heaven and earth, time and eternity, truth and grace – but he is also reconciling us, individually and collectively, on a detailed, difficult, nitty-gritty level, so that we who have been 'estranged and hostile in mind' can be reconciled and make 'peace through the blood of his cross'.

Maybe that's worth sharing with the PCC too!

Reflection by **Malcolm Guite**

Continuous:
Amos 8.1-12
Psalm 52

Related:
Genesis 18.1-10*a*
Psalm 15
Colossians 1.15-28
Luke 10.38-end

Proper 11

Luke 10.38-end

'Mary has chosen the better part' (v.42)

It is important to remember that this little story of Mary and Martha is set in the context of Jesus having set his face to go to Jerusalem. There is an urgency behind the text that is not always noticed when the story is isolated from its setting. The point is that the passion lies ahead. This helps make sense of Jesus' response to the two sisters, which otherwise could seem unfair. After all, it is Martha who welcomes him into their home, Martha who gets on with the housework while Mary listens to the Lord. Jesus' judgement of Martha is not a condemnation of her work, but more a comment on her distractedness. She prefers to let herself be taken up with necessary, but perhaps not absolutely vital, tasks rather than spending precious moments listening to what the Lord is saying. Mary, on the other hand, grasps the moment, perhaps recognizing that it will not come again.

One wonders whether he is talking to Mary about his impending suffering and death and the need for sacrifice on the part of his disciples. Perhaps this is the part that Martha cannot bear, and she is not alone. All of us baulk at the challenge of Jesus to take up our cross 'daily' (Luke 9.23) and follow him. How much of our schedule today is calculated to avoid the things that really matter?

Reflection by **Angela Tilby**

Proper 12

**Sunday between
24 & 30 July inclusive**

Continuous:
Hosea 1.2-10
Psalm 85 [*or* 85.1-7]
Colossians 2.6-15 [16-19]
Luke 11.1-13

Hosea 1.2-10

'... it shall be said to them, "Children of the living God."'
(1.10)

The prophet Hosea speaks in beautiful imagery about the love of God that will not let people go.

So often we name our children after people in our family. We try and keep names going because of family history, identity and story. Here, though, the Lord instructs Hosea to name his son 'Lo-ammi' – a name that means 'not in my name'. Yet in the very next verse, there is a gear change of direction. The Lord promises that at the very place where it was said the people were no longer God's, they would once again be called 'children of the living God'. It is as though the end of the covenant is too terrible to contemplate – the overarching love of God cannot be shut out even when the people break their side of the bargain.

Hosea is a striking figure. He takes upon himself something of the people's sin, something of their pain. Through his marriage to Gomer and the birth of the children, he enacts the long-suffering love of God, who bears with his erring people far beyond their deserving – who in the end opts for compassion and forgiveness as the way to life.

All of this matters because Hosea writes as if this is all about his family. Hosea reminds us that we often feel the strongest emotions for those who are closest to us. Things may happen that are 'not in my name' – but, ultimately, we are family, and we share the same name and bloodline.

Reflection by **Tim Sledge**

Genesis 18.20-32

Proper 12

Psalm 138
Colossians 2.6-15 [16-19]
Luke 11.1-13

Genesis 18.20-32

"Will you indeed sweep away the righteous with the wicked?' (v.23)

The announcement of a new beginning for Abraham and Sarah is followed immediately by the prospect of a destructive end for the city that Abraham, in his tent in the mountains, could see in the distance on the plain. The Lord deliberates about taking Abraham into his confidence and, when he does, the tables are turned, and Abraham becomes the Lord's questioner, putting God on the spot in an example of Middle Eastern bargaining. The question is not whether there will be judgement on the city, but what decides the extent of it: the wickedness of the many or the righteousness of the few?

Abraham presses hard until he receives the answer that a few innocent and righteous people are more important than many wicked people. Righteousness is the key concept here: Noah was righteous, but that quality has not (yet) been ascribed to Abraham. However, the Lord has chosen Abraham to lead his descendants in the way of righteousness and justice. So this is a testing both of God's purposes and of Abraham's commitment to, and understanding of, what it means to be righteous.

Pray today for people trying to live righteously in the midst of vice and wickedness. Can you be their advocate, as Abraham was?

Reflection by **Rosalind Brown**

Proper 12

Continuous:
Hosea 1.2-10
Psalm 85 [*or* 85.1-7]

Related:
Genesis 18.20-32
Psalm 138
Colossians 2.6-15 [16-19]
Luke 11.1-13

Colossians 2.6-15 [16-19]

'... you have come to fullness in him, who is the head of every ruler and authority' (v.10)

In his epistle, Paul urges the Colossians to a fuller appreciation of Christ. This is not simply for the sake of deepening their spiritual growth – yes, he very much desires their encouragement and common unity in Christ – but he is also concerned with their spiritual protection: 'See to it that no one takes you captive through philosophy and empty deceit'.

Paul doesn't at this stage elaborate further, but in his insistence that in Christ the Colossians had been circumcised 'with a spiritual circumcision', it may be that some people were insisting that non-Jews still needed to submit themselves to physical circumcision. This is no longer necessary, insists Paul, because Christ's victory on the cross has superseded any need for this distinguishing mark of membership. Stand firm, he says, in the Christ you have received, and 'continue to live your lives in him'.

We are encouraged to hold fast to what we know and have experienced of Christ, but we are also urged to exercise discernment. Now, as then, many things are said of Christ and taught in his name, and not all will necessarily ring true with the understanding of Christ growing within us. A similar sentiment expressed in the first epistle of John encourages us to 'test the spirits to see whether they are from God; for many false prophets have gone out into the world' (1 John 4.1).

Reflection by **Barbara Mosse**

Proper 12

Luke 11.1-13

'... everyone who asks receives' (v.10)

Today's passage reflects Luke's take on Jesus' teaching about prayer. What emerges clearly is that Jesus expects his disciples to pray with boldness, trusting God to take care of their daily needs. The disciples clearly sense that there is something about the way Jesus prays to the Father that they need to inhabit for themselves. The 'model' prayer he gives them is fairly unremarkable, full of phrases familiar to any pious Jew. The teaching that follows stresses the need for persistence. The friend at midnight who at first refuses to provide food for an unexpected visitor stands here for our constant experiences of setback in prayer; our projections onto God of our own impatience and lack of compassion. We are not born trusting God; trust has to be discovered and learnt, and we are to persist in spite of any damage to our image of God that arises from past experience or wounded memories.

God is not like the friend at midnight; yet we may sometimes feel abandoned and that our requests are not heard. Praying with persistence requires discipline and courage. Our spiritual muscles need developing and exercising before we can rely on them to carry us through barren times. Once again, Jesus prepares the disciples for his passion. To interpret his suffering, and the suffering they themselves will endure, requires the consoling gift of the Holy Spirit.

Reflection by **Angela Tilby**

Continuous:
Hosea 11.1-11
Psalm 107.1-9, 43 [*or* 107.1-9]
Colossians 3.1-11
Luke 12.13-21

Hosea 11.1-11

'I was to them like those who lift infants to their cheeks.'
(v.4)

In Chapter 11, it is as if Hosea makes a breakthrough in understanding the divine nature, or perhaps that God breaks through to Hosea. In other chapters of Hosea, God is a jealous husband, a frustrated artisan or farmer; here, God is a loving parent who has to let his wayward child go, but can hardly bear the pain. He has not only created and produced this child, he has adored and nurtured him, setting him on his way as a toddler who learns to walk and is guided by his parent and comforted when he trips up and bangs his knee.

We might ask why we should privilege this view of God over the others presented by the prophet. The answer is that Christians read the Hebrew Bible through the lens of the New Testament, and this is the view of God that is taken up by Jesus. It is most fully and poignantly developed in the story of the prodigal son in Luke 15, and it is edifying to read the two passages as a pair.

The son relies on his own strength, forgets the nature of his relationship with his father, travels to a foreign region, and becomes involved with immoral and unclean practices. He gets into trouble as a natural consequence of his actions rather than as a direct punishment for them. The rejected father awaits his homecoming, and when he sees his son return 'trembling', finds that he cannot 'execute anger' but is instead overcome with 'compassion'.

Reflection by **Joanna Collicutt**

Related:
Ecclesiastes 1.2, 12-14; 2.18-23
Psalm 49.1-12 [*or* 49.1-9]
Colossians 3.1-11
Luke 12.13-21

Proper 13

Ecclesiastes 1.2, 12-14; 2.18-23

'Vanity of vanities, says the Teacher ... All is vanity' (1.2)

The words of the ancient Teacher of Ecclesiastes are not meant for nourishment (according to one writer). They are meant instead as cleansing, as rebuke, for purging: a cold shower on a muggy day. We will not always agree with him. The preacher reminds us that there are no easy answers to the dilemmas of life and faith. The book provokes a reaction. Its words are a slap in the face for our own self-importance.

What projects and priorities are most dear to me this day? What am I most anxious about or most proud of this morning? Ecclesiastes invites me to see all things in the long perspective of the ages. The sun rises and sets again. The seasons change. The streams still flow to the sea. What has been is what will be. There is 'nothing new under the sun' (Ecclesiastes 1.9). Nothing I do (or cannot do) this day will change these facts.

This long perspective of the ages frames my own living in a different way. My pride is punctured, my self-importance winded. The things that occupy my time and attention diminish in size; most (if not all) are vanity and 'chasing after wind'.

Reflection by **Steven Croft**

Proper 13

Continuous:
Hosea 11.1-11
Psalm 107.1-9, 43
[or 107.1-9]

Related:
Ecclesiastes 1.2, 12-14;
2.18-23
Psalm 49.1-12 [or 49.1-9]
Colossians 3.1-11
Luke 12.13-21

Colossians 3.1-11

'... you have stripped off the old self' (v.9)

There are two images woven through this passage, both rooted in the baptism service. The first is the theme of death and resurrection. At baptism, the disciple goes down into the waters of death and rises to new life in Christ. This death is a once and for all event ('for you have died') but also a continual call to holiness ('Put to death, therefore, whatever in you is earthly').

In a similar way, resurrection and new life have already begun. The new self 'is being renewed in knowledge according to the image of its creator'. We look forward to the day when we will 'be revealed with him in glory'.

The second image from baptism is taking off one set of clothes and putting on another. At baptism, the disciple comes out of the water, strips off their old garments and is given a new white robe. This profound image is taken deeper. According to Colossians, 'you have stripped off the old self with its practices and have clothed yourselves with the new self'. It is one thing to take off your soiled old clothes. Christ's love penetrates even to peeling back layers of our very self so that we might be healed and renewed.

Each Christian is baptized only once, but the power and the symbolism of our baptism affects us every day as we seek to live our lives in Christ. Every day means death to the old self and awaking to new life. Every day means putting aside our old, soiled clothes and putting on the new self.

Reflection by **Steven Croft**

Continuous:	Related:	
Hosea 11.1-11	Ecclesiastes 1.2, 12-14;	**Proper 13**
Psalm 107.1-9, 43	2.18-23	
[or 107.1-9]	Psalm 49.1-12 [or 49.1-9]	

Colossians 3.1-11
Luke 12.13-21

Luke 12.13-21

'... life does not consist in the abundance of possessions' (v.15)

It's been said that in the West we spend money we don't have on things we don't want in order to impress people we don't like. Although we laugh at the accuracy, it should make us cry, because this circle of dissatisfaction ends up leaving us with lots to live *with* but little to live *for*. Jesus knew the spiritual shipwrecks that occur when greed takes over a life. He tells his followers to be on their guard and tells them a parable to bring home the point.

Jesus often taught with parables. They can infuriate because they don't always make easy sense. But this is the point. They were not intended to make easy sense but to make us, or rather *re*-make us, by way of an often puzzling but resonant story that reconfigures the heart by way of the mind. His parable of the man building more storage for yet more stuff is eerily relevant. It ends by asking us what it means to be 'rich towards God'.

All the things that matter most in this life – love, relationship, trust, wisdom, justice – these increase as you share them. If others win, so do I. Unlike wealth and power, where if you win I lose, the qualities of the kingdom that allow us to relate more deeply to God, ourselves and other people are all so rich that both the giver and receiver benefit in an exchange of sacred significance. To live within this economy, teaches Jesus, is to live as a citizen of God's kingdom and not just as a consumer of the world.

Reflection by **Mark Oakley**

Proper 14

**Sunday between
7 & 13 August inclusive**

Isaiah 1.1, 10-20

*'Your new moons and your appointed festivals
my soul hates' (v.14)*

The book of Isaiah engages deeply with social and political themes. The first chapter seems to be a miscellany of sayings by Isaiah from various points in his long career, which lasted for most of the second half of the eighth century BC. Verses 1 to 9 reflected the situation in 701 BC, when the Assyrians (based in what is now Iraq) invaded Judah and laid siege to Jerusalem; verses 10-20 reflect an earlier time, when all seemed well and prosperous in Jerusalem. Yet, for Isaiah, who believed in divine retribution for sin, it was the misdeeds of the inhabitants of Jerusalem in the earlier time that had led ultimately to their national disaster as the Assyrians invaded. Like all the prophets, he saw the lack of social justice among the upper classes as calling down the anger of God, which was then expressed through the agency of a foreign power.

Isaiah particularly concentrates on the way that the rulers of Judah cloak their oppression of the poor by assiduous religious practice. But God does not want 'religion' divorced from caring for those in need. True religion, as the Letter of James puts it, is 'to care for orphans and widows in their distress' (James 1.27), not to spend one's money on lavish offerings to God while ignoring the plight of desperate people or, worse, actually oppressing them.

Reflection by **John Barton**

Related:
Genesis 15.1-6
Psalm 33.12-end [*or* 33.12-21]
Hebrews 11.1-3, 8-16
Luke 12.32-40

Genesis 15.1-6

'Do not be afraid, Abram, I am your shield' (v.1)

It seems that God's promises to Abram – of vast lands and countless offspring (Genesis 13.14-17) – are wearing a bit thin. We can sense Abram's frustration that there is no sign of them being fulfilled. He is getting older, there's no prospect of a son and heir, and he wants some certainty about it all. So he complains to God and, wonderfully, God does not tell Abram off but takes him outside for an object lesson. On a clear, starlit night in the wilderness, Abram is invited to ponder the view and, through that, take in the magnitude of God's promise to him. It has the desired effect: Abram believes and the Lord reckons that to him as righteousness – the same right relationship with God that Noah had (Genesis 6.9).

What follows this is a strange covenant ritual that comes from an earlier tradition, with fire acting as the symbol of the holy presence of God (Genesis 15.17). This foreshadows the burning bush that Moses saw when slavery in Egypt was about to end.

We can take comfort from God's willingness to let Abram express his questions and his fears and then give him very vivid reassurance. It is better to be honest about our doubts than just abandon our hope. That way our faith can be strengthened.

Reflection by **Rosalind Brown**

Proper 14

Continuous:
Isaiah 1.1, 10-20
Psalm 50.1-8, 23-end
[or 50.1-7]

Related:
Genesis 15.1-6
Psalm 33.12-22
[or 33.12-21]

Hebrews 11.1-3, 8-16
Luke 12.32-40

Hebrews 11.1-3, 8-16

'If they had been thinking of the land that they had left behind ...' (v.15)

As Søren Kierkegaard, the Danish theologian, said: 'Life can only be understood backwards; but it must be lived forwards.' In today's reading, we are given the example of Abraham and other great figures of faith (vv. 4–7) who have lived forwards. They did not yearn for a return to where they had come from, but rather walked – by faith – into a new and uncertain future.

This is often the Christian vocation. But if this true, what are the next steps? How would you know you were called? How could you be sure? You can't of course, but there are two simple things to bear in mind.

First, have courage. Many journeys of faith and adventure with God never begin – because of fear. Fear of failure, or perhaps just of getting it wrong – suppose someone rumbles that I am just ordinary? Suppose I really make a mess of it? But failure is not the worst thing; letting it defeat you is. It takes a special kind of wisdom and courage to face failure and defeat, and then to try and move on from this.

Second, have patience. The Christian life is often lived more in waiting and hope than in results. Our journey of discipleship is measured over the entire course of a life. It takes a long time to appreciate just how much God has called us to. It takes daily devotion to see that our calling is not about affirmation or success at all, but rather faithfulness. Sometimes we are called not to win but merely, by faith, to walk with Christ.

Reflection by **Martyn Percy**

Continuous:
Isaiah 1.1, 10-20
Psalm 50.1-8, 23-end
[*or* 50.1-7]

Related:
Genesis 15.1-6
Psalm 33.12-end
[*or* 33.12-21]

Proper 14

Hebrews 11.1-3, 8-16
Luke 12.32-40

Luke 12.32-40

'Be dressed for action and have your lamps lit' (v.35)

After the serenity of Jesus telling his followers not to be anxious about their lives, the intense urgency of his subsequent teaching here, about being ready for his arrival at the end of time, comes as a shock. The phrase 'dressed for action' used to be translated as having 'your loins girded', that is, ensuring that your robes are pulled up and fastened high enough to allow your legs to run. Like a family at an airport arrivals lounge, they need to be ready to run with arms open – ready for a reassuring hug.

The first readers of Luke's Gospel may have been wondering why Jesus hadn't yet returned. Some may have been suffering as they waited. Contemporary readers may have similar questions as to why evil and pain are not brought to an end by the final reign of God on earth. Why is patience more virtuous than justice?

Jesus' teaching here reminds all of us that, for the Christian, all things are as yet unfinished. Our discipleship is a way, a journey, and it requires of us an alertness and readiness for discerning right decisions, movement and courage. The challenge is for us to be a continually expectant people, eager to have enough light in our lives to be able to see Christ when he comes to us in the frightened, hurting, oppressed and ignored. Unless we are ready to move towards such men, women and children living alongside us now, dressed for action with light shining, we may well miss him when he arrives at the 'unexpected hour'.

Reflection by **Mark Oakley**

211

Proper 15

**Sunday between
14 & 20 August inclusive**

Continuous:
Isaiah 5.1-7
Psalm 80.1-2, 9-end [*or* 80.9-end]
Hebrews 11.29 – 12.2
Luke 12.49-56

Isaiah 5.1-7

'... he expected it to yield grapes, but it yielded wild grapes'
(v.2)

The vineyard is a common symbol of Israel in the Bible. It stresses God's diligence in looking after his people, who need his constant care just as a vineyard needs continual attention, and also the flourishing and fruitfulness that is his desire for them.

Here, however, Judah and Jerusalem turn out to be an unfruitful vineyard, like the one in Jesus' parable in Mark 12.1-12. What begins by sounding like a song celebrating God's love for his vineyard thus turns out to be a prophecy of doom. The vineyard is unfruitful because of the people's lack of justice and righteousness, which are the standard prophetic terms for the way rulers ought to behave towards those they rule, with probity and social concern.

The obvious message for the Christian is that we often fail to respond to God's care for us: he provides opportunities and expects a response, but (like the third man in the parable of the talents) we do too little with what he gives us, and get in the way of our own flourishing by ignoring the needs around us. Fortunately for us, God's last word is one not of destruction but of re-creation, as he provides 'a shade by day from the heat, and a refuge and a shelter from the storm and rain' (Isaiah 4.6).

Reflection by **John Barton**

Related:
Jeremiah 23.23-29
Psalm 82
Hebrews 11.29 – 12.2
Luke 12.49-56

Jeremiah 23.23-29

'I have heard what the prophets have said...' (v.25)

God has certainly heard 'the prophets', but the question is, have they heard him?

The prophet's main task is to listen to God and then to report what they've heard. This listening can take the form of receiving auditory or visual stimuli from God, sometimes in very exact words, sometimes in dreams and symbols that need interpreting. The crucial question is whether these are from God or not. The fate of the whole nation depends on the answer.

Only those prophets who have 'stood in the council of the Lord' (23.18) are qualified to speak as if from him. Instead, the people are being deceived by self-styled prophets, communicating their own ideas. We should be particularly suspicious of those who tell us what we want to hear. Straw and wheat may seem similar, but only one is really nourishing. You will need to look more deeply to know the difference. God's word to us can be as fierce as fire or as destructive as a hammer. It's not soft gloop.

Do you know God well enough to know when a message is authentically from God? Now that God has poured out his gifts on his whole Church, a prophet or prophetess could be a member of your own congregation or family. If you listen to God and open up your spirit and dreams to him, it could be you.

Reflection by **Jeanette Sears**

Proper 15

Continuous:
Isaiah 5.1-7
Psalm 80.1-2, 9-end
[*or* 80.9-end]

Related:
Jeremiah 23.23-29
Psalm 82

Hebrews 11.29 – 12.2
Luke 12.49-56

Hebrews 11.29 – 12.2

'... let us run with perseverance the race that is set before us' (12.1)

Douglas Adams, in *The Hitchhiker's Guide to the Galaxy*, says that there is an art to flying. The knack lies in 'learning how to throw yourself at the ground and miss'. When we speak of falling, we can barely conceive of it in positive terms. To fall is dangerous ... I have had a fall and broken a bone. We speak of fallen leaders, fallen men or women. The Fall ends the creation story in Genesis, and a fall begins the final chapters of our salvation story – Jesus falls on the Via Dolorosa.

The list of heroes of the faith today is a mixed bag. Some have succeeded outright, but others have failed – and conspicuously too. Yet God can even do great things with failure, because what matters to God is not success or failure, but faithfulness. The race that God asks us to run is like no other. It is more of a marathon than a sprint, and with few laurels at the end. Points don't mean prizes, alas.

Christians are called to follow a servant, not a winner – the one who led not by dominating, but by serving; the one who led not by triumphing, but by being sacrificed; the one who led not by being first on the podium, but by falling to the ground and dying. It is from here we rise. For all discipleship requires us to give ourselves fully to God: to fall to and for him; to die with him, so that we might not only be raised, but also see the fruit grow from the many seeds that God is, even now, seeking to sow in his world.

Reflection by **Martyn Percy**

Continuous: *Related:*
Isaiah 5.1-7 Jeremiah 23.23-29
Psalm 80.1-2, 9-end Psalm 82
[*or* 80.9-end]

Hebrews 11.29 – 12.2
Luke 12.49-56

Proper 15

Luke 12.49-56

'... why do you not know how to interpret the present time?' (v.56)

It's been said that the heart of the human problem is the problem of the human heart. If to follow Christ means any change in that heart, and we claim readily that it does, it will entail significant consequences. These will lead us from time to time into conflict with the currents of society, the 'norms' that can be taken for granted by a generation, and even with those who are nearest and dearest to us. Jesus says that he has comes to bring fire to the earth, he has come to burn away human dross in a fire similar to that encountered by Moses, one that roars with the loving and eternal presence of God, defrosting the world of self-regard.

Jesus asks why we cannot interpret our own times. We might reply that there are too many people today interpreting and opinionating from every direction. Shouldn't the person of faith withdraw from them all and find a deeper stillness within? Yes, certainly, but only so that we can then discern with a fresh perspective the thoughts and actions that are controlling human motivations in our day and the ways in which people are being damaged or forgotten by them. Then comes the hard part. If we don't stand for something, we will fall for anything. Christians need to voice their challenge to the world, as well as to the Church itself of course. Christians will often be afraid to do this, but must do it anyway. Christian spirituality is a slow learning of speaking up for others, burning up with love whatever diminishes them.

Reflection by **Mark Oakley**

Continuous:

Proper 16

**Sunday between
21 & 27 August inclusive**

Jeremiah 1.4-10
Psalm 71.1-6
Hebrews 12.18-end
Luke 13.10-17

Jeremiah 1.4-10

'... I am only a boy' (v.6)

Jeremiah's response to God is one we know. How can I speak into this situation? What authority do I have? Will people listen? Will I find the words? It's not easy when you need to speak out on a principle; when you propose the unpopular but right way forward; when you are questioned, contradicted, and find yourself a lone voice. Jeremiah's commission to be a prophet to the nations came with the warning that 'They will fight against you ...' (Jeremiah 1.19).

How do we discern the will of God? By looking and listening, by interpreting the signs of the times. Jeremiah saw almond branches and boiling pots, and saw the will of God in such things. But where do we look? How do we discern what's the right thing to say or do? It should take time to make up our minds. Luther said 'Here I stand: I can do no other' only after long consideration and prayer.

We're not all called to be Jeremiahs, or Luthers, but every so often our response to the truth of the matter requires us to speak out, regardless of the consequences. If we don't, it can be hard to live with the regret. Claiming that we're too young, or 'slow of speech and slow of tongue' as Moses did (Exodus 4.10), won't wash.

'Do not worry about how you are to speak or what you are to say; for what you are to say will be given to you at that time; for it is not you who speak, but the Spirit of your Father speaking through you.' (Matthew 10.19-20)

Reflection by **Frances Ward**

Related:
Isaiah 58.9b-end
Psalm 103.1-8
Hebrews 12.18-end
Luke 13.10-17

Proper 16

Isaiah 58.9b-end

'... you shall be called the repairer of the breach' (v.12)

When a city has been destroyed by war or natural disaster, those who once lived there frequently set out to restore it. The television cameras have left, the journalists have moved on to the next story, but the slog of rebuilding begins. It is stone by stone, house by house, and street by street.

When the Jewish exiles returned from Babylon to Jerusalem in 539 BC, they found it devastated. It had been destroyed fifty years earlier by Nebuchadnezzar, and many of its inhabitants had been taken across the deserts to begin their lives as refugees in a strange land. It was Cyrus the Great of Persia who eventually gave the refugees a chance to return home, which many of them did. The temple and the city walls began to be rebuilt. It was a hard and demanding time. The people were spurred on by their fundamental belief that God was with them in all that they did.

The rebuilding of cities is one form of human resilience. At a more personal level, many people find that they too have to rebuild their lives after, for example, the death of a loved one, a divorce or a tragic accident. That rebuilding is also, as it were, stone by stone, house by house, street by street ...

To help in the rebuilding of walls is a Christian duty, isn't it? By doing so, we share in God's purpose of reconstructing a broken world.

Reflection by **Christopher Herbert**

Proper 16	*Continuous:*	*Related:*
	Jeremiah 1.4-10	Isaiah 58.9b-end
	Psalm 71.1-6	Psalm 103.1-8

Hebrews 12.18-end
Luke 13.10-17

Hebrews 12.18-end

'But you have come ... to the city of the living God' (v.22)

There are two different understandings of religion here. One is theatrical: exhilarating and frightening in equal measures. Its essence is an exciting experience, with a beginning and an end. It may be a communal experience, but people leave it awed and shaken, but not fundamentally changed.

The other is religion of daily holiness, whose mirror image is the vision of the heavenly Jerusalem, where the rejoicing hosts of heaven and earth live with God. The practices of this religion are designed to build parallels here and now with what we long for in the future.

So this religion values, above all, those virtues that build trust and fellowship. It abhors, above all, those vices that cause bitterness, suspicion and division.

These two pictures of religion do not have to be complete alternatives. Hebrews reminds us that our God is indeed a 'consuming fire', real, potent and all-consuming. But this God is not just a source of exciting personal experiences for us, but the God of the whole world. To serve this God is to be drawn out of ourselves and our own interesting religious urges, into God's purposes for creation. Our faith is not just for us, but to help us build a community that will be at home in 'the city of the living God'.

Reflection by **Jane Williams**

Continuous:
Jeremiah 1.4-10
Psalm 71.1-6

Related:
Isaiah 58.9b-end
Psalm 103.1-8

Proper 16

Hebrews 12.18-end
Luke 13.10-17

Luke 13.10-17

'... a woman with a spirit that had crippled her' (v.11)

Names are a vital part of our identity and self-worth. In this story, however, we meet someone who is simply known as 'the bent woman'. Her distorted back forced her to look at the ground. She was unable to look people in the eye, and presumably damage had been done to various organs of her body. The woman doesn't have an identity other than that of a victim. Her shoulders most probably carried a much heavier and isolating burden than anyone knew. She is there in the Gospel for everyone whose soul and beauty are not seen because of a label pinned on them – the 'gay', the 'Muslim', the 'immigrant', the 'pensioner'. We could extend the list ...

The healing from Jesus, this 'setting free', might be understood to be a physical one. Her back is put right and she can stand tall. But there is another healing given her. Jesus calls her a 'daughter of Abraham'. In all the Gospels, only here is this expression used. Jesus celebrates her as an heir to the one to whom, one starry night, a promise was given that a great and blessed people would come through him (Genesis 15.5-6). She is an heir to this blessing and is freed now to become a blessing herself to others. Once again, Jesus turns a person's full stop into a comma so she can begin a new life with herself, her neighbours and her God.

When the world tries to bury us, God makes us seeds. I wonder how her life took shape after this day, as she began to live and grow into God's dreams for her?

Reflection by **Mark Oakley**

Proper 17

**Sunday between 28 August &
3 September inclusive**

Continuous:
Jeremiah 2.4-13
Psalm 81.1, 10-end [*or* 81.1-11]
Hebrews 13.1-8, 15-16
Luke 14.1, 7-14

Jeremiah 2.4-13

'... my people have changed their glory' (v.11)

God's word to Israel begins gently and positively in chapter 2 of Jeremiah, as did their early relationship after the escape from Egypt. This was their honeymoon period: a time of devotion and love, when Yahweh (the Hebrew name of Israel's God, usually translated 'the Lord') and his bride Israel belonged to one another, exclusively and faithfully (Jeremiah 2.2).

It did not last. The prophets indict their nation for breaking the faithful, loyal relationship with Yahweh. While God was true to his word, the people and their leaders forgot him, no longer rehearsing the story of their deliverance and the gift of the Promised Land. The priests did not seek him; the judges did not embrace his justice; the prophets sought the words of other gods.

So, Jeremiah proclaims what the Old Testament scholar Walter Brueggemann calls the 'prophetic "therefore"': 'Therefore ... I accuse you, says the Lord'. First the indictment, then the declaration of judgement. It is for this, God declares, that disaster is coming upon you. There is no parallel to their crime. Even the heathen did not change gods, but Israel has abandoned Yahweh (its 'glory') for a pretend, nothing-deity. It has walked away from the source of all life, 'the fountain of living water', for a leaky, DIY-job of cowboy plumbing. The prophet and his God stand appalled.

Reflection by **Jeff Astley**

Proper 17

Proverbs 25.6-7

'Do not put yourself forward ... ' (v.6)

The two verses in this short reading are concerned with the need for personal humility, and in the New Testament we find numerous echoes of this teaching. In his parable of the wedding banquet, Jesus warns those who overestimate their own importance that 'all who exalt themselves will be humbled, and those who humble themselves will be exalted' (Luke 14.11). On another occasion he has to warn his own disciples not to adopt the competitive ways of the world (Matthew 20.20-27). Paul, also, urges the Romans not to think of themselves more highly than they should (Romans 12.3).

We don't find humility easy. We tend to confuse humility with a doorstep mentality, a kind of grovelling humiliation. We hit out because our pride has been wounded. However, true humility is not concerned with pride, but rather the need for a cheerful acceptance of our littleness in relation to God's greatness. If we get that right, our relationships towards one another naturally become more courteous and considerate.

Although the teaching is addressed personally, this passage from Proverbs is concerned with this wider application. Its context has been made clear with the mention of the king. Individual behaviour and relationships mattered, because the king was God's representative on earth, and under him, society was to be peaceful and well ordered. What steps might we take in order to live out this teaching within our own communities today?

Reflection by **Barbara Mosse**

Proper 17

Continuous:
Jeremiah 2.4-13
Psalm 81.1, 10-end
[*or* 81.1-11]

Related:
Ecclesiasticus 10.12-18
or Proverbs 25.6-7
Psalm 112
Hebrews 13.1-8, 15-16
Luke 14.1, 7-14

Hebrews 13.1-8, 15-16

'Do not neglect to show hospitality to strangers …' (v.2)

The theologian Mark Oakley says that 'Jesus is the body language of God'. The life Jesus leads expresses the wisdom of God. It is not just what he says; it is also what he doesn't say. It is not just what he does, but what he doesn't do. His silence speaks as much as his words. His wisdom is embodied. And that is our calling: to let the Spirit of God dwell in us – to become a people where God is truly at home. The houses and homes that Jesus lived and stayed in tended to be pretty busy places – ones that practised God's hospitality. But with Jesus present, these were no longer ordinary homes. Many people came into these spaces and places for Jesus' teaching and healing ministry. The conversations and encounters that ensued were utterly transformative; individuals and societies were changed. There is a sense in which our churches can also follow this – through gathering, convening and drawing all in, becoming an agent of God's gracious, proactive hospitality.

True Christian hospitality ought to make us a little uncomfortable; otherwise the dinner or lunch we offer is just like having friends over. The hospitality that Jesus exhorted his disciples to practise was one that broke down tribal barriers. It overcame divisions of race and gender, of age and class. Jesus welcomed all. That's why churches need to remember that it's not 'our altar' or 'our communion service'. It is Jesus' table; it is his meal. He desires to share with sinners. With the widow too, and the orphans, the prisoners, the lame, the leprous and the Samaritans. Jesus lives the hospitality of God. He now invites us to live and practise God's hospitable heart.

Reflection by **Martyn Percy**

Proper 17

Luke 14.1, 7-14

'For all who exalt themselves will be humbled, and those who humble themselves will be exalted' (v.11)

Throughout his ministry, Jesus used meals as signs of God's kingdom, where each has a place at the table and each enjoys the company with shared gifts and common purpose.

Jesus has taken up an invitation to a sabbath meal at the house of one of the leaders of the Pharisees. As he looks around, though, he sees that the company has made this meal exclusive and not inclusive. It is a meal that reflects their pride rather than humility, as they jostle for the best places. He shows them that a meal works best when your gratitude at being present outweighs any desire to push others aside. A meal becomes a feast when all feel welcome, all share the same foods and each looks to the other to make the occasion rich in friendship and hope. As in the meal, so in life. Those who exalt themselves miss out on the true shared beauty of the kingdom.

In Isak Dinesen's story called *Babette's Feast*, extraordinary transformations happen to ordinary people eating together. The two sisters who hosted the meal watch the guests make their way home at the end and comment that 'the stars have come closer tonight'. Heaven draws nearer when humility makes place for everyone.

Reflection by **Mark Oakley**

Proper 18

Sunday between
4 & 10 September inclusive

Continuous:
Jeremiah 18.1-11
Psalm 139.1-5, 12-18 [*or* 139.1-7]
Philemon 1-21
Luke 14.25-33

Jeremiah 18.1-11

'... he reworked it into another vessel' (v.4)

Like the potter who will not waste the clay he was using when a pot goes wrong, God too is willing to put it to a new purpose. God is a recycling God.

The language of God's infinite resourcefulness and responsiveness can seem very apt here, and it helps us to understand that we are in a relationship with God in which there is reciprocity. The things we do – whether to repent or to resist God – have consequences for how God relates to us. God's intentions can appear to alter when we – like the pot – 'spoil'. God will devise a new strategy to deal with the failure. 'I will change my mind', says the voice of God in this passage. Another pot will be made.

But we ought not to be misled by this bold statement into thinking of God as fickle. Read the text closely, and it is clear that the apparent changeability of God is really the result of the changeability of human beings in relation to God's purposes. If we change for good, God will not enact a promised destruction, and if we change for bad, God will not deliver a promised blessing. In the realm of human action, we have room to move, and as we move it will be as though God moves with us. But the realm of human action in its entirety is nevertheless held within the divine potter's sure and unerring hands.

Reflection by **Ben Quash**

Related:
Deuteronomy 30.15-end
Psalm 1
Philemon 1-21
Luke 14.25-33

Deuteronomy 30.15-end

' ... the Lord your God will bless you in the land that you are entering' (v.16)

For the Israelites, as a small, marginalized, nomadic people, the symbol of the Promised Land, where they could live in security and at peace with God and their neighbours, was a very potent one. The idea perhaps finds its most concentrated focus in Psalm 37, where trust in the Lord promises security in the land – inheritance for those who wait for the Lord, are meek, are blessed by the Lord and are righteous. The context of both today's passage ('If you obey the commandments ... the Lord your God will bless you in the land') and Psalm 37 ('Trust in the Lord ... so you will live in the land', Psalm 37.3), is one of *choice*.

The same theme of choice threads its way through the New Testament, using very different imagery. One of Jesus' parables involves two men who built their houses respectively on rock and sand (Matthew 7.24-27). We can choose to skim along on the sandy surface of life, never achieving anything of lasting worth; or we can make our decisions from a basis of firm foundations in God that will stand the test of time and lead us into eternity.

The message here is as relevant today as it was then. In our very different situations, we are urged to build our houses upon rock, so that we, too, may inherit the land that the Lord our God is giving us.

Reflection by **Barbara Mosse**

Proper 18

Continuous:
Jeremiah 18.1-11
Psalm 139.1-5, 12-18
[*or* 139.1-7]

Related:
Deuteronomy 30.15-end
Psalm 1

Philemon 1-21
Luke 14.25-33

Philemon 1-21

'... I would rather appeal to you on the basis of love' (v.9)

We live in a world that seems to believe that the louder you shout at someone, the quicker and more efficient they will be. Simple life experience belies this. Even standing in a queue waiting for a cup of coffee illustrates this. Those who berate the assistants for being slow seem to get their coffee even slower than those who smile, crack a joke and speak easily to the assistant. It is a fact that we all recognize, that crafting good relationships gets things done far more efficiently and effectively than simple commands.

Paul is probably not the person whom we most associate with this way of being. On other occasions, he seems all too willing to shout at people and berate them for their actions. It is, perhaps, a sign of how much he cared about both Philemon and Onesimus that, for once, he did not command Philemon (as he acknowledges he could have done) but drew on their relationship and their bonds of love to ensure that Onesimus' future was assured.

Telling people to do things can be the more simple thing to do, but loving them into good action, though taking longer, can be far more effective.

Reflection by **Paula Gooder**

226

Continuous:
Jeremiah 18.1-11
Psalm 139.1-5, 12-18
[*or* 139.1-7]

Related:
Deuteronomy 30.15-end
Psalm 1

Proper 18

Philemon 1-21
Luke 14.25-33

Luke 14.25-33

'Whoever comes to me and does not hate father and mother ...' (v.26)

When people refer to the hard sayings of Jesus, this is the passage they most often have in mind. And within this saying, it is the part about hating father and mother, wife and children, brothers and sisters that appals. Is Jesus truly asking me to *hate* (the Greek is *misein*: 'hate' is what it means) my parents who gave me life and first showed me love, who taught me the very expressions of my face? My spouse, the flesh of my flesh, along with my children, who carry my name and my face forward into time? My siblings, who share all my memories? 'Yes, and even life itself.'

If there were fine print on the bottom of your certificate of baptism, this is what it would say. This is the cost of discipleship spread over a lifetime, with interest.

Who makes up this massive crowd? Some of us are looking for a miracle: healing for myself or for my child. Some of us want to make sense of our lives. Some of us know a good show when we see it. Even the disciples are hoping for something: a Messiah who calls them by name. What matters to Jesus is the kingdom of God. Everything flows from that source. There are thousands of people here, pushing near to hear what Jesus is saying. He is walking upstream, against the current.

Reflection by **Alice Goodman**

Proper 19

**Sunday between
11 & 17 September inclusive**

Continuous:
Jeremiah 4.11-12, 22-28
Psalm 14
1 Timothy 1.12-17
Luke 15.1-10

Jeremiah 4.11-12, 22-28

'The whole land shall be a desolation; yet ...' (v.27)

The German Protestant theologian, Rudolf Otto, wrote of the experience of holiness as two-sided. The holy is entrancing, attractive. We speak of it – of him/her – as good. But there is dread and terror as well. Moses before the burning bush and the disciples witnessing the transfiguration were captivated and enthralled, but fearful too. Talk of judgement articulates this stormy side of God's love.

This is how it is: turning away from the light and warmth of grace, we stumble into the cold, dark side of holy fear. 'Do not be deceived ... you reap whatever you sow' (Galatians 6.7). A stroppy, defiant adolescent might respond to a parent's demand by shouting 'Or else what ...?' Israel and Judah, by betraying God's love, now face the answer to that question. Turn your back on God, and you face what is not-God, and must face it alone. God's love is personal. His 'wrath', however, sounds like an impersonal, unavoidable force – a cosmic catastrophe. God's dark side is the undoing of creation, its return to the chaos, darkness and emptiness that preceded the love of God's creative Spirit (Genesis 1.1-2).

Imagine the prophet spitting out these words. He is addressing not only the people, prophets and priests, but also the officials and the king himself. Jeremiah alone will face and name the terrible reality of God's inevitable judgement in response to his children's rejection.

And yet, is there no hope? A glimmer, at least? Perhaps an ambiguous whisper may be heard in verse 27: 'yet I will not make a full end'.

*Reflection by **Jeff Astley***

Related:
Exodus 32.7-14
Psalm 51.1-11
1 Timothy 1.12-17
Luke 15.1-10

Proper 19

Exodus 32.7-14

'... they have been quick to turn aside' (v.8)

Because worship can take many forms, so can idolatry. Few today would be tempted to make an idol in the shape of an animal, and bow down and worship it. And yet our cultural blindness can often lead us to affirm forces that we think serve us, but to which we are actually in bondage. For example, children exposed to relentless advertising for high-fat, sugary foods turn away from vegetables, fruit and balanced diets in favour of quick-fix snacks. The result is obesity. A relentless focus on acquisitions and commodities may lead to children knowing what they want to *have*, but not what they want to *be*, in terms of vocations and careers.

Here, of course, we may discover that less is more – that by reducing choice, we enhance our enjoyment of ourselves and one another. The illusion of endless choice, and sating our desires, can quickly turn our gaze away from God and the needs of others.

Moses is exasperated by what he sees – by a people who have just been delivered from one captivity only to take up another without any pressure. But he pleads with God for time. He pleads for his people, and God 'changed his mind' and let them live. One can only assume that God already knows that those who consume materialism – very much the idolatry described – will end in being consumed by it. God gives them time, even though he knows they will fail. But he also knows he will still forgive.

Reflection by **Martyn Percy**

Proper 19

Continuous:
Jeremiah 4.11-12, 22-28
Psalm 14

Related:
Exodus 32.7-14
Psalm 51.1-11

I Timothy 1.12-17
Luke 15.1-10

1 Timothy 1.12-17

'Christ Jesus came into the world to save sinners' (v.15)

Paul writes his letter to Timothy as his mentor, to instruct and encourage him in his leadership of the Church at Ephesus. The letter is full of sound advice about how lead the Church in 'love that comes from a pure heart, a good conscience, and sincere faith' (1 Timothy 1.5). Paul, however, does not set himself up as a faultless paragon of virtue. On the contrary, he wears openly his own shameful history as a persecutor of the very Christians he now seeks to build up.

It is exactly *because* Paul sees himself as the 'foremost' of sinners, rescued by the grace, faith, love and mercy of Christ, that he is able to offer himself as any kind of example. This is not an example of perfection but an example of redemption.

On the news yesterday evening, there was an interview with a man who had once been a drug dealer, addicted to heroin. He now works as a counsellor and advocate for those also struggling with similar addictions. What made him so effective was his understanding of the depths in which his clients now found themselves. He had been there too and so was able to offer effective help. Paul's knowledge of himself as 'chief amongst sinners' enables him all the more to recognize the overflowing effectiveness of God's mercy, and to encourage his young friend Timothy, as he holds out an offer of that same mercy to others.

Reflection by **Emma Ineson**

Continuous:
Jeremiah 4.11-12, 22-28
Psalm 14
     I Timothy 1.12-17
     Luke 15.1-10

Related:
Exodus 32.7-14
Psalm 51.1-11

Proper 19

Luke 15.1-10

'Rejoice with me, for I have found my sheep that was lost'
(v.6)

What do we do when we lose something?

Both these parables demonstrate an intense effort to regain something highly valued. The painstaking searches of the shepherd and the woman mirror God's active compassion for every person who runs into trouble. The faithful Creator is not indifferent, but seeks out with persistence and determination those who have strayed, to restore them to his loving care.

The joy of finding is highlighted as the crucial point of both parables. The solitary rejoicing of the shepherd on the way home and the celebration of the woman with her friends and neighbours are comparable with the joy of God over sinners who repent. The keynote is not the condition of repentance but the irrepressible desire of God for people to return to him and his overflowing gladness when they do.

Jesus contrasts sharply the judgemental attitude of his Pharisee critics with the welcoming outreach of God. Is God's covenant community a mutual admiration society for the virtuous or a place of refuge for failures? Every Christian and every church ought to ask themselves whether they genuinely share the divine passion to go out to those who have lost their way and the divine happiness when the lost return.

Reflection by **Christopher Jones**

Proper 20

**Sunday between
18 & 24 September inclusive**

Continuous:
Jeremiah 8.18 – 9.1
Psalm 79.1-9
1 Timothy 2.1-7
Luke 16.1-13

Jeremiah 8.18 – 9.1

'... no balm in Gilead' (8.22)

The tone of these verses is set by the tragic vocabulary of illness, pain, grief and death. These verses contain a lament – not only Jeremiah's lament but the lament of the Lord. The insertion of the phrase 'says the Lord' in the verse before today's passage indicates that we, as readers, must know that it is not just Jeremiah who weeps for the people; we are witnessing the grief of God. It is grief such as that of a parent for a sick child; somehow the pain of the child becomes the pain of the parent. All that both can do is watch the disease take hold and do its worst on the body of the beloved child.

We are told here of the Lord's rage, grief and despair; somehow the refusal of the people to repent has removed the power of God to save them. There are simply no more options left. We hear the isolation and desolation of God, pleading with the people to return to the one who has loved them from the beginning.

As with much of Jeremiah's prophecy, although it will have been said in a specific circumstance, the general underlying themes are universal and applicable to different situations in different centuries. We are left wondering what our lives look like to this pleading God, grief-stricken at the state of the world we have helped to create.

Reflection by **Lucy Winkett**

Related:
Amos 8.4-7
Psalm 113
1 Timothy 2.1-7
Luke 16.1-13

Proper 20

Amos 8.4-7

*'... you that trample on the needy,
and bring to ruin the poor of the land' (v.4)*

When faced with the wrath of Amos, there is nowhere to hide! Chapter 8 picks up on the themes and language of chapter 4. There the wealthy, self-absorbed women of Israel were the objects of Amos' ire; here it is the businessmen of the city. The time is one when business is booming; merchants are eager to capitalize on every investment and every chance to increase sales. Taking Amos 4 and 8 together, they represent the comprehensive scope of Amos' accusations.

The essential condemnation by God is not that money and wealth are bad in themselves, but that money has had a seductive and corrupting influence on those who possess it, so that they come to neglect those around them. Amos shows that it is greed that shifts our emphasis away from the poor and needy, away from basic concern for people and away from God.

Prophecy repudiates the idea of a dichotomy between faith and life. Amos rejects the notion of two lives lived under different rules or values. God is to do with the *whole* of life – not just about whether we go to church on Sunday or indeed give over part of each day to Bible reflections, as you are doing now! He compels us to examine our attitude towards possessions and wealth, with a reminder that in the ancient Church – and perhaps more than ever today – one of the seven deadly sins was greed.

Reflection by **Tim Sledge**

Proper 20	*Continuous:*	*Related:*
	Jeremiah 8.18 – 9.1	Amos 8.4-7
	Psalm 79.1-9	Psalm 113
	1 Timothy 2.1-7	
	Luke 16.1-13	

1 Timothy 2.1-7

'... a quiet and peaceable life in all godliness and dignity'
(v.2)

Paul's exhortation in these verses may appear somewhat daunting to those of us suffering from 'compassion fatigue' as a result of the relentless daily onslaught of bad news from the media. Paul here urges Christians to the work of intercessory prayer in all its breadth and depth. Prayers should be *offered for everyone*, he says, and especially 'for kings and all who are in high positions'. Is this realistic? How is it possible for us to take on the concerns of everyone in our prayer?

This seems to represent the opposite end of the spectrum to those prayers Jesus urges us to make for our own needs or the needs of those close to us (Matthew 7.7-11), but Paul's purpose and the context in which he is writing are all-important. Christian communities under persecution found it hard to gain acceptance within the societies of their time. They may have been tempted to pull up the drawbridge and withdraw into their own world, but Paul is urging the community to engage fully with that world, through prayer, even though it may be hostile to them. Christ's salvation was for all, and the Christians' prayers needed to reflect that reality.

Our own world, though distant in time, shares many resonances with the world of 1 Timothy. Are we able to pray for the forces opposed to Christ and his message, so that we, too, may live 'a quiet and peaceable life in all godliness and dignity'?

Reflection by **Barbara Mosse**

Continuous:
Jeremiah 8.18 – 9.1
Psalm 79.1-9
     I Timothy 2.1-7
     Luke 16.1-13

Related:
Amos 8.4-7
Psalm 113

Proper 20

Luke 16.1-13

'You cannot serve God and wealth' (v.13)

Business ethics are currently being questioned as global banking systems and entire countries buckle under the dynamics Jesus highlights in this parable: the shrewd and self-interested avoid their responsibilities and create indebtedness, caring nothing about justice or community wellbeing.

When mammon is the god being worshipped, much human ingenuity goes into designing systems that benefit a few at the expense of the many. And we help sustain systemic injustice whenever we avoid tax, tweak an insurance claim, gamble our wages, purchase goods made by exploited workers, turn a blind eye to dubious work practices, make wealth acquisition our life goal and fail to help the poor.

We might try to justify ourselves, but we know – and God knows – that we are reluctant to put all of our resources at God's disposal. Instead, we put our energy and time into whatever, superficially, makes us feel safe and successful. Beneath the surface however, we don't trust God's provision; perhaps we just don't know God well enough to believe that God wants us to be eternally rich – now.

True riches are the fruit of God's Spirit flourishing in the hearts of godly men and women of integrity. 'Love, joy, peace, patience, kindness, generosity, faithfulness, gentleness and self-control' (Galatians 5.22-23) cannot be purchased and cannot be sold, but multiply as God works in and among those who follow Jesus.

Reflection by **Sue Pickering**

Proper 21

**Sunday between 25 September
& 1 October inclusive**

Continuous:
Jeremiah 32.1-3a, 6-15
Psalm 91.1-6, 14-end
[*or* 91.11-end]
1 Timothy 6.6-19
Luke 16.19-end

Jeremiah 32.1-3a, 6-15

*'Houses and fields and vineyards shall again be bought
in this land' (v.15)*

Context is everything. There is nothing unusual about Jeremiah buying a piece of land from his cousin Hanamel to keep it in the family. The noteworthy fact is that the field is in the middle of a war zone and, given that the Babylonians have only temporarily withdrawn from besieging Jerusalem and will certainly be back, purchasing land is not necessarily a wise move. However, discerning that it is 'of the Lord', Jeremiah accedes, and the details of the transaction are carefully recorded for posterity in the presence of witnesses.

It is theology rather than economics that is needed to interpret this act. In the midst of losing the entire land to the Babylonians, and the crisis of the people being deported, there remains one field on which Jeremiah has staked a claim. It is a symbol of hope in the midst of a hopeless situation. Though the purchase deeds are put in a jar for long-term storage, one day trading will resume. Judah will suffer judgement, Jerusalem will be destroyed, but Jeremiah makes a practical investment in God's promise of future restoration, whenever that might be.

It is the spiritual equivalent of speculating to accumulate. Taking a risk of faith to enact a divine directive will yield unimagined blessings, however foolhardy others consider the action to be at the time.

Reflection by **Helen Orchard**

236

Related:
Amos 6.1a, 4-7
Psalm 146
I Timothy 6.6-19
Luke 16.19-end

Proper 21

Amos 6.1a, 4-7

'Alas for those who lie on beds of ivory' (v.4)

So you learnt how to drive years ago. You have never had any points on your licence, never been caught speeding, never even had a claim on your insurance. You think you are a wonderful driver. Until ... you get complacent, and something happens.

There are often so many areas of our life where we are confident. That is good, but confidence can move into complacency – which is not good – and then arrogance. Leadership, money, power, wealth – these are all incredibly seductive, but they also have by-products. In this passage, Amos cleverly places a mirror up against those who enjoy a high standard of living and leadership position. But rather than making us feel guilty, Amos goads us out of our complacency and indifference and towards a careful examination of our own actions.

There used to be a much-loved children's programme on the radio called *Listen with Mother*. It always began with the words: 'Are you sitting comfortably? Then I'll begin.' For Amos, his shot across the bows is that, if we are sitting comfortably, how can God begin with us? Throughout Scripture and the Christian tradition, God really works in people's lives when he takes them from one place and puts them in another more challenging place. That is where the real work of transformation begins.

Amos never makes comfortable reading; it's not meant to! Then and now, it is aimed to stir us and move us to a new and more fruitful place.

Reflection by **Tim Sledge**

Proper 21

Continuous:
Jeremiah 32.1-3a, 6-15
Psalm 91.1-6, 14-end
[or 91.11-end]

Related:
Amos 6.1a, 4-7
Psalm 146

1 Timothy 6.6-19
Luke 16.19-end

1 Timothy 6.6-19

*'... if we have food and clothing, we will be content
with these' (v.8)*

It would be easy to read this passage as a simple diatribe against money. But when we look more closely at it, we realize that Paul is writing with a deep pastoral concern for Timothy and the Church. He writes of the *oregomenoi* – those who are 'stretching themselves out', with deep hunger and unsatisfied desire, towards riches. Paul knows that trying to satisfy inner hungers with money can never work. In fact, trying to meet those inner needs with money proves to be damaging and destructive, plunging people down into debt and ruin, destroying relationships and 'piercing them with many pains'.

Instead, Paul urges his readers to cultivate contentment. He uses the word *autarkeia*, meaning 'a frame of mind viewing one's lot as "enough"'. Contentment, then, is a mindset. It's a way of seeing. This way of seeing can be developed through contemplating our beginning and our end: we came into the world with nothing, and we certainly can't take anything with us when we go.

There is another layer of meaning to *autarkeia*. It means 'being adequate in oneself'. That's not to encourage self-satisfaction. But it's to suggest that if our inner resources are there, we need very little else – with food and clothing we've got enough. The real riches are not found with external, material things but within, with Christ. Contentment is simply the enjoyment of that hidden wealth.

Reflection by **Sue Hope**

Proper 21

Luke 16.19-end

'There was a rich man ... And at his gate lay a poor man'
(vv.19–20)

Why should we care for the poor? This haunting passage begins with a Jewish version of an ancient folk tale about the reversal of fortunes in the afterlife. It fulfils the blessings and woes pronounced by Jesus and demolishes a theology – held by many Jews then and by some Christians today – that wealth is a clear sign of divine favour.

Instead, it is apparent that the rich man failed to use his wealth to help a starving and sick fellow human being on his own doorstep. Profoundly shocked to find himself thirsting in the torment of Hades, he is desperate to save his brothers from a like fate.

The second part of the story takes a provocative twist as Abraham confounds the rich man's assumptions about human motivation. If the consciences of the prosperous are hardened against biblical teaching on obligations to the poor, they will not be softened by warnings about hellfire – or even by a miraculous resurrection. Awareness of God's justice and compassion, with its potential to disturb and transform us, must be received on its own terms. Jesus, fulfilling the law and the prophets, draws us away from self-absorption and calls us to respond to human need because love demands it.

Reflection by **Christopher Jones**

Proper 22

**Sunday between
2 & 8 October inclusive**

Continuous:
Lamentations 1.1-6
Canticle: Lamentations 3.19-26
or Psalm 137 [*or* 137.1-6]
2 Timothy 1.1-14
Luke 17.5-10

Lamentations 1.1-6

'The roads to Zion mourn ... all her gates are desolate' (v.4)

I confess that I have a penchant for films that feature dystopias. I think of *Logan's Run*, a wonderful science fiction classic from 1976 starring Jenny Agutter and Michael York. Set a long time in the future, this unlikely couple escape the clutches of their pursuers, only to find that the sanctuary they reach is a 'wasted place' – a city in ruins. Its former glory is there to glimpse – but the city is now an uninhabited wasteland. This is an Aleppo, Palmyra, Benghazi and Tripoli.

It is no wonder that these verses also form part of the readings for Monday in Holy Week, as the evocative image of a desolate city prefigures the death and desertion of Good Friday. It is also a metaphor for inner grief, the death and destruction inside our souls. We mourn for the state we are in.

In this lamentation, the writer speaks for his people, but also echoes something of Jesus' experience of his final desolate hours – abandoned, scorned, an object of vilification and wrath. What has he done to deserve this? 'My God, my God, why have you forsaken me?' (Matthew 27.46).

Yet no matter how deserted we may feel, God never abandons us. We are ultimately raised up from despair and death. Jesus becomes the desolate one on our behalf, so that we might never be without God again. Jesus becomes forsaken so we might forever have eternity with God.

Reflection by **Martyn Percy**

Related:
Habakkuk 1.1-4; 2.1-4
Psalm 37.1-9
2 Timothy 1.1-14
Luke 17.5-10

Proper 22

Habakkuk 1.1-4; 2.1-4

'If it seems to tarry, wait for it; it will surely come' (2.3)

Habakkuk is perhaps one of the less well-known books of the Hebrew Scriptures, but it is a powerful book about the realization of God's purposes and will for his world, set in the context of the rise of Chaldeans as the new world power in the late seventh century BC. Habakkuk asks the question: 'Where is God when the world is in trouble?' He asks this not as someone sceptical about God but as a person of deep faith, constant prayer and intimate communion with God. We *can* have honest conversations with God! Indeed, Scripture has a long tradition of people arguing with God, including the Psalmists, Jeremiah and Moses.

Frustrated over the loss of law and justice and over his own helplessness in the situation, Habakkuk is not only willing to argue with God; he is also persistent in seeking the answer. He will watch from his tower on the city wall.

God's answer is brief and cryptic. He assures Habakkuk that his waiting will not be futile, but wait he must, if the vision seems to tarry. When we think that God is indifferent, he might actually be involved in a way we don't recognize.

Habakkuk does not propose a simple solution to the problem of injustice, but the 'righteous' become part of the solution. They will long and work for justice and righteousness. They 'live by their faith', which means that they will have the strength to go on through their faithfulness and vision. They will place trust in the vision they received from God rather than in the brute facts of existence.

Reflection by **John Perumbalath**

Proper 22

Continuous:
Lamentations 1.1-6
Canticle:
Lamentations 3.19-26
or Psalm 137 [or 137.1-6]

Related:
Habakkuk 1.1-4; 2.1-4
Psalm 37.1-9

2 Timothy 1.1-14
Luke 17.5-10

2 Timothy 1.1-14

'Do not be ashamed, then, of the testimony about our Lord ...' (v.8)

Timothy comes into focus in this chapter. It would appear that he had received the faith not in a dramatic conversion like Paul's, but through his family – his grandmother and his mother. It would also seem that he was a young man who lacked confidence. Nevertheless, he was the pastor of a church, and Paul's letters are full of encouragement to him to fulfil his calling. In particular, he is not to be ashamed to testify about the Lord. Later in the letter, Paul urges him to 'do the work of an evangelist' (2 Timothy 4.5).

It's sometimes tempting to think that it's only extroverts who are called to bear public witness to Christ and to share the good news. If these were things we could do in our own strength, there might be some truth in this. But, in fact, God's work can be done only in the power and strength of the indwelling Holy Spirit. And, sometimes, those who feel most vulnerable and uncertain are those whom God can use most. For when we feel weak, we lean on God for strength. We may not feel his power with us – even after prayer, we may still feel foolish, tongue-tied, awkward and stumbling – but, with his help, even our simple words may become carriers for his mighty acts.

Reflection by **Sue Hope**

Proper 22

Luke 17.5-10

'... we have done only what we ought to have done!' (v.10)

Humility is a slippery thing. If we think we've got it, then we probably haven't. False humility, whether in fictional characters such as Uriah Heep in Dickens' *David Copperfield* or in ourselves, is a particularly unattractive quality. True humility is rooted in an honest and unanxious self-knowledge. It is liberating, freeing us to serve and also to lead.

In this chapter, Luke has strung together sayings of Jesus like beads; the thread holding them together is the humility that shapes the lives of the disciples of Jesus.

Humble disciples live with a faith that changes the world. When the disciples ask for greater faith, Jesus replies with a picturesque challenge to contemplate the impossible – the mulberry tree being especially resistant to uprooting – and to believe that God can do it. The power of faith, like the smallest of seeds, does not stem from its greatness but from its ability to point us away from ourselves to God.

A life shaped by humility is a life that finds joy and freedom in service. In a typically provocative way, Jesus describes his disciples as slaves; they freely choose to serve and in doing so find liberation and life.

How might you find liberation today, living a humble life of faith and service?

Reflection by **John Kiddle**

Proper 23
Sunday between
9 & 15 October inclusive

Continuous:
Jeremiah 29.1, 4-7
Psalm 66.1-11
2 Timothy 2.8-15
Luke 17.11-19

Jeremiah 29.1, 4-7

'... seek the welfare of the city where I have sent you into exile' (v.7)

Jeremiah's letter to the exiles in Babylon reveals what a controversial, but also pastoral, prophet he is. While the prophets in Babylon are still encouraging the exiles to think they will be home in two years, Jeremiah prepares them for the long haul. His advice is a sound strategy for survival in a foreign land: settle down and make the best of it. Build, plant, eat, marry and multiply so that you may be in a good position to start again when you do return.

He goes a step further than practical instruction, however, by also issuing a revolutionary spiritual imperative: 'Seek the welfare (shalom) of the city ... and pray to the Lord on its behalf'. Is this just a recommendation based on political expediency? After all, things will go better for the exiles if they accommodate their imperial oppressors and contribute to peace and prosperity in Babylon. Or is there more to it than that? It places a responsibility on the exilic community to look beyond itself and its woes. Put into the language of Jesus, it also sounds rather like a command to love your enemies and pray for your persecutors.

When prompted to pray 'forgive us our trespasses', Judah refused. Now the exiles are given an even harder prayer to pray: 'forgive those who trespass against us'. Which is the more pressing for you today?

Reflection by **Helen Orchard**

244

Related:
2 Kings 5.1-3, 7-15c
Psalm 111
2 Timothy 2.8-15
Luke 17.11-19

2 Kings 5.1-3, 7-15c

'... his flesh was restored like the flesh of a young boy, and he was clean' (v.14)

Getting into God's healing zone often means getting out of our own comfort zone, as this story shows. A slave girl has to lift her head from cleaning floors to refer her sick master to the right consultant. A king has to turn from politics to ask one of his vassals to facilitate the healing of his leading general.

It is harder for Elisha, who has to learn how to be inclusive and generous to a threatening stranger without compromising his own faith and calling. He will indeed heal Naaman, but he has to seek that healing by a baptism in Israel's river and at the hand of Israel's God.

For Naaman himself, it is hardest of all. He has to go into an alien culture and submit himself to the ministry of a man whom he would have considered his natural enemy. He certainly does not like the prescription that is offered to him, with its claim that the rivers and the God of Israel have a saving power far beyond those of Syria. But the reward of such humiliation is more than healing – it is conversion to the living God.

Reflection by **Tom Smail**

Proper 23

Continuous:
Jeremiah 29.1, 4-7
Psalm 66.1-11

Related:
2 Kings 5.1-3, 7-15c
Psalm 111

2 Timothy 2.8-15
Luke 17.11-19

2 Timothy 2.8-15

'Do your best to present yourself to God as one approved by him' (v.15)

Timothy was under enormous pressure in the Ephesian Church. Here he was, the leader of a Christian community, and the Church was being infiltrated by false teachers. They were having an unsettling effect, causing controversy and disturbance. It's not quite clear what these teachings were, but they were possibly a form of early gnosticism – a way of viewing reality that drove a wedge between the spiritual and the material, encouraging a kind of super-spirituality and elitism.

For someone like Timothy – unsure of himself, not yet experienced in leadership – these false teachers would have posed a personal threat. He may have feared at times that they were more influential and convincing than he was, with strong and attractive personalities that his people responded to.

That's why it's heart-warming that Paul encourages him 'to present himself to God as one approved by him'. Whatever others say about him, his self-worth, his identity, is to be found in God's approval of him. Knowing God's affirmation of his ministry means he can keep on with renewed determination in the work that God has given him to do.

We all get knocks to our confidence and need to return to that sense of being known and valued by God. For it's his love that is the mainspring of our life and our ministry, wherever we serve him in the world.

Reflection by **Sue Hope**

Proper 23

Luke 17.11-19

'Get up and go on your way; your faith has made you well'
(v.19)

In recounting Jesus' healing of people with leprosy, Luke underlines the love of God for social and religious outcasts, isolated and stigmatized by their ritual uncleanness. Given the setting, near the region of Samaria, it is likely that he focuses on the man who was also a Samaritan (and hence a twofold outsider) to anticipate the coming of salvation to the gentiles. Here, as elsewhere, Jesus attends sympathetically to people on the edge and draws them back into society.

It has often been asked why Jesus criticizes the nine for obeying his command – to go and show themselves to the priests, as required by Leviticus to certify a cure. The point is rather that the Samaritan is commended for seeing the deeper significance of what had happened to him, returning to thank Jesus and praise God for it.

The verb 'made well' also means 'saved'. There may be an allusion in this incident to the historical precedent of Naaman the Syrian (see page 245), who was both healed of leprosy and converted to the worship of the God of Israel (2 Kings 5.1-15). The action of the Samaritan is a response of faith to the breaking in of God's kingdom. Sometimes the receptive outsider grasps the God-given meaning of events that jaded insiders miss or take for granted.

Reflection by **Christopher Jones**

Proper 24

Sunday between
16 & 22 October inclusive

Continuous:
Jeremiah 31.27-34
Psalm 119.97-104
2 Timothy 3.14 – 4.5
Luke 18.1-8

Jeremiah 31.27-34

*'I will put my law within them, and I will write it
on their hearts' (v.33)*

Jeremiah contains quite a few references to the human heart, most of them unfavourable. Specifically, 'the heart is devious above all else; it is perverse – who can understand it?' (Jeremiah 17.9). In biblical thought, the heart was not simply the seat of emotion but also of volition: it *knows* and *wills* as well as feels. When we learn that 'The sin of Judah is written with an iron pen; with a diamond point it is engraved on the tablet of their hearts' (Jeremiah 17.1), we realize that a significant cardiac intervention will be required for health to be restored.

In today's passage, we learn of the treatment plan: it is nothing less than a new covenant. Instead of a law chipped out on tablets of stone, a more delicate keyhole procedure is proposed. The law will be skilfully inscribed on the heart of each of God's people. As a result they will all 'know' God, a word that indicates the intimate personal knowledge shared by two parties who are committed wholly to one another in relationship.

How is your heart bearing up this morning: robust or fragile; tender or sclerotic? Sometimes it can be difficult to remember that God has written his law of love on our own hearts, but just remembering that can help to soften it. In Book IV of *Against Heresies*, the early Church Father St Irenaeus advises, 'Offer to him your heart in a soft and tractable state … lest you lose the impression of his fingers'.

Reflection by **Helen Orchard**

Related:
Genesis 32.22-31
Psalm 121
2 Timothy 3.14 – 4.5
Luke 18.1-8

Proper 24

Genesis 32.22-31

'Jacob was left alone; and a man wrestled with him until daybreak' (v.24)

In 1940 the sculptor Jacob Epstein was faced in his studio with an enormous block of alabaster weighing over two and a half tons. He must have gazed at it for many, many weeks before he set to work with hammer and chisel. Going with the grain of the material, rather than against it, and after expending huge amounts of physical energy (you can still see the chiselled gouges in the sculpture) the outline of two figures gradually emerged. They were locked in a wrestling embrace. It was Jacob and the angel.

Epstein himself had spent a good deal of time in the previous decade reading the Book of Genesis and, perhaps because of his own name, was particularly moved by the story. The resulting work is stupendous. Jacob rests, apparently defeated, in the arms of the angel whose bulging thighs and biceps strain to hold Jacob upright. Will the weight of Jacob drag the angel to earth or will the power of the angel lift Jacob to heaven? Which of the two forces, gravity or grace, will win? The sculpture does not tell us: it is poised, held in balance between the two.

Part of the message of the sculpture is about the dogged resistance of the materials with which Epstein was so strenuously working and part of the message is autobiographical, but part is spiritual – that with effort, discipline and concentrated attention, beauty and meaning can emerge out of recalcitrance.

Reflection by **Christopher Herbert**

Proper 24

Continuous:
Jeremiah 31.27-34
Psalm 119.97-104

Related:
Genesis 32.22-31
Psalm 121

2 Timothy 3.14 – 4.5
Luke 18.1-8

2 Timothy 3.14 – 4.5

'All scripture is inspired by God ...' (3.16)

'All Scripture is God breathed' is the more accurate translation. We need the intimacy of that image. After all, if you are close to someone's breath, you are close to their very being. To 'inspire' someone, in this sense, is to breathe life into them. And, without breath, we expire.

This suggests a relationship with God's word more like a deepening personal relationship than a manual of instruction or 'how-to' guide to be understood and obeyed. Through it, God breathes his life into us. It takes us back to the beginning of creation where God breathed into Adam's nostrils and he became a living being. And, through that God-breathed word, we too are formed, nourished and enabled to live as faithful disciples.

This will change the way we read it. We take breath into the depths of our being. Scripture must be drawn in deeply and regularly, entering something much deeper than our minds. Whether, like Timothy, we have long believed, or whether faith for us is newer or even still being explored, the call is to stay close to this God-breathed word and let it totally 'inspire' us.

Reflection by **David Runcorn**

Continuous:
Jeremiah 31.27-34
Psalm 119.97-104

Related:
Genesis 32.22-31
Psalm 121

Proper 24

2 Timothy 3.14 – 4.5
Luke 18.1-8

Luke 18.1-8

' ... [the] need to pray always and not to lose heart' (v.1)

The accepted social status and religious duties of widows and judges in Israel form the background to this parable. Widows were especially vulnerable, deprived of the support of a husband, whose estate passed directly to their children. If the children refused to support their mother, then a judge would be brought in to adjudicate. The sharp nub of this parable lies in the fact that this judge was unjust, and couldn't be relied upon to hear cases fairly and impartially.

But we completely miss the point if we take the picture of the unjust judge in this parable as representative of the way God responds to his children. Jesus is saying, look – if somebody as partial and patently unjust as this judge can be goaded into behaving well, how much more will your loving heavenly Father reach out in compassion to those who seek his help. There is a strong resonance here with a passage in Matthew's account of the Sermon on the Mount: 'Ask, and it will be given to you ... Is there anyone among you who, if your child asks for bread, will give a stone? ... If you then, who are evil, know how to give good gifts to your children, how much more will your Father in heaven give good things to those who ask him!' (Matthew 7.7-11).

Can we remember and trust that 'how much more' when we bring our own deepest and most heart-felt concerns to God?

Reflection by **Barbara Mosse**

Proper 25

Sunday between
23 & 29 October inclusive

Joel 2.23-end
Psalm 65 [*or* 65.1-7]
2 Timothy 4.6-8, 16-18
Luke 18.9-14

Joel 2.23-end

'Even on the male and female slaves, in those days,
I will pour out my spirit' (v.29)

Prophets take a look into the future and then report back. We don't know anything about Joel, probably living in the middle of the fourth century BC, but he was very much in this prophetic tradition of forcefully telling people to see what they have become and where it will all end. He shakes them to wake them up to the question of how selfish and indifferent human days stand in relation to, what he calls, 'the day of the Lord' (Joel 2.1).

At the heart of Joel's words, however, is the reassurance of God's care for his people. God will pour out his spirit and energy, and people will once again be able to see the world as God sees it. Dreams and distilled perceptions will help them re-imagine their world so that they will understand again that God is the source and destination of all that is.

What must have been shocking is Joel's report that such spiritual insight will be granted to slaves as well. In other words, a whole transformation of what we like to think of as our 'social order' is part of God's plan for us. It will feel as if the whole cosmos itself is in turmoil. The heart of the human problem is the problem of the human heart and therefore there needs to be an upheaval of human behaviours if God is to be God in our lives and not just a word we reverently use to legitimize injustice.

Reflection by **Mark Oakley**

Related:
Ecclesiasticus 35.12-17
or **Jeremiah 14.7-10, 19-end**
Psalm 84.1-7
2 Timothy 4.6-8, 16-18
Luke 18.9-14

Proper 25

Jeremiah 14.7-10, 19-end

'... we are called by your name; do not forsake us!' (v.9)

There are moments in Jeremiah's life where his desire to speak what he believes to be the truth becomes internalized into prayer. This is one such moment. His love for his people is absolute. Is not the hot anger of truth-telling sometimes born of desire to see improvement because what you love is under threat?

Now he addresses not his people but the Almighty. It is a prayer of heartfelt intensity. Jeremiah yearns for the right relationship between God and his people to be re-established. He sees around him the effects of a drought (described in haunting terms in verses 1-6), and interprets it as a sign of God's absence. He feels as desolate as the parched earth, so he calls to God: 'Yet you, O Lord, are in the midst of us, and we are called by your name; do not forsake us!'

The words spiral up into the air. A dialogue ensues, in which God answers that the people have been constantly disobedient, but Jeremiah courageously replies: 'Is it not you, O Lord our God? We set our hope on you ...'. He begs God to remember the closer-than-covenant relationship that he has with his people. And Jeremiah waits. He can do no more ...

Prayer of this kind is based on the belief that, in spite of all things, God remains faithful, true to himself, utterly holy, utterly compassionate. We meet it in the cry of the man who encountered Jesus and said: 'I believe, help my unbelief!' (Mark 9.24).

Reflection by **Christopher Herbert**

Proper 25

Continuous:
Joel 2.23-end

Psalm 65 [*or* 65.1-7]

Related:
Ecclesiasticus 35.12-17
or Jeremiah 14.7-10, 19-end
Psalm 84.1-7
2 Timothy 4.6-8, 16-18
Luke 18.9-14

2 Timothy 4.6-8, 16-18

*'As for me, I am already being poured out as a libation,
and the time of my departure has come' (v.6)*

Imagine a yacht, at the quayside, ready to leave. The ropes have been uncoiled from the buoys, loosened but not yet cast off. Everything has been done for departure; all that is needed is the word from the captain. Paul, writing from his prison cell, tells Timothy that this moment has come for him. He uses the Greek word *analusews* to describe his situation: a word which means 'to loosen in order to depart'. And he says that the moment is 'at hand'. He can read the signs – he knows his time has come.

Things have changed for Paul. Whereas others continue to be busy in the cause of the gospel, that part of his life is over. His life, once so full, so active, has narrowed down. He sees that a different vocation awaits him. In the solitude, he has also been remembering past hurts and betrayals. Paul, with his massive intellect, his passion, his energy, his leadership, shows us here a touching vulnerability and humanity.

But two things remain constant. The message of the gospel is still to be proclaimed under these most testing of circumstances. His trial will afford him yet another opportunity. And his faith, stretched and developed through his life, is holding him steady as he looks death in the face. The pattern and shape of his life may have changed but he knows that the Lord, who has been his strength in the past, will continue to be with him and to bring him home.

Reflection by **Sue Hope**

Continuous:	Related:	
Joel 2.23-end	Ecclesiasticus 35.12-17	**Proper 25**
	or Jeremiah 14.7-10, 19-end	
Psalm 65 [*or* 65.1-7]	Psalm 84.1-7	
	2 Timothy 4.6-8, 16-18	
	Luke 18.9-14	

Luke 18.9-14

' … who trusted in themselves that they were righteous' (v.9)

This passage follows on directly from last week's on the parable of the widow and the unjust judge, and continues Jesus' teaching on prayer. As with the earlier parable, today we are presented with a contrast: two men, a Pharisee and a tax collector, are praying in the temple. Again, there is an unevenness of status between the two. The Pharisee is one of the respected religious elite; the tax collector, a member of the 'tax collectors and sinners' class of outcasts.

Jesus reserved some of his harshest criticism for those who paraded their supposed virtue and importance in public, and the Pharisee here comes in for particularly scathing judgement. Jesus seems to be saying that the ultimate barrier between ourselves and God does not necessarily lie in the wrong attitudes we hold and the mistakes we make in life, but in whether or not we are able to approach God, ourselves and others with genuine humility. It is human nature to play up what we imagine are our strengths and underplay our weaknesses, and to compare ourselves to others, often to the others' detriment. Subversively, this is the tendency Jesus confronts us with, and with which he challenges us to face honestly our own behaviour and attitudes. I once heard of a preacher whose sermon simply consisted of reading this parable to the congregation and then saying, 'Hands up anyone who *didn't* think, "Thank God I'm not like that Pharisee!"…'

Reflection by **Barbara Mosse**

Isaiah 45.22-end
Psalm 119.129-136
Romans 15.1-6
Luke 4.16-24

Last Sunday after Trinity
if observed as Bible Sunday

Isaiah 45.22-end

'Turn to me and be saved' (v.22)

There seems to be no end to the human capacity for creating evil, whether that be the colossal suffering created by tyrants or the random barbarous cruelty of urban terrorists. Humans can be twisted out of shape by wickedness.

Within this dark maelstrom, the voice of the prophet can barely be heard; it is almost drowned out by the cacophony of malevolence. But not quite. The cry from God speaking through the prophet is a simple one: 'Turn to me and be saved...' This is not a voice that is heard among the self-fulfilment gurus, nor is it a voice that finds any space in social media, where personal virtue is constantly proclaimed. It is too angular for that, too hard edged. It is a battle cry. It has its own kind of stark singularity.

And the question is: 'saved from what?' To which the answer is: 'saved from our own innate wickedness', to be un-twisted, to be straightened out, re-formed, made whole.

There is, of course, a bewildering irony in this: that it required the insight of a prophet growing up among a people who thought of themselves as 'chosen', separated out, special, to see the universal nature of the divine. The divine was not limited, not exclusive. Quite the opposite. God offers to all humankind the deep beauties of his very nature, a nature that takes evil to itself (through death on a cross) and works to redeem it into love.

Reflection by **Christopher Herbert**

Isaiah 45.22-end
Psalm 119.129-136
Romans 15.1-6
Luke 4.16-24

Romans 15.1-6

'... the good purpose of building up the neighbour' (v.2)

Paul often urges his hearers and readers to be individually accountable before God in their actions. We are each answerable to God and our conscience. But he also urges us to be committed to each other in the Body of Christ. He wants us to support each other and live in harmony and with mutual flourishing. Paul isn't the extremist he is often painted as, except in one thing – that our task is to 'glorify the God and Father of our Lord Jesus Christ'. It was this that directed and energized his life.

In other words, Paul exhibited a passionate balance. He was passionate in his personal commitment to Christ ('For to me, living is Christ ...' Philippians 1.21), but at the same time he was balanced in wanting the whole diverse community to live together in mutual support and encouragement. There was in Paul a pragmatic tolerance of difference that we in the Church today would do well to emulate. God is infinitely bigger than our biggest ideas, and probably less concerned with our doctrinal salami-slicing than we think.

What God wants of us is Paul's passionate balance. The question then is – how passionate are we in our faith, and how balanced in our acceptance of difference?

Reflection by **John Pritchard**

Last Sunday after Trinity

Isaiah 45.22-end
Psalm 119.129-136
Romans 15.1-6
Luke 4.16-24

Luke 4.16-24

'... he has anointed me to bring good news to the poor' (v.18)

Twice in this section of the Gospel we are told that Jesus was going down well with the crowds (v.15 and v.22). It all goes wrong though. By verse 28 they are all in a rage and trying to throw him off a cliff. Why? What is it that Jesus does to our expectations that makes him such a threat?

We read here Jesus' first sermon. Using words from Isaiah 61.1, Jesus spells out God's priorities and how his own ministry is to embody these. Jesus defines the mission of God as speaking good things to the poor and marginalized, releasing the imprisoned, letting blindness give way to sight and, in the translation of the King James Bible, 'to set at liberty them that are bruised' (v.18). The truth may set us free, but before this it tends to really annoy us. The people wonder what's going on, but when Jesus tells them, his own neighbours, that their faith in this God is so lacking, so full of low expectation, that goodness cannot come of it, they turn on him.

What is clear from this passage is that, at the heart of Jesus' belief, God desires his people to be free from all the chains – mental, physical, past or future – that hold us down. His heart is with the oppressed, the vulnerable and those whose needs are too easily overlooked. Any group of Christians today need only read this passage to see whether they are really following the man from Nazareth or managers of a self-regarding institution. However, lest we get too hard on ourselves, Luke leaves out half a sentence in his Isaiah quotation – the reference to the 'day of vengeance of our God' (Isaiah 61.2).

Reflection by **Mark Oakley**

258

Daniel 7.1-3, 15-18
Psalm 149
Ephesians 1.11-end
Luke 6.20-31

All Saints' Day

1 November *Principal Feast*
(Sunday between 30 October & 5 November
if this is kept as All Saints' Sunday)

Daniel 7.1-3, 15-18

'... my spirit was troubled within me' (v.15)

A churning sea; four howling winds; four writhing beasts; and in verses 9-10 a vision of the Ancient of Days from whose presence issues a river of fire ... it is no wonder that Daniel was troubled! Such a hyper-coloured psychedelic vision was deeply disturbing. He needed a wise being to interpret it, so he turned to one of the angels for help in understanding, an angel who moved easily between heaven and earth ...

The usual way to analyse this kind of writing is to say that it stands in the apocalyptic tradition, but that is only a way of establishing the genre. And although this genre is filled with political symbolism, that too is not the entire answer to its meaning. What we need to do is to go beneath the genre into the heart of the matter. This is a form of theology: a way of trying to make sense of the brutal realities of the political world and to see those realities in the light of eternity. Raw human power is contrasted with the overarching purposes of God, a God who is terrifyingly holy and who is surrounded by a fiery mandorla of saintly beings.

This is language that is not literal. It is language pushed to breaking point, mysteriously metaphorical, impossible to comprehend. Designed to stretch our spiritual imaginations, it leads us to that place where language completely fails and all we are left with is an awe-filled, numinous silence.

Reflection by **Christopher Herbert**

All Saints' Day

1 November *Principal Feast*

Daniel 7.1-3, 15-18
Psalm 149
Ephesians 1.11-end
Luke 6.20-31

Ephesians 1.11-end

*' ... what are the riches of his glorious inheritance
among the saints' (v.18)*

Today, we celebrate All Saints' Day, but what *is* a saint, precisely? What, or who, do we think of when we hear the term? Perhaps we think of those rare individuals publically declared to be saints after a somewhat tortuous canonical process. Or perhaps our minds leap to any number of those spiritual giants of the past: Julian of Norwich, Teresa of Ávila, John Wesley, Cuthbert of Lindisfarne ... The list is endless. These are powerful witnesses, and our sense of spiritual connection with them across time and space enlivens our experience of the reality of the communion of the saints.

But today's passage from Ephesians talks about sainthood in a rather different way. When Paul commends the Ephesians for their 'love towards all the saints', he seems to be referring to contemporary fellow believers, not those who have gone before them. He seems to be using the term in quite an everyday kind of way, as shorthand for all those striving to follow Christ in company with their fellow believers.

On this reading, the way of sainthood belongs to us all. It comes automatically with the gift of being a unique member of Christ's Body, whatever our particular place in that Body may be. It comes with the joys and difficulties that accompany the struggle to become an authentic community, and with the challenge of journeying peaceably alongside one another as we all seek to follow the way of Christ.

Reflection by **Barbara Mosse**

Daniel 7.1-3, 15-18
Psalm 149
Ephesians 1.11-end
Luke 6.20-31

Luke 6.20-31

'... for yours is the kingdom' (v.20)

Here is the world turned upside down! A blessing on those who suffer what we quite reasonably try to avoid – poverty, hunger, sorrow, defamation – and then a corresponding 'woe' to those who have actually achieved the goals for which we are all supposed to be striving – wealth, satisfaction, happiness, reputation. What are we to make of it?

It is not in itself blessed to be poor or hungry; if it were, then Jesus would not be asking us, as he clearly does, to relieve the poor and to feed the hungry. Nor is it necessarily a blessing to weep. And yet, paradoxically, Jesus asks us to look deeper, to look beneath the veil of these present sorrows and privations, and glimpse a change, a reversal, a hidden glory waiting to be made manifest. Everything turns on the movement in these verses from 'now' to 'will', turns on the hinge of hope: you weep now, but you will laugh; you are deprived now, but yours is the kingdom. We must dare to see through the veil of the present, and dare also to tear aside the veil of the false fulfilment, the temporary satisfaction, the purchase of the world that lost us our souls. I recently reflected, in a sonnet on the Beatitudes, that Jesus speaks these words not to condemn, but to challenge and change, to lift the veil of time just enough to help us see that:

> *'... longing is the veil of satisfaction,*
> *And grief the veil of future happiness.*
> *We glimpse beneath the veil of persecution*
> *The coming kingdom's overflowing bliss.'**

*Malcolm Guite, 'Beatitudes', *Parable and Paradox*, Canterbury Press 2016

Reflection by **Malcolm Guite**

261

Fourth Sunday before Advent

**Sunday between 30 October &
5 November inclusive** *(For use if the
Feast of All Saints is celebrated on 1 November)*

Isaiah 1.10-18
Psalm 32.1-8
2 Thessalonians 1
Luke 19.1-10

Isaiah 1.10-18

'Come now, let us argue it out' (v.18)

Isaiah is read up to Christmas and prepares us for the celebration of the Incarnation, with the powerful twin themes of God's wrath and mercy, divine threat and promise. God is referred to as the 'Holy One of Israel' (Isaiah 1.4), showing both the holy transcendence of God and his immanence (immediate presence) to his chosen people. This recalls how God comes to the manger as both judge and saviour, intimate physical human but also hidden God.

The opening setting is a law court, with the heavens and earth as witnesses, and the Holy One is not to be placated by acts of worship. The case is argued out, and a reorientation of life is required: 'cease to do evil, learn to do good'.

Isaiah is addressing Israel, but the reading can be applied to us. The action of God in our lives brings a courtroom-style conviction – we fall short of the glory of God. However, we are not left to be condemned. The gospel we proclaim is one of freedom: we can accept forgiveness and are set free from the consequences of our actions – 'though your sins are like scarlet, they shall be like snow'. In the Christian Scriptures, Isaiah is the most quoted Hebrew prophet; like John the Baptist, he prepares the way of the Lord.

Reflection by **Paul Kennedy**

Isaiah 1.10-18
Psalm 32.1-8
2 Thessalonians 1
Luke 19.1-10

Fourth Sunday before Advent

2 Thessalonians 1

'... your steadfastness and faith during all your persecutions'
(v.4)

Faith is something that seems to thrive best in adverse circumstances and in hard ground. It appears to welcome wintry conditions. The faith of the Thessalonians is showing signs of real maturing. It's not only their faith that's growing but also love, and the result is a kind of 'enlargement', a generosity, a spaciousness of character. It all seems to be going towards shaping that mysterious future – the kingdom of God. But the growth is happening in the context of great trouble and hardship.

This enlargement in faith and love in adverse circumstances isn't something limited to the enthusiasm of first-century Christianity. Beside the body of a child in Ravensbrück concentration camp was found this prayer:

'O Lord, remember not only the men and women of goodwill, but also those of ill will. But do not remember all the suffering they have inflicted; remember the fruits we have bought, thanks to their suffering – our comradeship, our loyalty, our humility, our courage, our generosity, the greatness of heart which has grown out of all this. And when they come to judgement, let all the fruits which we have borne be their forgiveness. Amen.'

Reflection by **Sue Hope**

Fourth Sunday before Advent

Isaiah 1.10-18
Psalm 32.1-8
2 Thessalonians 1
Luke 19.1-10

Luke 19.1-10

'Today salvation has come to this house' (v.9)

The much-loved story of Zacchaeus has an ugly background, for the people are strongly hostile to the fraudulent tax-collector. He may have heard of Jesus as a friend of his class, and he tries to watch unseen by climbing a tree. His efforts to hide are foiled when Jesus looks up and invites himself to his house – a brave and astonishing act.

Jesus' visit provokes the usual complaints from those who consider it unfitting for him to associate with the unworthy; yet he comes not with tolerant indulgence but costly grace. Confronted by this, Zacchaeus is ashamed of his dishonesty and agrees to give to the poor and make restitution on a lavish scale. This is a climactic moment in the Gospel, evoking the ringing assertion that 'the Son of Man came to seek out and to save the lost'.

Sharing the good news of salvation is both breathtakingly powerful and genuinely risky. In coming together, both Jesus and Zacchaeus stand fast against the forces of social and religious condemnation. Today, the story is used as the pattern for a victim awareness programme for offenders. We must look to discern where salvation comes today, and what it costs – remembering that identifying with sinners took Jesus from the house of Zacchaeus to the Place of a Skull.

Reflection by **Christopher Jones**

Job 19.23-27a
Psalm 17.1-9 [*or* 17.1-8]
2 Thessalonians 2.1-5, 13-end
Luke 20.27-38

Third Sunday before Advent

Sunday between
6 & 12 November inclusive

Job 19.23-27a

'For I know that my Redeemer lives ...' (v.25)

What a difference a capital letter makes! In this verse from Job, 'Redeemer' has a capital letter. And that inevitably leads us to hear the music of Handel's great oratorio *Messiah* crashing around in our minds. Glorious.

But there is a problem. Hebrew does not have capital letters. So if one follows the Handelian tradition, the word 'Redeemer' (with a capital 'R') can lead to the implication that Job was a prophet, someone who foretold the good news of the Messiah, Jesus, who was to come. But if one follows the literal Hebrew tradition, the word 'redeemer' does not have a capital letter and refers simply to a *go'el* that is, a vindicator; someone, usually a close relative, who protects the vulnerable from exploitation or who requites a wrong.

So, two potential meanings for the word 'redeemer'. When faced with this kind of ambivalence, what are we to do?

Our natural reaction is to want to resolve the problem by worrying away at it – perhaps, trying other biblical translations or getting to grips with the Hebrew, or reading a variety of commentaries. But generations of biblical scholars have done this and have not solved the problem. Some opt for the capital letter; others do not. And here's the rub: both are right.

We may crave certainty, but we cannot have it. Living with uncertainty is part of our human condition ... but presumably that is how God our Creator designed us to be?

Reflection by **Christopher Herbert**

Third Sunday before Advent	Job 19.23-27*a*
	Psalm 17.1-9 [*or* 17.1-8]
	2 Thessalonians 2.1-5, 13-end
	Luke 20.27-38

2 Thessalonians 2.1-5, 13-end

'As to the coming of our Lord Jesus Christ ...' (v.1)

Reports have reached Paul and his companions that the Thessalonians are alarmed and shaken. The early Church believed that the coming of Christ was imminent. The Church therefore took very seriously the calls in the Gospels and the Epistles to keep awake.

There were some dangers as well, however. It was all too easy to be disturbed by rumours or false teaching that the coming of Christ as king had happened already and that the Thessalonians had been left behind and missed the kingdom.

Paul here seeks to counter these ideas and offer reassurance. He does so by a complex argument about a rebellion and a lawless one. This rebellion, Paul argues, must come first and therefore Christ has not yet returned. In other words, things are going to get much worse before they get better...

This imagery of the lawless one is complex. It builds on references in Daniel and other apocalyptic literature and is referenced again in the Gospels and Revelation. It is puzzling language for us today.

We need to remember that we live in a Church where the coming of Christ all too often does not seem imminent. Passages such as this challenge us to return to the creeds and remind one another that Christ will come again and that we too are called to keep awake.

Reflection by **Steven Croft**

Job 19.23-27*a*
Psalm 17.1-9 [*or* 17.1-8]   **Third Sunday before Advent**
2 Thessalonians 2.1-5, 13-end
Luke 20.27-38

Luke 20.27-38

'... they are like angels and are children of God' (v.36)

Who can say what heaven is like? It would be like asking a fish to describe the Milky Way. What we do know is that the word 'heaven' in Hebrew means 'with God'. Whatever God is like, whatever is the intimate and transcendent nature and being of God, then heaven is like that. We do know what God is like from the revelation of the sacred Scriptures. God is love. God is good, God is just, God is holy, God is everywhere. Therefore, heaven, as the reality of being in the being of God, has these characteristics as its essence. Any attempt to go beyond this revelation is speculation.

Jesus is well within these realities when he talks about the nature of marriage in heaven. He simply transcends the Sadducees' small-minded and legalistic question about heavenly realities and conditions with a remarkable image of freedom in resurrection, of the primacy of life over death and of the beautiful image of God's eternal love for God's children.

It has been said that death for a Christian is simply the extinguishing of a candle at the dawn because a greater light has come. Our life with its warmth and light, as well as its vulnerability and shadow, is to be utterly transformed, completely illumined in that resurrection light like a rising sun shining upon us. How then should we be afraid to die, to fall into the hands that made all things? The anxiety of the Sadducees is irrelevant.

Reflection by **David Moxon**

Second Sunday before Advent

**Sunday between
13 & 19 November inclusive**

Malachi 4.1-2a
Psalm 98
2 Thessalonians 3.6-13
Luke 21.5-19

Malachi 4.1-2a

'... the sun of righteousness shall rise' (v.2)

Malachi brings his prophecy to an end with a threat and a promise. The book is framed as six question-and-answer dialogues, all inviting the recently returned Jews to change their ways, in which case they can be assured of God's favour and protection. But here, finally, is the deal – arrogance and destruction, or repentance and blessing.

It's easy to know who the arrogant and evildoers are; it's them. It's not us. And the divine Terminator will come and sort them out on the Day of the Lord. So that's clear, then, and it makes us all feel a lot better. Except that it isn't, and it doesn't. There's so much 'them' in me, and I can't stay long on my moral high ground without feeling a fraud. The wheat and the weeds of which Jesus speaks in Matthew 13 are both part of me, and will continue to be so until the end of my life.

What gives us reassurance is that God's judgement is the only one that matters, and those dealings will be utterly fair and gracious in the hands of the One who loved us so much that he gave his only Son. Love, not fear, is the heart of our faith and is therefore what we need to embody today in our words and actions.

Reflection by **John Pritchard**

Malachi 4.1-2*a*
Psalm 98
2 Thessalonians 3.6-13
Luke 21.5-19

2 Thessalonians 3.6-13

'... keep away from believers who are living in idleness' (v.6)

Paul has addressed his first two themes of persecution and the timing of the coming of Christ. He now turns to the third report that has reached him: idleness in the Christian community.

The Church is called on in every generation to exercise mutual love and support and the practical sharing of goods. A strong work ethic is a necessary part of this culture of care for the poor. Without it, there is a danger of laziness and creating dependency. The kindness of Christian friends will be exploited by some, and the whole system of care will fall.

Most Christians finding time to read Paul's words in mid-November will probably raise their eyebrows at this point. The demands of family and working life and the extra demands of the coming Christmas season will probably mean there is too much to do and too little time to rest, let alone for idleness.

But there is a message here, even so, about the God-given importance of work, about the ingredients for human flourishing and about the way we build up our common life and responsibility: mutual care is not to be at the expense of individual dignity.

Everyone matters. Everyone's contribution matters. And that means your work and mine must be taken seriously today in itself and for the example we offer.

Reflection by **Steven Croft**

Second Sunday before Advent

Malachi 4.1-2*a*
Psalm 98
2 Thessalonians 3.6-13
Luke 21.5-19

Luke 21.5-19

'... do not be terrified' (v.9)

When we read this 'little apocalypse', we may well be thinking that it's all very well for Jesus to say 'do not be terrified', but the things he lists here are frankly terrifying. There has scarcely been a time between the day he said these words and our own when there have not been wars and insurrections, nations rising against one another and the even more dreadful civil and religious strife that divides nations and even families, the civil and religious wars through which intimacy is broken by persecution and betrayal. Why should we not be terrified?

What Jesus is calling for here is a kingdom vision that takes us through and beyond terror, a vision that meets terror with trust, faith and endurance. We can only rise to this if we rest and trust in that promise of life we heard earlier: the promise that even those who have met with death are alive to God, the God of the living; the promise that, in the final reckoning and new life inaugurated by the coming kingdom, we will indeed find that not a hair on our head has perished.

In light of that resurrection gospel, we can indeed discover, even in the chaos around us, even in persecution, not oppression, but what Jesus calls with beautiful audacity, a 'gift' of 'opportunity to testify'. What we testify to – what all the martyrs testify to – is the final triumph of Love, the final radiance of a light that no darkness can comprehend or extinguish.

Reflection by **Malcolm Guite**

Jeremiah 23.1-6
Psalm 46
Colossians 1.11-20
Luke 23.33-43

Christ the King

The Sunday next before Advent
Sunday between
20 & 26 November inclusive

Jeremiah 23.1-6

'I will raise up for David a righteous Branch' (v.5)

On the final Sunday of the Church's year we read a passage from Jeremiah that condemns the leaders of Israel and promises a righteous king. Jeremiah's original audience was Jerusalem under siege in the sixth century BC. The blame for the enslavement of the Israelites to Babylon he laid firmly at the feet of the kings of Judah who had failed to act justly and protect the weak (Jeremiah 22.3) and who had made themselves rich at the expense of the vulnerable (Jeremiah 22.13-14). The Babylonians would be Yahweh's instrument to end corruption and oppression in Jerusalem, so that he himself could raise up a righteous ruler who would govern justly.

The reference to the raising up of 'a righteous Branch' for David, however, has also been interpreted as a Messianic prophecy, fulfilled in Jesus. Unlike the self-serving 'shepherds' who still governed Israel in Jesus' day (like Herod, the collaborator with the Romans, whose magnificent palaces can still be seen today at Caesarea Maritima and near Bethlehem), the Messiah would be a just ruler who would deal wisely and even be known as 'The Lord is our righteousness'.

The feast of Christ the King thus reveals God as a God of justice who is on the side of the oppressed, and Christ as the one leader who can stand the judgement. All other leaders are called to turn from their self-serving ways and serve the poor and the vulnerable instead.

Reflection by **Jane Leach**

271

Christ the King
The Sunday next before Advent

Jeremiah 23.1-6
Psalm 46
Colossians 1.11-20
Luke 23.33-43

Colossians 1.11-20

'... in him all things hold together' (v.17)

This great hymn to Christ in Colossians has the same cosmic resonance – indeed hints at the same final coherence – as the prologue to John's Gospel. It lifts us out of our littleness. The next time your PCC is bogged down in a discussion of stationery, or the minutiae of the coffee rota seems to loom larger than it should, it would be well to recite, in awe-struck tones these verses of Colossians: all-inclusive, and all-transforming, that great phrase 'all things' is repeated again and again. Nothing and no one is beyond God's presence, or the reach and scope of his concern.

But there is more: this passage is not only about presence and coherence, about all things holding together in Christ; it is also about peace and reconciliation. It is not only that Christ reconciles things on a cosmic scale, bringing together, as he does, the very things we contrast and oppose – heaven and earth, time and eternity, truth and grace – but he is also reconciling us, individually and collectively, on a detailed, difficult, nitty-gritty level, so that we who have been 'estranged and hostile in mind' (v.21) can be reconciled and make 'peace through the blood of his cross'.

Maybe that's worth sharing with the PCC too!

Reflection by **Malcolm Guite**

Jeremiah 23.1-6
Psalm 46
Colossians 1.11-20
Luke 23.33-43

Christ the King
The Sunday next before Advent

Luke 23.33-43

"If you are the King of the Jews, save yourself!' (v.37)

In the Anglo-Saxon poem, *The Dream of the Rood*, Jesus embraces the cross as a warrior king engaging in mortal combat. It was considered degrading for an Anglo-Saxon king to display weakness and suffer humiliation in battle. So, while Jesus is 'strong and unflinching', the poet makes the cross itself experience the torment of crucifixion. Is this unrealistic? Not for Luke, who leaves us in no doubt, even here at this point of utter human vulnerability, of the kingship of Jesus.

In the verses just before today's reading, we have a mirror image of the triumphal entry into Jerusalem: not arriving, acclaimed as king, but leaving, accompanied by tears. Not a mounted king, but a beaten man going to a criminal's death, too weak to bear the physical weight demanded of him. All aspirations of kingship are surely utterly shattered.

And yet ... we also hear echoes of the Song of Songs, the bride addressing the 'daughters of Jerusalem' (Luke 23.28), summoning them to come out and see King Solomon, crowned, passing by. We hear Jesus speak, evoking the prophet Hosea's words of judgement from God on his idolatrous people. With 'king' and 'Messiah', the leaders think they mock, but there is truth in the plea of the second criminal: the kingdom is near. In the face of cruelty and shattered hopes, we are not to lose sight of the sovereignty of God.

Reflection by **Jane Maycock**

273

Dedication Festival

If date not known, observe on the First Sunday in October or Last Sunday after Trinity.

I Chronicles 29.6-19
Psalm 122
Ephesians 2.19-22
John 2.13-22

1 Chronicles 29.6-19

*'For all things come from you,
and of your own have we given you' (v.14)*

This familiar refrain, often used in services at the presentation of the offering, is taken from the passage describing what David did after the extraordinary response to his request for gifts for the temple. Immediately after the free-will offerings had been pledged, David broke into a spontaneous paean of praise to God, including this statement of faith in the divine source of all things.

In spite of the opulence of the gifts and the magnificence of the plans for the temple, David questions his right even to make such offerings to God. He voices his conviction that he and the assembled officials are 'aliens and transients' before God and that all their days on earth are 'like a shadow'. It is a remarkable statement in the midst of what was manifestly an extremely successful fundraising event. In expressing the fragility of the human position in relation to the eternal Being of God, David exposes the illusory nature of worldly security and wealth. He brings the focus right back onto God, and reminds himself and everyone present that all they own, all their great riches and possessions – everything comes from God.

Even as David anticipates the glory of the temple, he acknowledges that God's delight is in the joyful and open response of human hearts. While accepting the necessity of earthly riches, David remains firmly fixed on the values of eternity.

Reflection by **Christina Rees**

I Chronicles 29.6-19
Psalm 122
Ephesians 2.19-22
John 2.13-22

Dedication Festival

Ephesians 2.19-22

'So then you are no longer strangers and aliens' (v.19)

If you could travel back in time to Paul's Ephesus, you would notice, like any Mediterranean city of the day, that it was buzzing with cultural and ethnic diversity – much like our cities today. But there were some crucial differences. It was difficult to keep order in such cities. Magistrates and other officers handed out justice, but a person who was not a citizen of that city could ask to be tried by their own people under their own laws.

Cities, to be well ordered, were governed by assemblies. These were sometimes called *ekklesia* – an ancient secular word from which we derive the term 'church'. And to help keep order in cities, ethnic groups who were non-citizens often lived in neighbourhoods or ghettoes. Indeed, even in modern times, we find 'quarters' of a city reserved for the Spanish, French, Chinese – and sometimes for groups that are marginalized.

In ancient times, the areas reserved in a city for non-citizens were known as *paroikia* – from which we get the English word 'parish'. This is where the resident aliens lived – those who lived in the city, contributed to its welfare, but had no voting rights. In Paul's Church, we find Jews, Greeks and Romans; slave and free; male and female. All one in Christ. And in this 'assembly' of non-citizens, all are equal.

The parish church, then, is the inside place for the outsider. Or, as Archbishop William Temple once put it, the only club that exists for non-members. This is what it means to be one in Christ: built together to be the dwelling place of God.

Reflection by **Martyn Percy**

Dedication Festival	I Chronicles 29.6-19
	Psalm 122
	Ephesians 2.19-22
	John 2.13-22

John 2.13-22

'Stop making my Father's house a market-place!' (v.16)

Jesus ate with social outcasts, healed the sick, gave hope to the poor and forgave sinners. The only people he treated harshly were the religious. He drove the animals out of the temple with a whip, overturned the tables of the money-changers, and poured out their coins. He lashed the Pharisees and lawyers with his tongue, accusing them of breaking their own law by their hypocrisy, pride and manipulation of the poor. He said that he had come not to save the righteous but those who were regarded with contempt and indifference.

It is rather ironic that we have constructed a religion around Jesus; that many have become financially rich through religion; and that we have hierarchies of clergy in prominent seats and costly clothing. What can we do about it?

Jesus did not want to destroy the temple, but he subtly pointed out that his body was a temple that would be destroyed and raised again. When it was raised, the body of Christ would be the community of those who feed the hungry, heal the sick and comfort the bereaved, the hands and heart of the risen Christ.

Whatever the outward reality, it is when we are Christ's body, living as he lived, living in him, that we are truly the house of God.

Reflection by **Keith Ward**

Deuteronomy 26.1-11
Psalm 100
Philippians 4.4-9 *or*
Revelation 14.14-18
John 6.25-35

Harvest Thanksgiving

Deuteronomy 26.1-11

'A wandering Aramean was my ancestor ...' (v.5)

The closing chapters of Deuteronomy reiterate compelling themes from the entire Pentateuch, reminding God's people of their roots, and rehearsing a rich manifesto for life in the new covenant community.

Chapter 26 grounds this new way of life in two telling liturgies – the presentation of first-fruits to God in today's reading, followed by the dedication of the third year tithe to the poor and disadvantaged (in verses 12-15). Through both rituals, the people's expression of gratitude and celebration prompts a holistic response of obedience, generosity, and praise.

At the heart of the liturgical action is a deeply moving account of Israel's story, beginning with a wandering Aramean. In our own days of mass migration, we are acutely aware of the threat to life and livelihood, faith and identity, faced by countless thousands of displaced people across the world.

If we belong to the privileged community of those who are free to 'possess' a home, and to feel 'settled' in it, then Deuteronomy reminds us that our human good fortune is a very precious gift of God. We have a corresponding duty to be good stewards of his manifold grace (1 Peter 4.10), seeking ways to serve one another with whatever gift each of us has received.

What basket of blessings do you have to lay before the altar of your God?

Reflection by **Margaret Whipp**

Harvest Thanksgiving	Deuteronomy 26.1-11
	Psalm 100
	Philippians 4.4-9 *or*
	Revelation 14.14-18
	John 6.25-35

Philippians 4.4-9

'... whatever is pure, whatever is pleasing' (v.8)

'You are what you eat.' This is true of what we contemplate too. People talk about 'eye candy', and it's hardly a wholesome long-term diet. The decisions we make every day about what we will dwell longest on, think most deeply about, chew over most thoroughly, are decisions that will have profound long-term effects on the sort of people we become.

Paul is not, of course, telling us only to contemplate attractive or consoling things. 'Pleasing' is accompanied by 'true', 'honourable', 'pure', and more – all of which may also be challenging to face.

During the period of the centenary of the First World War, St Paul's Cathedral in London is displaying the astonishingly lovely altar frontal woven by the trembling hands of 140 shell-shocked soldiers as part of their occupational therapy. They were trained up by members of the Royal School of Needlework and did the work in various hospitals around the country. Their eyes had seen barely imaginable horrors; their heads were colonized by unwanted memories. But quietly, steadily, stitch by stitch, they were helped to consider beauty again as well, and to become part of its transmission to others.

To contemplate their achievement is to understand a little more about what Paul might have been calling the Philippians to do – and us too. Not to look away from the world's violence and trauma, pretending it isn't there, but to look insistently for the deeper and more enduring 'excellences' that can nourish and heal it. The altars from which Christians feed remember brutality but proclaim love.

278   *Reflection by* **Mark Oakley**

Deuteronomy 26.1-11
Psalm 100
Philippians 4.4-9 *or*
Revelation 14.14-18
John 6.25-35

Harvest Thanksgiving

Revelation 14.14-18

'... the hour to reap has come, because the harvest of the earth is fully ripe' (v.15)

No one knew the day nor the hour of the coming of the Son of Man, but it has arrived. This is the moment of judgement anticipated in the Gospels: the harvest at the end of the age, which represents the culmination of all things. In this vision we witness two stages of judgement: the harvest of the grain, followed by the grape.

In the first, Christ raises his sharp sickle and reaps the righteous with one clean swing. This is an image of salvation – the gathering up of all God's people – and a cause for rejoicing. But then it is the turn of the vintage of the earth, ripe with unrighteousness. If we read on to the end of the chapter, setting the swing of the second sickle in its proper context, we discover that this is a sour vintage indeed. The grapes are gathered up and trodden in the wine press of wrath, from which flows a torrent of blood.

Harvest is traditionally and rightly a time of thanksgiving for the gifts of the earth, but it is also a good time to reflect more broadly on farming and food production: to ask ourselves whether the choices we make in shops and markets support fair trade for all God's people and the flourishing of the earth, or whether they are contributing to that sour vintage of unrighteousness and oppression.

Reflection by **Helen Orchard**

Harvest Thanksgiving

Deuteronomy 26.1-11
Psalm 100
Philippians 4.4-9 *or*
Revelation 14.14-18
John 6.25-35

John 6.25-35

'I am the bread of life' (v.35)

In the words of biblical scholar John Marsh, Jesus 'is the gift he brings'. 'The bread of life' is the bread that is the source of life, and also the 'living bread'. It nourishes us, fills us, satisfies us, enlivens us. The symbolism chimes with the Church's eucharistic practice, in which the body of Christ is ingested and becomes part of us, part of our life.

In the period between the Old and New Testaments, 'the manna in the wilderness' was interpreted as God's wisdom, which was itself the word of life and the fulfilment of the Law. In taking to himself the divine word of revelation, 'I am', Jesus presents himself as this work of God's self-disclosure.

The bread is what God does: a gift that feeds the hungry, one that requires nothing of them but their acceptance that it is food and that it will indeed fill them. All we have to do – the only 'spiritual labour which makes it possible' to earn this food (as Anglican Franciscan scholar Barnabas Lindars put it) – is to accept and trust Jesus. John and Paul are at one in this.

To have this bread is to have life, life that is never going to be lost. The bread that 'comes down from heaven and gives life to the world' will not be lost, nor will any whom the Son has been given. Why? Because this filling up and making full, this *fulfilment*, is what God intends – and will ensure.

Reflection by **Jeff Astley**

REFLECTIONS FOR DAILY PRAYER

If you enjoyed *Reflections for Sundays (Year C)*, why not consider enhancing your spiritual journey through the rich landscape of the Church's year with *Reflections for Daily Prayer*, the Church of England's popular daily prayer companion.

Covering Monday to Saturday each week, *Reflections for Daily Prayer* offers stimulating and accessible reflections on a Bible reading from the lectionary for *Common Worship: Morning Prayer*. Thousands of readers value the creative insights, scholarship and pastoral wisdom offered by our team of experienced writers.

Each day includes:

- full lectionary details for Morning Prayer
- a reflection on one of the Bible readings
- a Collect for the day.

This book also contains:

- a simple form of Morning Prayer, with seasonal variations, for use throughout the year
- a short form of Night Prayer (also known as Compline)
- a guide to the practice of daily prayer by Rachel Treweek.

Each annual volume contains reflections for an entire year starting in Advent and is published each year in the preceding May.

For more information about Reflections for Daily Prayer, visit our website: www.dailyprayer.org.uk

REFLECTIONS FOR DAILY PRAYER
App

Make Bible study and reflection a part of your routine wherever you go with the Reflections for Daily Prayer App for Apple and Android devices.

Download the app for free from the App Store (Apple devices) or Google Play (Android devices) and receive a week's worth of reflections free. Then purchase a monthly, three-monthly or annual subscription to receive up-to-date content.

REFLECTIONS ON THE PSALMS

Reflections on the Psalms provides original and insightful meditations on each of the Bible's 150 Psalms, from the same experienced team of distinguished writers that have made *Reflections for Daily Prayer* so successful. The author team comprises:

Ian Adams
Christopher Cocksworth
Joanna Collicutt
Gillian Cooper
Steven Croft
Paula Gooder
Peter Graystone
Malcolm Guite
Helen-Ann Hartley
Barbara Mosse
Mark Oakley
Martyn Percy
John Pritchard
Ben Quash
John Sentamu
Angela Tilby
Lucy Winkett
Jeremy Worthen

Each reflection is accompanied by its corresponding Psalm refrain and prayer from the *Common Worship Psalter*, making this a valuable resource for personal or devotional use. Specially written introductions by Paula Gooder and Steven Croft explore the Psalms and the Bible and the Psalms in the life of the Church.

£14.99 • 192 pages
ISBN 978 0 7151 4490 9

Also available in Kindle and epub formats